Dante's Aesthetics of Being

Dante's Aesthetics of Being

Warren Ginsberg

Ann Arbor

THE UNIVERSITY OF MICHIGAN PRESS

Copyright © by the University of Michigan 1999
All rights reserved
Published in the United States of America by
The University of Michigan Press
Manufactured in the United States of America
⊗ Printed on acid-free paper

2002   2001   2000   1999   4   3   2   1

A CIP catalog record for this book is available from the British Library.

Library of Congress Cataloging-in-Publication Data

Ginsberg, Warren, 1949–
    Dante's aesthetics of being / Warren Ginsberg.
        p.   cm.
    Includes bibliographical references and index.
    ISBN 0-472-10971-5 (acid-free paper)
    1. Dante Alighieri, 1265–1321—Aesthetics.   2. Aesthetics,
Medieval.   3. Ontology in literature.   I. Title.
PQ4390 .G485   1999
851'.1—dc21   98-25520
                                                        CIP

*For my father
and
in memory of my mother*

Preface

At the nadir of the universe, Dante confronts Satan. As the source of all evil stands rooted before him, Dante struggles to represent the depravity he sees face to face.

> S'el fu sì bel com' elli è ora brutto,
> e contra 'l suo fattore alzò le ciglia,
> ben dee da lui procedere ogne lutto.
>
> (Inf. 34.34–36)

> [If he was once as beautiful as he is ugly now, and lifted up his brows against his Maker, well may all sorrow proceed from him.]

At first, Dante seems to imply that we can grasp how the most luminous of angels became the "point to which all weights are drawn from every part" ("punto / al qual si traggon d'ogne parte i pesi," *Inf.* 34.110–11) by constructing an analogy between Lucifer's past beauty and his present ugliness. We quickly realize, however, that no ratio can relate what the devil is now to what he once had been. Against common usage, Dante repeats the pronoun "he," "el" and "elli," to indicate the unbridgeable separation between a loveliness so lost it can be evoked only as a supposition and the hideous absence of grace and proportion that has replaced it. In similar fashion, Dante uses the "passato rimoto" of "fu" to divorce absolutely the instant before the seraph raised his eyebrow in rebellion from the instant after. Consigned perpetually to the chaotic gap between two moments that not even time can coordinate, Satan is frozen forever in the disjunction between his angelic and infernal natures, of which the former has been entirely obliterated.

It may perhaps seem strange that Dante invokes the beautiful in order to delineate a creature who has become the unintelligible principle of nonexistence. Beauty, however, was one of God's transcendental attributes; Dante's impulse to bring the "bel" and "brutto" of Satan into analogous relationship was in fact the most appropriate way to limn the devil. The fact that Lucifer's comeliness cannot be correlated with Satan's grotesquery makes the fiend the antiphrastic inversion of Jesus, whose joining of human and divine is the unity that all harmonious proportions in the *Comedy* take as their form. Satan's triple-headed brutishness parodies the perfect consonance of Father, Son, and Holy Spirit, which makes God "'l sommo piacer," the highest beauty, as Bernard calls him at the summit of paradise (*Par.* 33.33).

By discerning beauty at the core of either extreme of the universe, Dante signals that the aesthetic was something more than a form of knowledge that existed between the particulars of sense experience and the abstractions of the intellect. Indeed, precisely because the soul derived its beauty in part from the analogies that related its affects to its knowledge, Dante came to think of the aesthetic as the domain in which the love that moved the sun and the other stars expressed itself in human terms. He considered not only matters of form and proportion under its purview but questions of love, perfection of the self, identity, and existence. For Dante the aesthetic was a discourse of being.

Another way to say this is that the development of Dante's poetic vision coincided with the growth of his aesthetic imagination. In the following chapters I explore the implications of this claim by focusing primarily on the *Vita nuova* and the *Comedy*. In different ways in both works, Dante's meditation on Beatrice, her beauty, and the pleasure he experienced in perceiving it prompted him to appropriate for his poetry subjects that hitherto had been under the jurisdiction of theology, metaphysics, ethics, psychology, and the liberal arts. In the largest sense, then, the aesthetic for Dante was a form of cultural contestation; it provided an arena where the authority of Latin learning could be challenged, translated, and reformed by the vernacular.

These are the central contentions of *Dante's Aesthetics of Being*. Before I turn to them, however, I should add a word about its organization. The book ends as it begins, with a discussion of the aesthetics of Hell. Some readers will wonder why it does not conclude in the heaven of Mars with Cacciaguida, whom Dante acknowledges as the true progenitor of "lo bello stilo" that has done him honor. My reason is this: the "ordo" I have given the text follows the progress of intellection, an act I place at the heart of Dante's aesthetics. Understanding begins with the specific and sensible and proceeds by analysis to the universal. This essential form then becomes the starting point of a deductive synthesis that fully accounts for a particular object being what it is. In paradise Dante ascends to the cause and origin of his aesthetics; by ascending with him first, we can better grasp the principle that guided Dante when he constructed the aesthetics of damnation out of the dead matter that endures in the depths of the inferno.

Acknowledgments

It is a real pleasure to acknowledge the insight, advice, and kindness of a number of colleagues. At Albany I have profited from discussions with Richard Goldman, Colbert Nepaulsingh, and most especially Berel Lang; from other institutions I have had the good fortune to be able to share ideas with Robert Hanning, Teresa Kennedy, and Helen Lang. Each has read either a portion of or the entire manuscript; all have improved it by their comments. There are two friends and scholars to whom I owe a special debt of gratitude. Winthrop Wetherbee has supported this project early and late; his encouragement and criticism, which he offered both when some of these chapters were first written and then as a reader of the finished manuscript, were always indispensable. Most of all I want to thank Giuseppe Mazzotta. Nearly fifteen years have passed since our unforgettable weekly lunches at Yale. Many of the ideas in this book originated from these talks; a number of years later I was able to offer some of them in a more developed form in a lecture sponsored by Yale's Department of Italian; when I had completed a first version of the manuscript, Giuseppe offered crucial suggestions that enabled me to revise and strengthen it. For all this I can only say "mille grazie."

Finally, to my wife, Judith Baskin, and to our children, Samuel and Shira: there are no words that can express how indebted I am to you for your support or how blessed I am by your love.

A somewhat different version of the first two sections of chapter 5 appeared in *Traditio* 46 (1991): 205–33. I acknowledge with gratitude the permission of the editors to reprint.

Contents

Note on Dante's Texts

Unless otherwise stated, all quotations from Dante's texts and their English translations (at times somewhat altered for the sake of literalness), are drawn from the following editions. When no English version is listed, translations are my own.

Convivio. 2 vols. Edited by Giovanni Busnelli and Giuseppe Vandelli. 2d ed. Edited by A. E. Quaglio. Florence: Le Monnier, 1964.

Dante's Lyric Poetry. 2 vols. Edited and translated by Kenelm Foster and Patrick Boyde. Oxford: Clarendon, 1967.

De vulgari eloquentia. Edited by Pier Vincenzo Mengaldo. In *Opere minori,* vol. 2. Milan-Naples: Riccardo Ricciardi, 1979.

De vulgari eloquentia. Translated by A. G. Ferrers Howell. London: Kegan Paul, 1890.

La Divina Commedia secondo l'antica vulgata. 4 vols. Edited by Giorgio Petrocchi. Società dantesca italiana. Milan: Mondadori, 1966–67.

The Divine Comedy. Translated by Charles Singleton. Princeton: Princeton University Press, 1970–76.

Il Fiore e Il Detto d'Amore (attribuibili a Dante Alighieri). Edited by Gianfranco Contini. Milan: Mondadori, 1984.

Vita nuova. Edited by Domenico de Robertis. Milan and Naples: Riccardo Ricciardi, 1980.

1

Introduction:
Dante's Aesthetics of Being

The alphabet is not often a source of irony; that aesthetics is the first of Raymond Williams's key words is one instance when it is.[1] Williams's project, of course, was to show that the semantic history of certain words cannot be separated from the cultural history that conditioned their meaning. Our understanding of aesthetics, Williams notes, begins with Baumgarten's *Aesthetica* (1750–58), in which he argued that beauty is a perfection we apprehend through the senses. Though Kant protested because he thought that aesthetics should be defined in the "original and broader Greek sense of 'the science of the conditions of sensuous perception,'" Baumgarten's idea has dominated the subsequent history of the word. We associate aesthetics today chiefly with beauty, especially in its visual aspect, as apprehended by "subjective sense activity." Williams notes that with the triumph of this meaning, aesthetics reflects the modern tendency to empower the isolated subject; his responses determine art and beauty, "as distinct from *social* or *cultural* interpretations."[2]

More recently Terry Eagleton has offered a comprehensive critique of philosophical treatises on aesthetics from Baumgarten to Marx to postmodern thought.[3] Contrary to common usage, philosophers generally followed Kant: they considered aesthetics a form of knowledge that goes beyond the particularities of sensible experience but does not participate in the abstraction of rational deliberation. For Eagleton, however, the social always determines the epistemological, not only in subjective interpretations of beauty but even when beauty has been assigned a place in a seemingly objective ordering of knowledge.

---

1. Raymond Williams, *Keywords* (Fontana: Croom Helm, 1976).
2. Williams, *Keywords*, 27–28.
3. Terry Eagleton, *The Ideology of the Aesthetic* (Oxford: Blackwell, 1990).

Eagleton shows how in Kant, for example, despite appeals to classical Greece, the aesthetic actually presupposes bourgeois concepts of self and society, wherein an autonomous subject enters into communal relations by obeying laws it gives itself. Not until Marx does bodily sensation come to be truly valued; only with the appearance of *The Eighteenth Brumaire* could aesthetics begin to realize its potential as an emancipatory political force.

Both Williams and Eagleton rightly emphasize that the aesthetic is a historical formation. Yet for many readers it will seem ironic that the history each gives leaves out so much history. In both writers, we jump from a foundational moment, the Greek word "aisthesis," which meant sense perception, to the Enlightenment. Since Williams and Eagleton are concerned with the modern development of aesthetics, they are certainly justified to say that Baumgarten's use of the word was new and to begin their critiques with him. But long before the eighteenth century people responded in equally complex ways to the epistemological and cultural challenges of aesthetic experience. When Suger, rapt to a "strange region" by the exquisite adornments of St. Denis, found himself "transferring that which is material to that which is immaterial" [de materialibus ad immaterialia transferendo], he, no less than Baumgarten, was moved by a kind of knowing that coincides with neither the eyes nor the mind.

> then it seems to me that I see myself dwelling, as it were, in some strange region of the universe which neither exists entirely in the slime of the earth nor entirely in the purity of Heaven; and that, by the grace of God, I can be transported to that higher world in an anagogical manner [ad illam superiorem anagogico more].[4]

Similarly, when Aquinas says those things are beautiful that please when seen ("pulchra enim dicuntur quae visa placent"), his observer is neither autonomous nor bourgeois, yet he, as much as the subject in Kant, is someone whose empirical experience very much plays a part in constituting his status as a being in the world.

---

4. Suger of St. Denis, *De rebus in administratione sua gestis,* chap. 33, translated in Edwin Panofsky, *Abbot Suger on the Abbey Church of St.-Denis and Its Art Treasures* (Princeton: Princeton University Press, 1979), 63–65.

Beauty has to do with knowledge, for those things are beautiful which please us when they are seen. This is why beauty consists in due proportion, for the senses delight in rightly proportioned things as similar to themselves, the sense faculty being a sort of proportion itself like all other knowing faculties.[5]

In Suger, the compass that circumscribes the boundaries of the territory he envisions is the imagination; for Thomas analogies of proportion link the perceptible world to the realm of essences. In establishing a connection between well-formed objects and the pleasure with which we react to them, both the abbot and the theologian acknowledge the prerogatives of the physical sensation. At the same time, however, each takes care to remove delight from the domain of the sensual by making it a form of knowledge. These attempts to discipline beauty, Aquinas's by rationalizing it, Suger's by beatifying it, are in effect corroborations of its potential power as a social force. Without proper safeguards, dignifying a quality so rooted in the flesh by raising it almost to the level of ideas could seem an open invitation for the discourses of the earthly world to assert their own authority. As in the Enlightenment, the aesthetic consequently did its principal cultural work throughout the Middle Ages by offering a placatory ideology of political identity. Again and again we hear that the classes were united in the harmonious hierarchies of the three estates. Medieval clergy, however, comprehended the social dimensions of the beautiful in terms of the very language they used to discuss it, unlike Baumgarten or Kant, who predicated the communal on the autonomy of the individual. The danger Aquinas and Suger labor to foreclose is the possibility that they would hear the vernaculars speak truths hitherto heard only in Latin, that they would see love poetry sit down at the same table as metaphysics. For them, the peril of the beautiful was that it might create its own public.[6]

---

5. *Summa Theologiae*, I.5.4 ad 1, quoted in Umberto Eco, *The Aesthetics of Thomas Aquinas*, trans. Hugh Bredin (Cambridge, Mass: Harvard University Press, 1988), 56–57.

6. Certainly, as Robert Hollander says, Aquinas's review of figurative language in the Bible, and his consequent depreciation of poetry, stemmed in part from his dissatisfaction with previous theological discussions. And Hollander is right to point out how defensive contemporary "apologiae" of poetry were in the face of such opposition. But Mussato's claim that poetry was a second theology was a symptom of the age that preceded him as well a harbinger of humanism. His position would have made theologians anxious, I think (and I think Hollander would agree), at least from the time of Guinizzelli. See "Dante "Theologus Poeta,'" in *Studies in Dante* (Ravenna: Longo, 1980), 39–89.

How quickly this day was approaching we can see from the following "jeu d'esprit" Cino da Pistoia sent to Dante sometime before 1306.

Poi ch'i' fu', Dante, dal mio natal sito
fatto per greve essilio pellegrino
e lontanato dal piacer più fino
che mai formasse il Piacer infinito,
io son piangendo per lo mondo gito
sdegnato del morir come meschino;
e s'ho trovato a lui simil vicino,
dett'ho che questi m'ha lo cor ferito.
Né da le prime braccia dispietate,
onde 'l fermato disperar m'assolve,
son mosso perch'aiuto non aspetti;
ch'un piacer sempre me lega ed involve,
il qual conven che a simil di beltate
in molte donne sparte mi diletti.[7]

[Dante, ever since heavy exile has made me a stranger from my native city and separated me from the most exquisite beauty that Infinite Beauty ever made, I have gone weeping about the world, a poor wretch disdained by death; but when I have found near me a beautiful woman, I have said it was my beloved who wounded my heart, for *that* woman's beauty was the similitude of hers [literally, when I have found near me any beauty similar to *that* one, I have said that *this* one has wounded my heart]. Nor, though I expect no help, have I ever left those first pitiless arms, from which a well-grounded despair releases me: for it is always the selfsame beauty that binds and trammels me; it is this beauty that necessarily delights me in whatever is like it in beauty in many different women.]

---

7. I quote Cino's text from *Dante's Lyric Poetry*, ed. K. Foster and P. Boyde, 2 vols. (Oxford: Clarendon, 1967), no. 88a. On the dating of the poem, see 2:312. As Foster and Boyde note (2:62), "piacer" frequently denotes the objective beauty of a lady that causes joy. (See further n. 10.) Here and throughout I have followed the excellent translations in this edition. On occasion, I have slightly altered their versions, hoping to gain in literalness what I lose in tone and fluency.

Cino organizes this condensed encyclopedia of medieval ideas about beauty so that it can be read in two directions at once. By invoking "il Piacer infinito" he expects Dante to recall early scholastic arguments that beauty is a transcendental (that is, one of the metaphysical conditions, like unity and goodness, that accompany being);[8] by saying that this Beauty is the form of his lady's, even as hers is the essence of everyone else's, he also plays on Albertus Magnus's definition of it as a splendor of ordered form.[9] The sonnet derives its brio, however, from the turn Cino gives to Aquinas's contention that beauty is a property that is disclosed to a knowing subject. For Cino, this subject has a body fully ready to use the resources of reason to accommodate the contradictions of desire. On the one hand, his "Selvaggia's" cruelty has been so unrelenting, he has fallen out of love with her; since he no longer feels pain from her rebuffs, he turns his attention elsewhere. On the other, he maintains that it is her beauty that still and always will command his love. To prove that even when he loves another woman he remains faithful to the lady who is her form, Cino therefore enlists all the intellect's power to comprehend the analogies that join heaven and earth in beauty. This is an argument that does not strive to persuade us it is true, only that it is witty. Metaphysics doffs its transcendental cap to a carnally minded rhetoric. By the poem's end, "piacer" has grounded beauty in its sensible Provençal roots, which entirely dominate its abstract counterparts and the faculties that discern them.[10]

At the same time, however, the sonnet also traces an ascent through the hierarchies of being. It opens with the fact of exile; before Cino establishes the analogy between his removal from his "natal sito" and the distance that separates all souls from God, he anchors it in personal grief and the fallen politics of the City of Man. For Dante, this association would seem both bitter and ironic, since the city in which the banished Cino had taken refuge was the Florence that had driven him out. By the time Cino is through making his inconstancy a paean to his

8. On beauty as a transcendental, see Eco, *The Aesthetics of Thomas Aquinas,* 20–48; see also H. Pouillon, "La beauté, proprieté transcendentale chez les scolastiques (1220–1270)," *Archives d'histoire doctrinale et littéraire du moyen âge* 15 (1946): 263–327.

9. On Albertus's *De Pulchro et Bono,* see Eco, *The Aesthetics of Thomas Aquinas,* 44–46.

10. "Piacer" is related to Provençal "plazer," which carried definite overtones of physical beauty. See Michele Barbi, "Con Dante e coi suoi interpreti: II: Francesca da Rimini," *Studi danteschi* 15 (1932): 10–11.

steadfastness, however, exile has been so associated with idealized perceptions of beauty that it no longer designates an experiential reality so much as it has become a floating metaphor for the disappointed lover's alienation from himself (an alienation echoed by Selvaggia's loss of gender, folded as she is into an inclusive masculine "piacer"), for the more permanent estrangement of death, or for the vagrancy of a mind remote enough from its proper operations to occupy itself by spinning out clever sophistries.

In Cino's poem, as in the "stil novo" generally, the aesthetic negotiation between the epistemological ideal and the material culture that the senses not only admit but speak for is weighted in favor of the mind; time and place have little bulk in the *Vita nuova*. Of course I do not mean to imply that the emergence of the "stil novo" is unrelated to the rise and fall of Guelf and Ghibelline fortunes and the shifting constellations of communal power in "duecento" Bologna and Florence; the elevation of the "donna angelica" to the metaphysical sublime and the certainty of "the one and the other Guido" that love and the noble heart are the same thing are expressions of social ideology as much as poetic conviction.[11] Nevertheless, these texts are unremittingly self-reflexive: like Suger's and Aquinas's speculations on beauty, they tend to mask their historicity by equating the strategies of representation they foreground with the ageless operations of the intellect.[12] This is the perspective from which they ask to be read; for the most part it is the perspective I adopt in this book. Even though history will mean literary history in these pages, however, my approach to Dante still owes more

---

11. See, for instance, the important article by Susan Noakes, "Hermeneutics, Politics, and Civic Ideology in the *Vita Nuova:* Thoughts Preliminary to an Interpretation," *Texas Studies in Language and Literature* 32 (1990): 40–59.

12. As Contini says, although "the experience of love is minutely analyzed and its elements subsequently hypostasized, this analysis does not proceed with reference to the empirical individual but goes beyond his initiating adventure to man considered as a universal . . . the entire experience of the stilnovist is depersonalized, transferred to a universal order" [è il fatto amoroso minuziosamente analizzato e poi ipostatizzato nei suoi elementi, quest'analisi non va già referita all'individuo empirico, ma di là da questa sua avventura iniziale, a un esemplare universale di uomo . . . l'intera esperienza dello stilnovista è spersonalizzata, si transferisce in un ordine universale]. *Poeti del duecento,* ed. Gianfranco Contini (Milan, Naples: Riccardo Riccardi, 1960), 2:443. However, the work of John Ahern does situate even early texts like the *Vita nuova* firmly in late thirteenth-century Florence and is an important counterbalance. See "The Reader on the Piazza: Verbal Duel in Dante's *Vita Nuova,*" *Texas Studies in Language and Literature* 32 (1990): 18–39; "The New Life of the Book: The Implied Reader of the *Vita Nuova,*" *Dante Studies* 110 (1992): 1–16.

to the social critics I have mentioned than to intellectual historians like Croce who deny that the aesthetic existed as a meaningful category of thought in the Middle Ages.[13] It is of course true that there are no sustained medieval treatises that discuss the essence of the beautiful and how we apprehend it. Bernard's hostility to church ornament was well known and sanctioned by long-standing tradition. Even Suger's effusions, exceptional in themselves, occupy only half of *De rebus in administratione sua gestis*, which is a general account of what he did as abbot of St. Denis. But De Bruyne, Glunz, Balthasar, Eco, and many others have shown that thinkers did concern themselves with aesthetic matters in the Middle Ages—indeed, perhaps never more than then. Whether people contemplated the order of the heavens or the constitution of their own bodies, whether they delighted in the harmonious concordances of music and color or rejoiced in the splendor of form that made all creation beautiful, they considered not only the nature of the pleasure they felt but how that pleasure was related to the God who was its source and cause.[14] Beauty was everywhere; within its precincts one considered not only form and proportion but questions of love, perfection of the self, identity, and being. Aesthetics was thus the domain where all these issues could converge. Indeed, in the last years of the thirteenth century, Dante and the other practitioners of the "dolce stil novo" seem to me nothing less than theorists of the aesthetic. By emphasizing the marriage of matter and spirit, they appropriated subjects and discourses that schoolmasters had previously reserved to themselves. In light of such poetic activity, the absence of philosophical tracts that explicitly treat beauty and its pleasures seems less an indication of a want of interest than evidence of the same anxiety Aquinas

---

13. Benedetto Croce, *Aesthetic*, trans. Douglas Ainslie (New York: Noonday Press, 1955).

14. Among the many studies of medieval aesthetics I have consulted and learned from, the most helpful have been the following: Hans Urs von Balthasar, *The Glory of the Lord: A Theological Aesthetics*, 3 vols., ed. Joseph Fessio and John Riches (San Francisco: Ignatius Press, 1982); Eco, *The Aesthetics of Thomas Aquinas*; see also his *Art and Beauty in the Middle Ages*, trans. Hugh Bredin (New Haven: Yale University Press, 1986); Hans H. Glunz, *Die Litterarästhetik des europäischen Mittelalters*, (Frankfurt: Klostermann, 1963); Geraldus van der Leeuw, *Sacred and Profane Beauty: The Holy in Art*, trans. David Green (Nashville: Abingdon Press, 1963); George Santayana, *The Sense of Beauty: Being the Outline of Aesthetic Theory* (New York: Dover, 1955); E. J. M. Spargo, *The Category of the Aesthetic in the Philosophy of St. Bonaventure*, Philosophy Series 11 (New York: Franciscan Institute of St. Bonaventure, 1953). For a good review of medieval aesthetic ideas in Dante, see J. F. Took, *"L'etterno piacer": Aesthetic Ideas in Dante* (Oxford: Clarendon, 1984).

addressed when he derogated the value of poetry. Because the aesthetic could generate a psychology and a physics, an epistemology and an ethics of its own, it had to be a continuing preoccupation for metaphysicians of the church. Once beauty had been admitted among the attributes of God, poets not only could claim an access of vision until then reserved for mystic contemplatives, they could say, against the theologians, that their poems, by making sensible and intellective love analogies of one another and of the Spirit that is Love, were the most appropriate medium to represent the human experience of the incarnate divine.

A number of Dantists, Giuseppe Mazzotta preeminent among them, have argued that Dante in fact makes this claim in the *Comedy*.[15] He lived in the century when beauty's status as a transcendental was vigorously debated; as a young man he became the most famous practitioner of a style of poetry that described a state of being, brought about by love, in a language that incorporated the sentiment of Provençal, Sicilian, and Tuscan poets, the precision of an Aristotelian philosophy of intellection, and the pneumatology that the Middle Ages inherited from the Stoics. As a stilnovist, Dante was aware from the start of his career that, far from being peripheral, the aesthetic was the venue in which he could best express the "amoroso usa di sapienza"[the amorous exercise of wisdom], as he would call the project of the *Convivio* (4.2.18).

In his early writings, Dante, like Cino, was chiefly concerned with the aesthetic as an epistemology. In chapter 2, "Medieval Aesthetics: The Analogies of the *Vita nuova*," I propose that Dante's first major work is an extended meditation on the conditions that enable his poetry to represent adequately the sensible perception of universal beatitude. By coordinating his deepening apprehension of Beatrice with his discovery of different ways to write about her, the *Vita nuova* inaugurated Dante's lifelong attempt to justify the truth of aesthetic discourse by representing it as the language of the mind in love.

For Dante, that language was necessarily a language of analogy. Like Cavalcanti before him, Dante locates love in the sensitive soul. Unlike

---

15. Giuseppe Mazzotta, *Dante's Vision and the Circle of Knowledge* (Princeton: Princeton University Press, 1993). See especially his concluding chapter, "Theologia Ludens," 219–41. See as well "Why Did Dante Write the *Comedy*? Why and How Do We Read It? The Poet and the Critics," in *Dante Now: Current Trends in Dante Studies*, ed. Theodore Cachey (Notre Dame: University of Notre Dame Press, 1995), 63–79.

Cavalcanti, however, Dante insists that because the operations of that soul are proportionate with those of the intellect, the writing that expresses love fully can capture what is ideal in the experience analogously; because intellection, as we shall see, ends in the production of language, its procedures will underwrite Dante's contention that the prose and poems of the *Vita nuova* reflect Beatrice's perfections. Indeed, Dante makes the very relationship that affiliates the activities of the sensible and intellectual souls an analogue of Beatrice, who is both a living woman and the essence of beatitude. She is, in fact, a miracle—a being whose effects only the full articulation of the rational soul can adequately describe, yet whose essence transcends the capacity even of the intellect to comprehend. Dante therefore constructs the *Vita nuova* about a hierarchy of proportioned knowledges, each of which has its own mode of expression: as the sensitive soul, with its poetry of the natural spirit and the imagination, stands to the rational, so the rational soul and its articulation in the "stilo de la loda" stand to Beatrice's nature. Each kind of knowledge and mode of expression participates in the higher order by analogy, and analogy itself becomes for Dante the mark of the aesthetic's coordination of the sensible and the metaphysical.

Analogy, of course, had served precisely this function in medieval physics, epistemology, ethics, metaphysics, and theology.[16] In the *Timaeus*, Plato established the unity of the cosmos, its "spirit of friendship" (*Tim.* 32c), by postulating a double analogy in which the terms are at once relational and qualitative: as fire is to air, so air is to water; as air is to water, so water is to earth (31b).[17] Analogy here is both interstice and framework: it is the bond that correlates the elements of the

---

16. In the following brief discussion of analogy in the Middle Ages I have relied chiefly on the following works: David Burrell, *Analogy and Philosophical Language* (New Haven: Yale University Press, 1973); Wilfried Fiedler, *Analogiemodelle bei Aristoteles*, Studien zur antiken Philosophie 9 (Amsterdam: B. R. Gruner, 1978); Bernard Landry, *La Notion d'Analogie chez saint Bonaventure et chez saint Thomas d'Aquin* (Paris: Loinvain, 1922); Hampus Lyttkens, *The Analogy between God and the World* (Uppsala: Almqvist and Wiksells, 1952); G. E. L. Owen, "Logic and Metaphysics in Some Early Works of Aristotle," in *Aristotle and Plato in Mid-Fourth Century* (Gotenburg: Symposium Aristotelicum, 1960), 163–90. For a suggestive essay on Dante and analogy, see Maria Corti, "Il modello analogico nel pensiero medievale e dantesco," in *Dante e le forme dell'allegoresi*, ed. Michelangelo Picone (Ravenna: Longo, 1987), 7–20.

17. For the *Timaeus* I quote from the Loeb Library edition of *Plato opera* VII, ed. R. G. Bury (Cambridge, Mass: Harvard University Press, 1941). I have also consulted Francis Cornford, *Plato's Cosmology* (London: Routledge and Kegan Paul, 1952).

universe, and it is the structure of their harmony. Centuries later Alan of Lille would write: "the whole of creation is like a book and picture for us, and a mirror as well."[18] His similes seek to show that everything on earth reveals the hand of its craftsman; whatever exists owes its coherence, however, to an analogy of attribution that ultimately goes back to these passages in Plato. Either directly through Chalcidius's translation of the *Timaeus* or indirectly through commentaries on its Neoplatonic elaborations, medieval theologians learned that they could specify the ways in which God was connected to the cosmos he created without sacrificing the essential differences between them by assigning to many things the name that designated the primary being they all shared in one way or another.

In the *Republic*, Plato had also made epistemology analogous. In the allegory of the line, the sensible world and the world of ideas, as well as being and becoming and knowledge and perception, are first distinguished from one another by the unequal division of a line but then affiliated to each other by subdividing each portion of the line by the same proportion as the first division. The four hierarchies of being (images, visible things, mathematics, and ideas) and the corresponding hierarchies of knowledge (imagination, belief, thinking, and intelligence) are thus related by analogy—in this case not because they share reality in common but because the degree of reality they possess is comparable. These notions will again pass to medieval Europe through the Neoplatonists and through a passage in the *Timaeus* (290) that prefaces the "likely story" of the creation;[19] the relation between Dante's "book of memory" and the *Vita nuova* is in part defined by them. Like most thinkers in the age of scholasticism, however, Dante learned of Plato's ideas primarily in the form of Aristotle's critique of them.

If Plato made analogy central to his account of the relations of the one to the many, Aristotle's definition of first principles explored the

---

18. "Omnis mundi creatura / Quasi liber et pictura / Nobis est et speculum," *Rhythmus alter*, PL 210.579.

19. The passage from the *Timaeus* (290) reads as follows.

Accordingly, in dealing with a copy and its model, we must affirm that the accounts given will themselves be akin to the objects which they serve to explain; those which deal with what is abiding and firm and discernable by the aid of thought will be abiding and unshakeable . . . whereas the accounts of that which is copied after the likeness of that Model, and is itself a likeness, will be analogous thereto and possess likelihood; for as Being is to Becoming, so is Truth to Belief.

ways in which the many are related to the one. Because causes, if they are truly first, must be present in every category, Aristotle contends that "the principles of different things are all in a sense different, but in a sense, if one speaks universally and analogically, they are the same for all" (*Met.* 1070a31). That is to say, though "specifically different things have specifically different elements," they all share three metaphysical principles: form, privation, and matter. But these differ in each species of thing: in color, for instance, white is form, black is privation, and surface is the matter, but in day, the triad consists of light, darkness, and air respectively. As principles, therefore, form, privation, and matter can be the same only analogically (*Met.* 1070b17–21). So too the four causes and actuality and potentiality are analogously common to all things, but again, they "are not only different for different things, but apply in different ways to them" (*Met.* 1071a5).

At its heart, the issue Aristotle addresses here is semantic: in order to save terms like "being," "one," or "actual" from utter equivocality, since they mean different things in different cases, Aristotle would deduce a subset of uses that points to one primary signification. But then, in the face of such differentiation, how does one determine which sense is primary? Plato had said by participation, the affinity of the object of knowing with the knowing subject; for Aristotle, however, this was a metaphorical maneuver that sidesteps the problem. Instead he argued that a word can have many senses that point in many ways to a central sense, but the scope and power of this insight can only be understood by use and not by definition.[20]

For Aristotle, the virtue of analogy was precisely its capacity to mediate between supervenient principle and practical experience. Use and practice are fundamental both to ethics and to art, yet both also transcend a local here and now. This is why Aristotle argues in the *Nicomachean Ethics* that virtues are not forms of prudence, as Socrates held—not because knowledge is unnecessary but because all virtue is realized in practice. Virtue consequently has its being in a habitual disposition that conforms to a rational principle. In ethics this principle is the mean between excess and defect, determined both in relation to the object and relative to us. The constitution of social interactions, which grow out of personal relations, is also governed by analogy; in friendship, the bond that joins equals is numerical, whereas the bond that

---

20. This is the conclusion of Owen, "Logic and Metaphysics," 189.

joins superior and subordinate in amity is proportional; similarly, if two people of the same station come before a judge, justice requires that he restore amounts according to an arithmetic mean; when there is a difference in rank, equality is preserved if restitution is made in proportion to the standing of each person.

As a kind of virtue, art is comprehended by analogy as well. In its mode of existence, art is a disposition acquired by habit; in its mode of operation, however, it is an efficient cause of coming to be. Art is empirical, arising from a knowledge of particulars, but it is also principled and resembles nature, inasmuch as each brings things into being in accord with a purpose. No art fully exists until "a single universal judgment is formed with regard to like objects" (*Met.* 981a24–b7). So much does Aristotle insist on this dimension of universality that he would base his analysis of change in the physical world on the analogy of the artisan and his work (*Phy.* 193a32–36; 194a21). In the world, however, as in art, universality can be understood only analogously.[21]

From Aristotle, therefore, the Middle Ages could discover how analogy constitutes the most comprehensive category to express the correlations among objects that cannot be directly compared or qualities of things that language has no name for (cf. *Post. An.* 2.98a20). Analogy could also discover likenesses of different genera, expressed as a similarity of relations or, by extension, as a likeness of properties; it could serve as well as a link that joined different categories, demonstrating that various properties exist in different subjects in like ways, without designating exactly what constitutes the similitude.

Throughout Christian Europe these modes of thought continued to be employed, especially in Dante's time, which it is not an exaggeration to call an age of analogy. God and transcendentals like beauty were continually spoken of "per analogiam," even though this sort of speech constantly ran the risk of lapsing into metaphor. Indeed, in the *Topics* (140a6; 158b10), Aristotle, again troubled by terms like "being," had looked to metaphor as a way of establishing some concepts as less equivocal than others. Only later did he see that analogy was a better

---

21. For a reading that resolves the contradictions between the *Convivio* and *Monarchia* very much in accord with these ratios, see Albert Ascoli, "Palinode and History in the Oeuvre of Dante," in *Dante Now: Current Trends in Dante Studies*, ed. Theodore Cachey (Notre Dame: University of Notre Dame Press, 1995), 155–86. Since rhetoric is an art as well, I think Dante would endorse what Ascoli calls here (and in his other essays) a rhetorical reading of him.

instrument than metaphor for identifying an element of univocality in variety. This modification had important consequences in the scholastic reexamination of figurative speech in Scripture; it is implicit in Aquinas's demotion of poetry. But the poet for whom love was an experience of body, mind, and spirit might not think embracing an Aristotelian sense of analogy automatically degraded the value, cognitive or otherwise, of a language of the aesthetic imagination. To the contrary, he might well say that it in fact sponsored the worthiness of such a language, for all discourses and knowledges would participate in the beauty it encompassed.

For Dante, this language was the "dolce stil novo."[22] He was not alone in seeing this new style as one in which analogy enabled the aesthetic to appropriate the liberal arts, moral philosophy, and theology. When, for instance, Bonagiunta of Lucca attacked Guido Guinizzelli, the "father" (*Purg.* 26:97) of the rhymes that had "changed the manner of elegant poems of love from the form of being they once had" [Voi, ch'avete mutata la mainera / de li plagenti ditti de l'amore / de la forma dell'esser là dov'era], his critique rested on two objections. The first was ethical; Bonagiunta charges Guinizzelli with unmerited self-aggrandizement. The second, though, was epistemological: he taxes Guido for making audacious incursions into learning unsuited to poetry: "è tenuta gran dissimigliansa, / ancor che 'l senno vegna da Bologna, / traier canson per forsa di scrittura." The most recent English

---

22. In his introductory essay to his edition of the *Vita nuova*, Francesco Mazzoni anticipates many of the arguments I make here and in the course of my next chapter when he relates Dante's development to the scholastic idea of "analogia entis."

. . . che proponeva all'uomo la presa di coscienza degli attributi di Dio creatore muovendo dalla attenta analisi delle perfezioni e della bellezza delle creature, di ogni causa seconda e mortale: la quale, in quanto "effetto," partecipa necessariamente d'una certa somiglianza con la sua "causa prima."

[which provided for human knowledge of the attributes of God the creator by proceeding from the careful analysis of the perfections and beauty of created things, of every secondary and mortal cause, which, as effect, necessarily shares a certain similarity with its primal cause.]

Mazzoni goes on to say that when analogy operates as a mode of epistemology, it permits us to grasp an object's form, which is what makes it similar to God; as a mode of metaphysical knowing, it is what enables us to know God through the transcendentals, such as unity, truth, goodness, and beauty, that are predicated of him. (*Vita nuova*, ed. Francesco Mazzoni [Tallone: Alpignano, 1965], xxii.)

translation, by Robert Edwards, renders these lines as follows: "It's thought a curious thing, though learning comes from Bologna, to drag song by force out of writing."[23] This nicely captures Bonagiunta's tone, but the paraphrases miss the directness of his barbs. Poems like "Al cor gentil rempaira sempre amore" did change the nature of poetry ("la forma dell'esser," as Bonagiunta slyly phrases it) not merely because they rummaged about in the conceptual closets of scholasticism but because they used analogy the way philosophers had, to make claims for the universal beauty of their lady. In the fifth stanza of "Al cor gentil," to cite an instance that had to have provoked Bonagiunta, Guinizzelli develops a comparison between the instantaneous metaphysics of angelic knowledge of God and the immediate conception in the lover of a desire to obey his lady as soon as he sees her. God himself cites the impropriety of this and Guido's other analogies; he tells the poet, "You passed beyond the heavens and came in the end to Me, and tried to compare Me to an empty love" [Lo ciel passasti e 'nfin a Me venisti / e desti in vano amor Me per semblanti]. Guinizzelli's God, however, seems decidedly more bemused than Bonagiunta by Guido's "dissimigliansa," which, expanding Contini's gloss of the term, we might paraphrase as the strangeness that results from making disproportionate things proportionate.[24] Guinizzelli ends his "canzone" by defending his analogy before God; his answer is an equally effective response to his detractor from Lucca: "she had the likeness of an angel of Your realm; I'm not to blame if I fell in love with her" [Tenne d'angel sembianza / che fosse del Tuo regno; / non me fu fallo, s'in lei posi amanza]. The daring way Guido expanded the beauty of "la bella donna" was exactly what made the "nove rime" new for Dante.

Underlying Bonagiunta's animadversions is his adherence to rhetorical precepts of convenience and the "genera dicendi," precepts which critics of Dante's poetics such as Barański have shown Dante entirely rethinks and revises throughout his career.[25] From the *Vita nuova* on,

---

23. *The Poetry of Guido Guinizelli,* ed. and trans. Robert Edwards (New York: Garland, 1987).

24. *Poeti del Duecento,* Contini, 2:481.

25. Among many essays, the following are especially noteworthy: Zygmunt Barański, "The Poetics of Meter," in *Dante Now: Current Trends in Dante Studies,* ed. Theodore Cachey (Notre Dame: University of Notre Dame Press, 1995), 3–41; "'Significar *per verba*': Notes on Dante and Plurilingualism," *Italianist* 6 (1986): 5–18; "Dante's Biblical Linguistics," *Lectura dantis* 5 (1989): 105–43; "Dante's (Anti-)Rhetoric: Notes on the Poetics of the *Commedia,*" in *Moving in Measure: Essays in Honour of Brian Moloney,* ed. Judith Bryce and Doug Thompson (Hull: Hull University Press, 1989), 1–14; "Allegoria, storia e letteratura

Dante made the art of composition an explicit subject in his works;[26] in contrast to most medieval literary theory, however, he never limited his conception of poetry to merely an activity of the practical intellect. In addition to mastery of forms and technique, Dante always sought to invest his poetic vernacular with a universality comparable to that of Latin. In the *De vulgari eloquentia*, he forges that universality by joining together the various dialects of Italy. The harmonious unity of such a discourse endows it with nobility and beauty; the very principle that makes Dante's Italian eloquent is both analogous and aesthetic. Conjugated in accordance with the grammar of Aristotle's hylomorphism (the importance of whose emphasis on the embodied existence of form cannot be overstressed), the analogies of the aesthetic constitute Dante's poetics as an art; in the *Vita nuova* they enabled him to combine the proportions that relate matter and intellect, intellect and spirit, in a vision of beauty.

When Dante came to write the *Divine Comedy*, however, he radically expanded the purchase and scope of aesthetics. In the twenty-fourth canto of the *Purgatorio*, Dante revisited the "stil novo" of the *Vita nuova* and significantly revised it. In the company of Forese Donati, with whom he had exchanged a series of vituperative sonnets, Dante meets the same Bonagiunta who had attacked Guinizzelli. The poet from Lucca asks if he sees before him the man who brought forth the "new rhymes, beginning with *Donne ch'avete intelletto d'amore.*" Dante responds by defining himself as much as a human being as a poet: "I' mi son un che, quando / Amor mi spira, noto, e a quel modo / ch'e' ditta dentro vo significando" [I am one who, when Love inspires me, takes note, and in the manner he dictates within goes signifying]. Perhaps the main argument of this book is that with this declaration, analogies become elements of identity; "like" is translated into "is." In the *Vita nuova*, the aesthetic offered a form of knowledge between sensation and intellection that made Dante and the poetry he copies from the book of his memory similar to Beatrice. In the *Purgatorio*, however,

---

nella *Commedia*," in *Dante e le forme dell'allegoresi,* ed. Michelangelo Picone (Ravenna: Longo, 1987), 79–97; see also Lino Pertile, "Canto—Cantica—Comedia e l'epistole a Cangrande," *Lectura Dantis* 9 (1991): 105–23. On Dante and the "genera dicendi," see Amilcare Iannucci, "Dante's Theory of Genres in the *Divina Commedia*," *Dante Studies* 91 (1973): 1–25.

26. As Contini says, "una costante della personalità dantesca è questa perpetuo sopraggiungere della reflessione tecnica accanto alla poesia," *Un'idea di Dante* (Turin: Einaudi, 1970), 4.

the aesthetic becomes a form of existence. In place of the ratios that made the various stages by which Dante knew Beatrice like her, Dante now asserts that his life is intelligible as an analogy: he is man and poet insofar as he moves signifying through the world in embodied proportion to the inner articulations of Love's promptings. The aesthetic has been transformed into the style of God's writing in heaven and on earth; it has become nothing less than a discourse of being.

In chapter 3, "From the *Vita nuova* to the *Comedy*," I examine the nature of this transformation both from the standpoint of style and in terms of the existential claims Dante makes for his new "modo di dire." When Cino or any stilnovist read the *Purgatorio*, he would have immediately understood why Dante reconfigured himself as poet in response to a question from someone like Bonagiunta. Even though in his own poetry Bonagiunta was no less concerned than Dante with the relation of nature, art, and love, as follower of Giacomo da Lentini and Guittone d'Arezzo, he was, as we have seen, no friend of the "new style."[27] That Dante would make such a man suddenly grasp the pith and marrow of the "stil novo" from what he says is therefore dramatically apt; what, however, Cino and others like him may indeed have found surprising is the fact that Dante's answer is not in that style.

In Purgatory, old forms of social relations and the love that reconstitutes them coexist in the same act. To comprehend such a place quite literally requires a new sort of aesthetic understanding, one that can accommodate proportions like those that prompt the fasting souls of gluttons simultaneously to weep and sing "Domine labia mea aperies" [O Lord, open my lips], a line from the Miserere whose irony serves not to negate but to reinforce the penitents' fervor. To depict ratios such as these requires a comparable form of writing, one whose elements are the letters of existence, like the "M" of mankind that Dante reads in the shape of Forese's eye sockets. Dante's definition of poetic selfhood is his explanation of the formal constitution of this new aesthetic discourse, which leaps beyond the "stil novo's" operations of spirit and phantasm to capture and reform in the same moment the antagonisms that separated men and women from themselves, from one another, and from God. Dante constructs the style of this unheard of manner of expression by interweaving reminiscences both from Bonagiunta's quarrel with Guinizzelli and from his "tenzone" with Donati through-

---

27. See Maria Simonelli, "Bonagiunta Orbicciani e la problematica dello stil nuovo (*Purg.* XXIV) 65–86," *Dante Studies* 86 (1968): 65–84.

out their colloquy. By knitting these voices into unexpected intertextual harmonies, Dante signals that the same breath of Love that informs him reforms literary history as well. As he goes signifying, Dante enunciates a style that does not belong to a particular kind of poetry but to its essence, a poetry that draws its beauty from the aesthetics of being in the afterlife.

In the following chapters I extend this argument to heaven and hell. In chapter 4, "The Aesthetics of Eternity: Forese, Cacciaguida, and the Style of Fatherhood," my thesis is that Dante's interactions on the sixth terrace of the *Purgatorio* become a key point of reference in his overall exemplification of the state of souls after death. I therefore seek to demonstrate that Forese and Bonagiunta occupy middle ground in that extraordinary process of transmutation that has as its extremes the damned in hell, who are matter without animating form, and the redeemed in heaven, who are pure form awaiting the regenerated body of the Resurrection. Thus when Dante meets his spiritual father, Cacciaguida, in Paradise, the quarrel with Forese serves as a backdrop that enables us to discern the stylistic unity of blessedness. This unity does more than reconcile the differences that set stilnovists apart from the "Guittoniani," as in the *Purgatorio*; it bridges the historical and cultural divide that separates Latin from all the vernacular languages descended from it. Donati was not the only poet who heard Dante's manifesto on the terrace of the gluttons; Virgil and Statius witnessed it as well. Just prior to Dante's encounter with Bonagiunta, Statius recounts how he had engaged in a "tenzone" of his own with Virgil when he turned Polydorus's curse against "auri sacra fames" into an exhortation to convert to Christianity. When Cacciaguida greets Dante, he also speaks Virgil's Latin.

O sanguis meus, o superinfusa
gratïa Deï, sicut tibi cui
bis unquam celi ianüa reclusa.

(*Par.* 15.25–27)

[O my blood, o grace of God infused from above and beyond measure! To whom as to you was ever the gate of heaven opened twice?]

In Paradise, however, love marries the stately rhetoric of the *Aeneid* to the vocabulary of Christian theology and enseams both into the pattern of Italian "terza rima." The transformation is so complete that Cacciaguida's "O sanguis meus" seems the original statement and Anchises's welcoming words to Aeneas in Virgil's underworld its echo. Dante establishes Cacciaguida's Latin as the source of that "bello stilo" that he says he drew from Virgil and that has done him honor. In the heaven of Mars Dante's ancestor speaks a language in which father and mother tongue speak at once; in Cacciaguida's words Dante asks the reader to hear the peace that is the Word, of which the broken harmony and cracked image are the history of poetic faction on earth.

Long before Dante composed his encounter with his great-great-great grandfather, however, he had staged another "tenzone" in the seventh "bolgia" of the *Inferno*. His ostensible rival was Ovid; after claiming the Roman poet cannot offer anything to match the metamorphoses of the thieves he has described, Dante in fact explicitly silences him. But Dante's real opponent, I contend in chapter 5, "Ovid, the Transformation of Metamorphosis, and the Aesthetics of Hell," was not Naso himself so much as the allegorized versions of him that were common in the Middle Ages. Such interpretations lent to changes of form that were entirely superficial an inner depth Dante felt they could not sustain. He therefore linked Forese's cantos and Statius's disquisition on the generation of the aerial body of the soul in 25 *Purgatorio* both to the specific transformations in cantos 24 and 25 of the *Inferno* and to the comprehensive metamorphosis it epitomizes, the loss of being that unforms all the damned. By articulating the proportions that make these metamorphoses of unbecoming parodies of particular and general justice, Dante shows why Ovid's style was too thin to hide truly substantive transformations like the Incarnation or Eucharist within its folds.

The most striking alteration of Ovid in the *Inferno*, however, was not Dante's rejection of the commentary tradition on him, even though that tradition included the *Convivio*. Dante's greatest revision was to make Ovid the titular forebear of his own unredeemed poetry, even as he made Virgil the spiritual father of his poetry of salvation. Dante does this by linking both his altercation with Forese and perhaps the last "canzone" he wrote, "Amor da che convien pur ch'io doglia," to the transformations of the thieves. By placing both the "stil novo" and the "tenzone" under the sign of metamorphosis, Dante suggests that whenever contentious sonnets or amorous songs present themselves as the reified objects of their own narcissism, they are Ovid's offspring. For the "stil novo" and the "tenzone" to transform a life, they must become Virgil's stepchildren. Only when they take on the substance of history and the polysemy of revelation do they become the poetry that expresses Dante's aesthetics of being.

2

Medieval Aesthetics:
The Analogies of the *Vita nuova*

The *Vita nuova* is a book of analogies: in it Dante conscripts precepts from the literature, philosophy, and culture of the late thirteenth century and organizes them into ratios that establish likenesses and preserve differences between the poet, his book, and the woman whose life and death made both new. In the first three sections of this chapter I discuss the idea and structure of memory and experience, of translation, of sensory and intellective knowing, of faculty psychology and pneumatology; my purpose is to show how Dante made each a contextual element of the aesthetics of the *Vita nuova*. I then turn to the formal analogies that Dante forged between the various kinds of poetry he writes about Beatrice and his developing perception of her significance. The remainder of the chapter, in other words, is devoted to the proportions that give Dante's "libello" its internal integrity, clarity, and beauty.

I

Perhaps the cardinal fact about Dante's *Vita nuova*, certainly the first thing we learn about it, is its constitution as a book.

> In quella parte del libro de la mia memoria dinanzi a la quale poco si potrebbe leggere, si trova una rubrica la quale dice: *Incipit vita nuova*. Sotto la quale rubrica io trovo scritte le parole le quali è mio intendimento d'assemplare in questo libello; e se non tutte, almeno la loro sentenzia.[1]

---

1. I quote from Dante Alighieri, *Vita nuova*, ed. Domenico de Robertis (Milan and Naples: Riccardo Ricciardi, 1980).

[In that part of the book of my memory before which little can be read, there is a rubric that says "Incipit vita nuova." Under this rubric I find written the words that I intend to copy into this little book, and if not all of them, then at least their meaning.]

Various critics, most notably Singleton and de Robertis, have called attention to the implications of this alignment of remembrance and literature as texts.[2] By stressing the finished quality of the events, Singleton underlines what one might call the theological dialectics of Christian autobiography. Since what has happened to Dante already is inscribed in his memory, his life is made subject to retrospective interpretation even as the narrative unfolds the incidents that comprise it in chronological sequence. As past and present, occurrence and understanding, are juxtaposed, actual disjunctions in time and perception take on the appearance of simultaneity and suggest a unity that then is translated into human terms; Dante the protagonist who experiences verges toward Dante the narrator who knows. A number of analogies are created in the process: just as memory resolves the differences between "was" and "is," so the book copied from it reconciles the several subjectivities—Dante the participant, the narrator, and the glossator—which those differences produced. The *Vita nuova* is, in this sense, Dante's book of genesis, wherein his words create the world of his personal and authorial identity.

For de Robertis, the idea of the book expresses itself more as the facticity of the *Vita nuova*. In the dialogue between prose and poetry Dante re-creates his life as the chronicle of his poetic development through interactions with the literature of his own and past ages. Poems that Dante had written for earlier occasions or to different women are now repositioned by means of a prose commentary so that they become chapters in the new book of his love for Beatrice. To a large extent, the subject of the *Vita nuova* for de Robertis is not "Dante-personaggio" but the intertextuality of the book he has written. For him, the miracle that is Beatrice is precisely the history of the poetry Dante writes in praise of her.

Each of these readings in fact points to the need for the other.[3]

---

2. Charles Singleton, *An Essay on the Vita Nuova* (1949; reprint, Baltimore: Johns Hopkins, 1977). Domenico de Robertis, *Il libro della Vita Nuova* (Florence: Sansoni, 1961).

3. For a perceptive critique of the shortcomings of both critics, who can stand as representatives of Italian and American modes of approaching Dante, see Robert Harrison,

Dante specifically authorizes the intertextual construction of both the formal unity of the *Vita nuova* and his own identity by the relationship he draws between the "libello" he has written and the "book of his memory" he has copied it from. The nature of this relationship, however, is hard to specify precisely. For one thing, while both remembrance and the literary work are, as we shall see, textual systems, the elements that constitute the textuality of each exhibit tendencies that seem to move in opposite directions. The memory image, for instance, in one respect was understood to be simply a duplication, unmotivated in itself, of some sensible event, just as the words of the *Vita nuova* to some degree simply mirror its events. But image and word were also held to be representations; both actively gave their material a shape in accordance with definite intentions. In fact, I will argue that one way memory and the *Vita nuova* are alike is that each comprehends its unity through a similar back-and-forth movement between mere iteration and dynamic reconfiguration. They are related, in other words, because they make meaning analogously, which is one way Dante indicates that the final provenance of his book is aesthetics.

The analogy between memory and a book, as Curtius has shown, was long-standing even in Dante's day;[4] Mary Carruthers has revealed the ideas that underwrote the association.[5] One of the inner senses, memory was not thought to be just a warehouse where information was stored; memory rather coordinated and arranged past impressions, such that any one could be tracked down by another thing associated with it. As an act of recollection, memory was therefore a heuristic process; "only those impressions," in Carruthers's words, "that have been ordered so that they are *readable* have truly entered the memory."[6] For this reason, rote repetition fell outside the scope of true memory, at

The Body of Beatrice (Baltimore: Johns Hopkins, 1988), 1–13. For a concise and very good description of the various ways the *Vita nuova* has been read, from spiritual or intellectual autobiography to mystical, hagiographical, and metaphysical approaches, see Michelangelo Picone, "La *Vita nuova* fra autobiografia e tipologia," in *Dante e le forme dell'allegoresi,* ed. Michelangelo Picone (Ravenna: Longo, 1987), 59–69.

4. See Ernst Robert Curtius, *European Literature and the Latin Middle Ages,* trans. W. Trask (1953; reprint, New York: Harper and Row, 1963), 326–32.

5. Mary Carruthers, *The Book of Memory: A Study of Memory in Medieval Culture* (Cambridge: Cambridge University Press, 1990).

6. Carruthers, *The Book of Memory,* 30.

least in the view of Albertus Magnus: matter one recites by heart has not been found out by any system of discovery.[7]

Moreover, the images we recall when we do remember are themselves as much representational as they are eidetic. In the *De memoria*, Aristotle had said that the "phantasmata" that are stored in memory could be considered in two ways: as pictures of things and as signs (450b11–20). In the first case we may regard any mental image in itself by comparing it with the object of which it is a picture: such a process one properly calls recognition. But when we remember, we regard the image as a likeness of something else; it is a sign whose recollection stands for a thing that no longer is present. As such, a memorial image is a reminder that enacts an ontological break and a temporal gap: when it is physically present, it declares itself a simulacrum, a ghost of an originating experience that has entirely passed. Such apprehension of the "pastness" of its own images was also part of memory: as Albertus Magnus saw, recollection is both "interrupted" *(interruptus)* and "differentiated" *(diversificatus)*.[8] Remembering consequently was considered a "reconstructive" process throughout the Middle Ages; it was, as Carruthers says, "analogous to reading letters that 'stand for' sounds *(voces)* that 'represent' things in a more or less adequate, fitting way" (25).[9] Recollection, in short, was an exercise in intertextuality, a kind of reading.

When Dante indicates that his memory has rubricated chapters, therefore, he is not only pointing to a formal correlation between the divisions that give a book its order and the loci that give memory its structure.[10] He is announcing as well that the *Vita nuova* is similarly descriptive and rhetorical, that its words will both copy those in his

---

7. *Liber de memoria et reminiscentia*, tract. II, cap. I, in Albertus Magnus, *Opera Omnia*, vol. 9, ed. August Borgnet and Emile Borgnet (Paris: Ludovicum Vives, 1890), quoted by Carruthers, *The Book of Memory*, 20.

8. *Liber de memoria et reminiscentia*, tract. II, cap. I, quoted by Carruthers, *The Book of Memory*, 25. Carruthers reviews the medieval development of Aristotle's distinction between picture and likeness on pp. 24–26.

9. As Carruthers points out, the comparison of memory images to letters to be read was a common one in the Middle Ages; see *The Book of Memory*, 21–33.

10. On the analogy between the rubrics of Dante's memory and medieval book production, see further Ahern, "The New Life of the Book," 1–16. The place of the divisions themselves in the *Vita nuova* has elicited much commentary. The most recent treatment, which has a good summary of previous scholarship, is Thomas Stillinger, *The Song of Troilus* (Philadelphia: University of Pennsylvania Press, 1992), 44–117.

memory and read them: "se non tutte, almeno la loro sentenzia." For all their deference, then, Dante's opening words are also reconstructive. With them he signals that his earlier poems, prompted by diverse occasions and for divergent ends, truly were "rime sparse"; by "recollecting" them now both in memory and in the *Vita nuova,* Dante has a priori redefined their status as literature. They have been given the standing of experience, as Aristotle had defined it in the last book of the *Posterior Analytics.*

Aristotle thought that all our sensory perceptions have an inherent potentiality for order because "the act of perception involves the universal." That is to say, what we perceive in a thing is, in David Ross's words, what "it shares with other things."[11] Such perceptions give rise to memories, and repeated memories "constitute a single experience." Experience thus is "the universal," the unity that is identically present in "all the memories": from it comes the principle for art and science (*Post. An.* 2.19.100a5–9).[12] In the *Vita nuova,* Dante's experience is Beatrice: she becomes the heuristic principle who from the start gives his memories their unity and the poems that are their counterparts their art.

Nevertheless, for all the enormous effect her presence in Dante's mind has had, Beatrice and his memory of her cannot be the same thing. As Dante will soon say, Beatrice is a beatitude that certainly is beyond the powers of his memory to comprehend fully. From the start, therefore, Dante intentionally makes the words that will "re-present" his beloved analogous to the "ontological break and temporal gap" we find inherent in memorial images by subjecting them to the double (and opposing) demands of reportage and invention. That Dante does

---

11. Sir David Ross, *Aristotle* (London: Methuen, 1966), 55.

12. The rest of the paragraph is of interest as well: Arts and sciences

arise from sense perception . . . As soon as the one individual percept has "come to a halt" ("stantos") in the soul, this is the first beginning of the presence there of a universal (because although it is the particular that we perceive, the act of perception involves the universal, e.g. "man," not "a man, Callias"). Then other "halts" ("istatai") occur among these (proximate) universals, until the indivisble genera or [ultimate] universals are established. (*Post. An.* 2.19.100a10–b5).

Quoted in Wesley Trimpi, *Muses of One Mind* (Princeton: Princeton University Press, 1983), 91; see also J. H. Lesher, "The Meaning of "NOYS" in the Posterior Analytics," *Phronesis* 18 (1973): 44–68. Aristotle repeats the idea that experience is constructed out of many memories at the beginning of the *Metaphysics* (1.1.980b25–981b1).

so may seem surprising, since he presents himself as the scribe who duplicates his exemplar with undeviating faithfulness. Indeed, "assemplare," the word Dante uses to designate his copying, probably bears the technical meaning of *exemplar*, a final product that the scribe submits to the public.[13] Yet even this profession, with its implicit avowal of writerly submissiveness, carries a hint of potential innovation. The fair scribal copy, as Carruthers tells us, was usually remanded to the author (or his agent), who made a final corrective collation.[14] Since Dante is author of the *Vita nuova* as well as its scribe, the term he uses for its assemblage suggests the possibility of correction, even if only in a muted, mechanical sense. But when Dante adds that his "libello" will contain all the significance, if not all the words, that is in his mind, what he says is unquestionably revisionary, for it labels his book not only a copy but a translation as well.

The extraordinary history of the idea that the "fidus interpres" will render not word for word but sense for sense has recently been excavated by Rita Copeland.[15] She argues persuasively that classical oratory in Rome and curricular commentary on classical texts during the Middle Ages recognized the contestatory logic of translation, whereby the mastery and authority of a source are paradoxically affirmed by another text whose different language both displaces that of the original and makes it subject to cultural appropriation. Since translations and commentaries of this sort were increasingly written in the vernacular languages, the vernaculars themselves more and more became an object of academic attention; with increased notice there came as well a rise in the status of those who composed in them. Ultimately, the same interpretive protocols that were applied to classical "auctores" were applied to vernacular translations. Like the Roman orator, the medieval translator was invested with the power of independent rhetorical invention to "discover his text anew in his new language"; the texts he produced came to be considered authoritative, canonical, original.

Dante not only subscribed to but developed some of these notions; for him the prose commentaries and poems of the *Vita nuova* are kinds of translations, the former of the latter and both together of the book of his mind. In each case, translation brings to discourse the same dialec-

---

13. On this meaning of "exemplar," see Carruthers, *The Book of Memory*, 195–96.

14. Ibid.

15. See Rita Copeland, *Rhetoric, Hermeneutics, and Translation in the Middle Ages* (Cambridge: Cambridge University Press, 1991).

tic between iteration and renovation that memory enacts in its operations. It was altogether fitting, therefore, that when, as was customary in the academic prologue, Dante contemplated the textuality of the *Vita nuova* in his "proemio," he associated its "modus scribendi" with learned traditions of translation and commentary and with the book of memory.[16] In so doing, Dante implicitly announced his book's rhetorical program of authorial reinterpretation even as he explicitly sought his readers' goodwill by making a commonplace bow to the conventions of scribal humility. With its suggestion that it is both preamble and palinode, with its simultaneous denial and assertion of selfhood, the beginning of the *Vita nuova* proposes that because its writing is like the writing of the mind, the analogies and proportions that make them similar will recognize rupture and difference even as they create structures of continuity and recovery.

II

The analogy between book and memory, of course, is an analogy of means: Dante emphasizes what is ordered and contingent in each to establish the likeness and difference of both to the dual nature of the woman the *Vita nuova* takes as its intentional and referential object. Since Dante presents his "libello" as a tactile counterpart to the intellectual experience it records, it can be compared to Beatrice, who appears as living woman and the essence of beatitude. These two aspects of Beatrice are implicit in the first glimpse we get of her.

> Nove fiate già appresso lo mio nascimento era tornato lo cielo de la luce quasi a uno medesimo punto, quanto a la sua propria girazione, quando a li miei occhi apparve prima la gloriosa donna de la mia mente, la quale fu chiamata da molti Beatrice li quali non sapeano che si chiamare. (2.1)

> [Nine times already since my birth had the heaven of light returned nearly to the same point in its own circling, when the glorious lady

---

16. The "modus scribendi" and "modus tractare" were explicitly treated in academic prologues to curricular texts. For a full treatment, see A. J. Minnis, *Medieval Theories of Authorship* (London: Scolar Press, 1984). Picone, "La *Vita nuova* fra autobiografia e tipologia," sees the practices of the "accessus" as a model for Dante's juxtaposition of biographical and allegorical events in his "libello." I would call the unity he finds in the *Vita nuova* aesthetic.

of my mind first appeared to my eyes, who was called Beatrice by many who did not know what her name was [or what it meant to call her this].]

The celestial revolutions not only introduce time and the material world, since they measure Dante's age, but also establish a supernal context we will associate with his donna's suprasensible qualities. They find an analogue in Beatrice herself, who is fleshly—she can be seen and spoken of—and intellectual and spiritual: she is the "gloriosa donna de la mia mente." For Dante, though, the sensible leads beyond itself: while "mente" here can carry the technical meaning of memory, it looks past this faculty of the sensible soul to the intellect.[17] Indeed, by qualifying the motion he describes, by saying "quanto a la sua *propria girazione*," Dante pointedly refers not to the rotation of the sun around the earth but to the circling that belongs to the "cielo de la luce" itself; we are being prompted to recall that this heaven, like all the others, is moved by its angel's intellection.[18] This signal, combined with the theologically pregnant phrase "glorious lady of my mind," prepares us for the revelation in "Donne ch'avete intelletto d'amore" that Beatrice is indeed more than merely the object of Dante's apprehension:[19] she is the light of illumination that makes understanding possible. Ultimately, in fact, the heaven's turnings forecast Dante's final conviction that the material world can hardly serve even as a trope for Beatrice's nature: as he says in his explanation of "Oltre la spera," the last poem of the *Vita nuova*, were he to contemplate his lady in glory, his mind would be dazzled like our weak eyes before the sun (*VN* 41.6). But that is in the future; here we learn what Beatrice is only from what people called her.

The fact that Beatrice's first appearance is public emphasizes Dante's view that to encounter her is to be impelled to express what she means. And "Beatrice," it is clear at once, is the lady's proper name and the abstract condition of blessedness her name is homologous with. In this initial attempt to define her, Dante invokes an elementary principle of

---

17. de Robertis cites *Convivio* 4.14.11 (*Vita nuova*, 29): Dante says here that one can use the word *mente* to designate "la nobile parte de l'anima nostra."

18. *Convivio* 2.14.15; this gloss is noted by de Robertis in his edition of the *Vita nuova* (28).

19. As Branca notes, "glorioso" is properly used only of the saints. See Vittore Branca, "Poetics of Renewal and Hagiographic Tradition in the *Vita nuova*," *Lectura Dantis Newberryana* 1 (1988): 147.

signification. According to Lambert of Auxerre, who in this can stand for a host of medieval logicians from the twelfth century on, four things are required for signification: a thing, a concept of the thing, an utterance, and the union of the utterance with the concept of the thing. The thing exists outside the soul; the concept of the thing is the idea or likeness of the thing that exists inside the soul. Signification is actualized by the production of an utterance that is joined to the concept of the thing and becomes its sign.[20] To say "beatrice," then, is to point equally to Beatrice and to the concept of beatitude, for even those who did not know her name properly designated the woman they saw as the form of blessedness through her effects.[21] From this moment, as a meaningful utterance, "beatrice" will be understood by reference to the way that the universal was received in the mind.[22]

As we shall see, the affiliation of the transcendent with intellection was for Dante the central proposition that the "stil novo" was founded on; the processes whereby the universal can be received in the mind from the particulars of sense will increasingly become the subject matter of his descriptions of his love. For him, of course, Beatrice is far more than the word that names her; she could never be adequately equated with the signification of a term in logic. Dante will come to see Beatrice as the living essence of beatitude; only the fully articulated response of the intellect she has taken possession of can be likened to her. To speak of her is to speak of how and how much we know her.

What people who saw her said, therefore, is an inaugurating response, a "terminus ad quem"; at this elementary level, however, what they meant is less important than their having been inspired to say something, since Dante will base his claim that some likeness exists between his knowledge, his poetry, and his beloved on the fact that sig-

---

20. Lambert of Auxerre, *Property of Terms,* translated in *The Cambridge Translations of Medieval Philosophical Texts,* ed. Norman Kretzmann and Eleonore Stump (Cambridge: Cambridge University Press, 1988), 104–5.

21. This is why the phrase "li quali non sapeano che si chiamare" can mean both "those who did not know what her name was" (de Robertis's preference) and "those who did not know what it meant to call her by that name" (Contini's preferred gloss: see *Letteratura italiana della origini* [Florence: Sansoni, 1970], 307 nn. 4, 5). As de Robertis notes (ad loc., 29–30), both interpretations have strong support.

22. As Branca notes, saints' lives in general, and the Franciscan hagiography he thinks influenced Dante in particular, often start by etymologizing the saint's name. See "Poetics of Renewal," 134–35. At the start of the *Vita nuova,* however, Dante stages a drama of signification, not of etymology: the difference is important.

nification ends in utterance.[23] For cognition also culminates with the production of language; according to Aquinas, it ends as "a synthesizing act of apprehension expressed in a proposition."[24]

Corporeal objects act upon the human senses in such a way that the imagination fashions an image ("phantasma") of an object that the senses perceive. This phantasm, however, is still of a form individualized by matter; it presents an image of Rover, another of Spot. The intellect, however, bears upon the universal; from the particulars produced in sensation it therefore abstracts the essential form, that which makes Rover and Spot both dogs, or dogs and foxes both canines.

The faculties that allow this activity to take place are the passive and the active intellects. The active intellect illuminates the particular thing that is represented in the phantasm and renders it intelligible by abstracting its essential form from the matter and the conditions that individuate it. The resulting universal likeness, called the "intelligible species," is then impressed on the passive intellect, which in response forms its own likeness of the abstracted nature. This is the "verbum mentis" (or, in the Augustinian tradition, "verbum cordis"), the universal concept in the full sense.[25] The abstract concept, expressed by a single word, determines how we know anything with respect to its nature.[26]

Because human beings, however, are a compound of body and soul, the universal concept is not, in and of itself, the object of cognition ("id quod intelligitur"); rather it is the means by which ("id quo intelligi-

---

23. Clearly I think Dante foreshadows the circumstances that inspired him to write "Donne ch'avete intelletto d'amore" in this opening tableau.

24. See Joseph Owens, "Faith, Ideas, Illumination, and Experience," in *The Cambridge History of Later Medieval Philosophy*, ed. Norman Kretzmann, Anthony Kenny, and Jan Pinborg (Cambridge: Cambridge University Press, 1982), 452.

25. The quotation is from Frederick Copleston, *A History of Philosophy*, vol. 2, *Medieval Philosophy*, part 2 (Garden City: Doubleday, 1962), 110. See *S.T.* 1a.79; see also appendix 7 of vol. 11 of the Blackfriars' edition. On Aquinas's theory of knowledge, see Copleston, *History*, 108–17. In Dante, as Bruno Nardi notes, the agent intellect seems affiliated more closely with the Neoplatonic and Augustinian notion of divine light than with Aquinas's idea that it is a faculty of the human soul. See *Dante e la cultura medievale* (Bari: Laterza, 1983), 149–54. One should therefore emphasize that in Augustine the confrontation of the mind with ideas gave birth to the concept, the mind's representation of the idea, which Augustine calls the "verbum." This word came to be called the "verbum cordis." See Owens, "Faith," 443–44, 453. In either case, however, what is important for my argument is that intellection ends in the production of language.

26. See Owens, "Faith," 452.

tur") we come to know the material object, which is the proper goal of human understanding. Knowing something with respect to its nature alone is not enough, for if understanding stopped here, one could not know anything particular. To comprehend a thing as it exists therefore requires that the soul return to the phantasms ("se convertere ad phantasma"), armed, as it were, with the abstracted concept, through which it can now form a judgment of the discrete object as true or false. This judgment takes the form of a proposition: not a single word, such as "dog" or "human," but the concept embedded in a statement of the form $a = b$, such as "Rover is a dog," "Socrates is a man."

When the people who saw her said "beatrice," therefore, the word they uttered, with reference to Beatrice herself, is an expression of her essential quality, which Dante will discover can be understood only by means of intellectual cognition. The miracle of Beatrice adumbrated here, however, is that her essence, like that of the Virgin Mary, with whom she is continually associated, is twofold: insofar as we consider Beatrice an individual woman, her intelligible species is womanhood, but she is also beatitude, the good as such, a first vision of what Dante will later call a "primal object of desire" (*Purg.* 18.57). This union of essences transcends reason; ultimately, Beatrice confounds earthly knowing. With reference to their own knowledge, however, the word the people spoke is a metaphor for the material utterance of the sensible soul: it is the delighted communal response to the sight of a particular woman, the effect of a cause whose full nature they remain unaware of. While hardly the result of intellection, what the people say is, as we shall see in a moment, an analogue of the intellect's operations.

A similar but not identical pattern of response marks Dante's initial reaction to Beatrice upon seeing her, "vestita di nobilissimo colore, umile e onesto, sanguigno, cinta e ornata a la guisa che a la sua giovanissima etade si convenia" [dressed in the most noble color, humble and dignified in red, bound and adorned in a manner suited to her youth].

> lo spirito de la vita . . . cominciò a tremare sì fortemente . . . e tremando disse queste parole: "Ecce deus fortior me, qui veniens dominabitur michi."

> [The spirit of life began to tremble so violently and shaking said these words: "Behold a god stronger than I who comes to rule over me."]

In the same way, the animal spirit says, "Apparuit iam beatitudo ves-tra" [Now appears your beatitude], and the natural spirit says, "Heu miser, quia frequenter impeditus ero deinceps!" [Alas wretched one, how frequently shall I be impeded from now on]. These utterances tes-tify to Beatrice's divinity by virtue of the tissue of scriptural allusions that underlies them.[27] That the spirits speak Latin may well be a form of cultural acknowledgment of Beatrice's elevated station; what matters most here, however, is not the language they speak but the fact that they speak in sentences.[28] The effect of Beatrice culminates in a series of inner statements. All the poetry and prose that follow are extensions of these pronouncements: together they constitute the proposition of the *Vita nuova*, which is Dante's apprehension that "Beatrice is beatitude," incarnate as a living woman.

Though intellection subtends Dante's reactions, his turn within is not fully mature, as befits a nine year old who sees his beloved for the first time. The responses are of Dante's sensitive spirits; at this begin-ning point, Dante will therefore be primarily concerned with the kind of knowledge sensation produces. In fact, from the thirteenth century on, with the recovery of Aristotle through the intermediaries of Avi-cenna and Averroes, philosophers in the Latin West were preoccupied precisely with the role the senses and imagination played in under-standing. Although the issue chiefly contested concerned the nature and indeed the existence of an agent intellect, the whole debate really took its impetus from the prior question of how the material senses could be the ground of knowledge at all if intellection itself was imma-terial and the concepts it had as its object were completely separated from all individualizing matter.

Both Albertus Magnus and Thomas Aquinas, the most important influences on Dante, claimed that material things act as objects of sen-sation and, ultimately, knowledge. When we know a thing via sensa-tion, however, we do not know it as it actually exists, as a form united with its matter. Rather we know it by means of an "intention" (cf. *Conv.* 3.9.7), which is an image of the material object that its form produces in the sense organ. The first level of sensation thus involves the generation

---

27. Analogous passages from Isaiah, Luke, Matthew, Galatians, and Titus have all been adduced; for a typical reading, see Branca, "Poetics of Renewal," 147.

28. Compare Charles Singleton, "The Use of Latin in the *Vita Nuova*," *MLN* 30 (1946): 108–12. The sheer volume of talk Dante's spirits produce is worth noting. Even in Caval-canti, who seems to have invented their use, the spirits generally sigh; far more rarely than in Dante do they say something.

of the "intentio" through the abstraction of the sensible form from the matter of an existing thing. We do not sense the stone itself, but a "similitudo" or likeness of it, which, in Aquinas's words, is not stony.[29]

The next stage of knowing occurs in the internal senses, which were thought to be four or five in number, depending on whether one followed Averroes, as Thomas did, or Avicenna, as did Albertus.[30] The common sense ("sensus communis") enables us to be aware that we hear and see; it also allows us to compare sounds to textures, scents to sights.[31] The imagination, also called the phantasy, formed and stored images called phantasms. Like the images of the outer senses, phantasms are the forms of sensible objects; unlike the outer senses, however, the imagination is able to retain its image of a sensible thing even when it is no longer present. Phantasms therefore are a second grade of abstraction; they are the forms that the intellective faculties of the soul use to arrive at rational knowledge. There are two other internal senses: the estimative or cogitative power and memory. In animals the estimative sense perceives phantasms that are not directly known to the external senses and moves them to instinctive judgments: it causes the sheep to sense danger in the presence of the wolf and to flee from it. Aquinas calls this sense in humans the cogitative power since it makes some

---

29. In this discussion, I am following chiefly *The Cambridge History of Later Medieval Philosophy*, ed. Norman Kretzmann, Anthony Kenny, and Jan Pinborg (Cambridge: Cambridge University Press), 602–22. See also Nicholas Steneck, "Albert on the Psychology of Sense Perception," in James Weisheipl, ed., *Albertus Magnus and the Sciences: Commemorative Essays, 1980*, Pontifical Institute of Medieval Studies (Toronto: University of Toronto Press, 1980), 263–90. Aquinas, one should note, agrees with Albert in his account of this aspect of sensation. For sense knowledge in Dante, see Nardi, *Dante e la cultura medievale*, 138–41. Nardi generally accepts Dante's own testimony that he undertook a serious study of philosophy only after Beatrice's death, that is, coincident with the writing of the *Convivio*. It would be hard to understand, however, how Dante could have read and admired Cavalcanti, especially "Donna me prega," without a thorough understanding of sensible knowledge. In this regard, see J. E. Shaw, *Guido Cavalcanti's Theory of Love* (Toronto: University of Toronto Press, 1949).

30. Albertus followed Avicenna: because the imagination and the fantasy were separate, there were five internal senses. Aquinas followed Averroes; for him there was only the imagination. The difference carries no weight in my reading. On the internal senses, see Nicholas Steneck, "Albert the Great on the Internal Senses," *Isis* 65 (1974): 193–211. For their use in Chaucer, see V. A. Kolve, *Chaucer and the Imagery of Narrative* (Stanford: Stanford University Press, 1984), 9–58.

31. Steneck, "Albert," 197. Aquinas differs from Albertus in that he feels the common sense, like the other internal senses, abstracts its intention completely apart from a physical object; for Albertus, the common sense made its abstraction as the external senses did, in the presence of the object.

rational comparisons among intentions and acts. Finally, memory stores all this information for reference to past time.[32] Because all the internal senses make use of intentions abstracted from sensible things even when those things are no longer present, they all utilize some form of memory.

Clearly, these operations of the sensitive soul share a structure that is continuous with and analogous to the operations of reason, which begins with the abstracting of a second phantasm from the form of the object that the imagination has produced. The difference between them, though, is the role that the spirits play in nonintellective knowing.

As Nardi, Klein, and Agamben have shown, by the twelfth and thirteenth centuries the phantasm of Aristotelian psychology had been firmly joined to the idea of the warm breath or spirit that the Middle Ages had inherited from Stoic and Neoplatonic pneumatology.[33] In its earliest form, the pneuma was a substance physicians thought caused health and illness. Generated from the exhalation of blood, this invisible "hot breath" flowed through the arteries to all parts of the body, vivifying it and making it capable of sensation. If the equilibrium between its circulation and that of the blood through the veins was maintained, a person remained well; if it was disrupted, he or she developed a fever.

The Stoics extended these notions; for them the pneuma was nothing less than a material principle of life. Identical to fire, this subtle and luminous body pervaded the universe and penetrated every living thing; besides enabling corporeal reproduction and growth, it also was the "matter" in which the phantasy impressed its images. As such the pneuma functioned as an intermediary between sensation and thought. Neoplatonic philosophers developed this idea; for them

---

32. For Albertus, the imagination stores intentions without reference to past time. See Steneck, "Albert," 197.

33. See Nardi, *Dante e la cultura medievale*; Robert Klein, "Spirito Pellegrino," in *Form and Meaning*, trans. Henri Zerner (New York: Viking, 1979), 62–85; originally published as *La forme et l'intelligible* (Paris: Gallimard, 1979); Giorgio Agamben, *Stanze* (Turin: Einaudi, 1977), 71–155; a good English translation, from which I take all my citations, is *Stanzas: Word and Phantasm in Western Culture*, trans. Ronald Martinez, Theory and History of Literature 69 (Minneapolis: University of Minnesota Press, 1993), 61–131. See also Patrick Boyde, *Perception and Passion in Dante's Comedy* (Cambridge: Cambridge University Press, 1993), 144–54; and Mary Wack, *Lovesickness in the Middle Ages* (Philadelphia: University of Philadelphia Press, 1990). Further citations from Albertus Magnus are in de Robertis, *Vita nuova*, 29–30; see also Shaw, *Guido Cavalcanti's Theory of Love*, 57–58. In the subsequent paragraphs I generally follow Agamben.

the pneuma became the agency through which the material touched the spiritual.

By the time these doctrines reached Avicenna, medieval doctors had generally distinguished three kinds of spirits. The natural spirit empowered growth; it was formed from exhalations of the blood and administered in the liver. When the natural spirit underwent a series of digestions or purifications in the heart it became the vital spirit, which animated the body as it coursed through the arteries. The animal spirit was distilled from the vital spirit when it passed through the three cells of the brain; once purified by the phantasy and memory, it filled the nerves and thus was responsible for sensation and movement. Even though the animal spirit was the most subtle of the three, however, Dante gives pride of place to the vital spirit in the heart. In this he followed a common distinction of medieval physiology. The heart is the seat of life; because the soul animates the whole body from there, the heart was also the "principle and origin of those powers [such as the nutritive, the imaginative, and the memorial] whose action finds their instruments elsewhere."[34] When the "spirito de la vita" in the *Vita nuova* sees a god coming to rule over it, the place from where Amore exercises his dominion is the common seat of all the spirits.

This pneumatic circulation animates the entire process of perception; it makes both external and internal sensation a dynamic system. Despite the fact that the spirits rationalize the sensitive soul, however, they still differ from reason, chiefly because reason ends in the production of language.[35] Although Aristotle had said that the phantasm is what distinguishes the human voice from mere sound, scholastics specifically denied that anything but the "verbum mentis" made a word meaningful. They agreed with Galen: the voice was a pneumatic current that originated in the heart and excited the motion of the tongue as it passed through the larynx. But from Boethius on they vigorously disputed the notion that the phantasm that speech signified was the image of the "spiritus phantasticus."

It is perfectly possible to think with Agamben that the stilnovists broke ranks with the philosophers by holding that the poetic sign arises

---

34. Agamben, *Stanzas*, 85. Agamben quotes a passage from Averroes's *Colliget* (bk 2, chap. 20) that perfectly elucidates how the heart and vital spirit can in a general sense house the others.

35. See, for instance, Albertus Magnus, *De Interpretatione*, treatise 2, chap. 1, quoted by Agamben, *Stanzas*, 126.

from the spirit of the heart; Cavalcanti especially seems driven by this conviction. But even in Dante's "primo amico," intellection becomes the means whereby Guido realizes that his love, which must remain in the sensible soul "dove sta memoria," cannot rise to the level of the transcendental beauty that caused it.[36] In the *Vita nuova*, however, Dante can represent the miraculous dual nature of Beatrice only by audaciously joining intellection to the workings of love in the sensible soul. In a manner similar to the way a cause is responsible for the form and quality of its effect even though it is not materially present in it, Dante therefore refashions the utterances of the "spiritus phantasticus" as analogies of the intellect's utterance upon its "conversion to the phantasms." As in Cavalcanti, love in the *Vita nuova* remains the history of the responses of Dante's sensitive spirits. Dante transcribes the poems of the book itself, which are the forms these responses have been given, from the book of his memory. Just as events reside as experiences in memory, so the poems of the *Vita nuova* reflect the collective conceivings of the inner senses.[37] But the underlying principle that accounts for their being poems—the ordered disposition of words—is the determination of intellection in a proposition. Love, as Dante will soon say, never ruled without the faithful counsel of reason. The poems, in other words, cannot be understood apart from intellection, apart, that is to say, from the discourse of the prose commentary, which explains through its discursive translations how the formal disposition of the sonnets, "ballata," and "canzoni" makes each a more or less fitting response to Beatrice, whose essence is beatitude.

Similarly, the gatherings of people, Florence itself, are public analogues to the communal constructions of the inner senses that memory stores.[38] But the substantive principle that accounts for the sensible form of the people's reaction to Beatrice—the uttering of her name—is the "verbum mentis." As Dante says in the *Convivio* (1.5.12), when he

---

36. See, for instance, Guido's sonnet "Chi è questa che vèn, ch'ogn'om la mira" and the fine analysis of it in conjunction with Dante's "Tanto gentile" in Harrison, *The Body of Beatrice*, 69–74.

37. The connection between the opening of the *Vita nuova* and Cavalcanti's "Donna me prega" is made by Mazzotta, *Dante's Vision and the Circle of Knowledge*, 60–62; his reading of the differences between Cavalcanti and Dante informs my reading here. See also Harrison, *The Body of Beatrice*, 69–90.

38. The strange vagueness that marks all the events of the *Vita nuova*, as well as all references to Florence, which as Mark Musa notes (101–2) is never referred to by name, is meant, I think, to correspond to the degree of abstraction that pertains to the inner senses. See Mark Musa, *Dante's Vita nuova* (Bloomington: Indiana University Press, 1973).

discusses the virtue of language: "Così lo sermone, lo quale è ordinato a manifestare lo concetto umano, è virtuoso quando quello fa, e più virtuoso quello che più lo fa" [So language, whose purpose is to manifest the concept humans have, shows its virtue when it does this, and that language is most virtuous that most does this]. "Lo concetto umano" should, I think, be understood precisely in the technical sense of the universal as perceived in the human intellect; from this point of view, the exposition of the *Vita nuova* is the record of how Beatrice enables any language that expresses her to become ever more "virtuous" and noble.[39]

III

By the end of his first two chapters, Dante has established the principles that allow us to call the *Vita nuova* an "estetica nuova" as well. The compounding of then and now that turns retrospection into a form of renovation makes memory almost metaphorical in its constitution.[40] When Dante remembers, the incidents stored in his "libro de la memoria" are not copies so much as "digested" analogies of their experienced counterparts—they have begun to be both dematerialized and codified.[41] My argument is that Dante introduces these operations of memory as an exercise of the dialogical vision of the aesthetic, in which the physical and transcendent also are assimilated as analogies of each other. The purchase of Dante's aesthetic vision, however, is not limited to the composition either of the book of memory or the "libello" he makes from it. Beyond allowing him to present his autobiographical development, poetical, philosophical, and spiritual at once, as an analogy of

---

39. In this respect, it is significant that Dante describes the ennobling effect of Beatrice on all who come into contact with her precisely during that time between his discovery that his poetry should praise her and her death. The fact that Dante reconceives this commonplace of courtly love largely in terms of potency and act (beginning with "Donne ch'avete" and running, to a greater or lesser extent, through "Amor e 'l cor gentil," "Ne li occhi," and each of the other poems of praise) indicates another shift in the level of discourse toward the intellect.

40. Cf. Giuseppe Mazzotta, "The Language of Poetry in the *Vita nuova*," *Rivista di studi italiani* 1 (1983): 3–14.

41. What I have called the "digestive" aspects of memory, its initiation of a process of "denuding" objects from their materiality and making them ever more legible, was fully recognized in the medieval concept of intention. When Dante returns to the metaphor of digestion in the *Convivio* and, as we shall see, in the *Comedy* (*Purg.* 25), he elevates the concepts he identifies here to the level of metaphysics.

Beatrice's life,[42] Dante's aesthetic imagination has determined how he organized the literary and cultural formations that are the backdrop of this analogy. The moralizing inquiries into the nature of love by Guittone d'Arezzo, Giacomo da Lentini, and their followers; the inner itineraries that lifted mystical contemplatives through the hierarchies of being;[43] Franciscan hagiography, especially of Saint Margaret of Cortona:[44] these traditions affected intellectual life in late thirteenth century Florence, and the *Vita nuova* certainly is driven by the same ascetic urgency that impelled each of them. But however much Dante charts his progress from fleshly passion to spiritual charity, his love always remains rooted in his body; operating in conjunction with the impulse to sublimation is the influence of Aristotle's hylomorphism. According to the retrospective testimony of the *Convivio*, when Dante was writing the *Vita nuova* he was preoccupied precisely with this new science of the soul, which he found chiefly in responses (heterodox as well as orthodox) to the *De Anima* and *Nicomachean Ethics*.[45] Even before the "thirty months" he devoted to philosophical study following Beatrice's death, however, Dante could hardly have read Cavalcanti without working knowledge of Aristotelian epistemology.[46] Alongside Augustine's "liber memoriae," therefore, and the books of memory that initi-

---

42. Beatrice's life, as Branca says, is presented not as a "vita" but as an epiphany (129). See Branca, "Poetics of Renewal," 123–52.

43. The chief spokesperson for this reading of the *Vita nuova* is Aristide Marigo, *Mistica e scienza nella Vita nuova di Dante* (Padua: Drucker, 1914). Cf. Barbara Nolan, "The *Vita Nuova* and Richard of St. Victor's Phenomenology of Vision," *Dante Studies* 92 (1974): 35–52. Marigo stresses that the mystic contemplatives and scholastic philosophers looked to the same end: both undertook itineraries of the *mind* to God. Apart from Marigo's overemphasis of the mystical tradition, there are real differences one should note between Bernard's "consideratio," or the psychology of Hugh or Richard of St. Victor, and the epistemology of Albertus Magnus and Aquinas, which is based on Aristotle's hylomorphism.

44. For the most forceful reading of the influence of Franciscan hagiography, see Branca, "Poetics of Renewal."

45. See *Convivio* 2.13. On Dante's study during this time, see especially Maria Corti, *La felicità mentale: Nuove prospettive per Cavalcanti e Dante* (Turin: Einaudi, 1983), 72–155.

46. In addition to finding a paraphrase from Homer in Albertus Magnus's *De intellectu et intelligibili* (see note 48), the Averroistic tract "Quaestio de felicitate," which Jacobus de Pistorio dedicated to Guido Cavalcanti, seems to me a strong indication that scholastic philosophy already has begun to inform the retrospective perspective of the *Vita nuova*. See Paul Oscar Kristeller, "A Philosophical Treatise from Bologna Dedicated to Guido Cavalcanti: Magister Jacobus de Pistorio and His *Quaestio de felicitate*," *Medioevo e Rinascimento: Studi in onore di Bruno Nardi*, 2 vols. (Florence: Sansoni, 1955), 1: 425–63. See also Corti, *La felicità mentale*, 5–7.

ate the spiritual ascents of the Victorines, alongside Cicero's emphasis on the importance of remembering in friendship, Dante has memory function as an independent faculty of the sensible soul.[47] To Hugh of St. Victor, memory and the senses were still primarily hindrances of the flesh, a beginning point to be gotten past in the uplifting of the spirit; in the *Vita nuova* they are that as well, but at the same time they are indispensable adjuncts of human nobility. By stressing the analogies that make the sensible and rational souls proportionate but not identical to each other, and the human intellect a similitude (but only a similitude) of the divine, Dante was able to locate the aesthetic at the center of the quest for what Maria Corti has called "la felicità mentale."

From the start, then, Dante composes the *Vita nuova* as Beatrice's likeness by making it the site wherein he represents the sensible reception of a universal. The materiality of his book of memory, the redness of whose title we have been enjoined to notice ("rubrica" is repeated twice in the two sentence prohemium), becomes an analogy of Beatrice, the woman he sees dressed in "sanguigno." With the utterances of the spirits, Love takes possession of Dante by taking possession of his imagination; for the next nine years, prompted by its inner compositions, Dante seeks to see Beatrice. Yet, as Dante says, however much Love ruled his outer acts and inner senses, reason stood close by.

nulla volta sofferse che Amore mi regesse sanza lo fedele consiglio de la ragione in quelle cose là ove cotale consiglio fosse utile a udire. (*VN* 2.9)

[Love never ruled without the faithful counsel of reason in those matters in which such counsel was useful to hear.]

For Dante, "la ragione ragiona"; reason speaks: once again it has left its signature in the form of an utterance about Beatrice that stands as a

---

47. On the "book of memory" see Branca, "Poetics of Renewal," 123–24. Often memory is treated from an Augustinian, or more generally, from a figural perspective; in addition to Singleton, *Essay*, see, for instance, Antonio d'Andrea, "Dante, la mémoire et le livre: Le sens de la *Vita Nuova*," in *Jeux de mémoire*, ed. Bruno Roy and Paul Zumthor (Montreal: University of Montreal Press, 1985), 91–97. I obviously do not discount these readings; I do, however, think Dante would have conceived of memory primarily in terms of its role in faculty psychology. For an account that acutely notes the differences between Augustine's conception of memory and Dante's, see Marziano Guglielminetti, *Memoria e scrittura* (Turin: Einaudi, 1977), 42–100. On the importance of memory in Cicero's tract *Laelius de amicitia*, see de Robertis, *Il libro della Vita nuova*, 21–24 passim.

summary of this phase of his sentimental education: "Ella non parea figliuola d'uomo mortale, ma di deo" [She did not seem the daughter of a mortal man, but of god]. These words, significantly borrowed from Homer through the intermediary of Albertus Magnus's *De intellectu et intelligibili*, are appropriate, considering Dante's age, precisely because they are both a translation and a quotation.[48] The product of an imagination not his own, the line nicely conveys the gap between Dante's perceptions and his own ability to express them poetically: it is a counterpart to the utterances of the spirits insofar as each is a calque of a biblical verse. As a statement about Beatrice, however, the words are less an admission that her claim to divinity is only Dante's opinion than they are a foreshadowing of the revelation that she is beyond the mind's capacity to understand, which Dante will proclaim in "Donne ch'avete," the "canzone" that established his identity as a poet. For in that "canzone" we will learn that Beatrice does not just appear to be an angel, like Guinizzelli's donna ("Tenne d'angel sembianza / che fosse del Tuo regno"), but is "la speranza de' beati," the light that so shines in the divine intellect it causes even an angel to exclaim in wonder and desire:

Angelo clama in divino intelletto
e dice: "Sire, nel mondo si vede
maraviglia ne l'atto che procede
d'un'anima che 'nfin qua su risplende."

(15–18)

[An angel cries out in the divine intellect and says: "Lord, on earth one sees a living miracle which proceeds from a soul which shines even here above."]

Beatrice is the illumination that enables understanding to occur.

Until her death, therefore, the utterances of the three sensitive spirits themselves become rubrics that structure Dante's development in the *Vita nuova*. To describe the effects of love, as registered primarily in the "spirito naturale," will be the burden of the first stage of Dante's book: everything that happens from Beatrice's greeting when he was eighteen, through the deflections of the first screen lady, her departure, and

---

48. Marigo shows that the text Dante found this paraphrase in was Albert's *De intellectu et intelligibili* (3.9); see *Mistica e scienza*, 95.

the death of Beatrice's friend (chaps. 3–8), is a gloss on the statement "Heu miser, quia frequenter impeditus ero deinceps." The appearance of Amore to Dante in his imagination, his counsel that he take a second screen lady, which leads to the denial of Beatrice's greeting, the second vision of Love, the ladies' mockery of Dante, and the poems he writes to explain Beatrice's effects on him (chaps. 9–18) all provide an anatomy of the sensitive spirits in love; each event elaborates the implications of the declaration "Apparuit iam beatitudo vestra." And the comprehensive spirit of life, which says, "Ecce deus fortior me, qui veniens dominabitur michi," informs the discovery that Dante's happiness lies not in her greeting but in the words that praise Beatrice and celebrate her divine nature (chaps. 19–28).

As in any hierarchy that is governed by analogy, not only will each higher spirit contain the knowledge of the lower but the very shape and function of the lower will operate as a signature of the higher. Aristotle had said each successive function of the soul contains potentially its predecessor, just as the square contains the triangle—a passage Dante will quote in the *Convivio* (4.7.14–15).[49] Boethius concurred; indeed, in resolving the apparent contradiction between free will and predestination, Lady Philosophy offers a paradigm of knowledge that I take as one model for the analogies of the *Vita nuova*.

A man himself is comprehended in different ways by the senses, imagination, reason, and intelligence. The senses grasp the figure of the thing as it is constituted in matter; the imagination, however, grasps the figure alone without the matter. Reason, on the other hand, goes beyond this and investigates by universal consideration the species itself which is in particular things. The vision of intelligence is higher yet, and it goes beyond the bounds of the universe and sees with the clear eye of the mind the pure form itself. In all this we chiefly observe that the higher power of knowing includes the lower. (*De Consolatio Philosophiae*, book 5, prose 4)[50]

Thus when the lovestruck Dante retires to his solitary room after Beatrice greets him, and he is overcome by his first vision of Love, though

49. *De Anima*, 2.3. 415a1.
50. I quote from Boethius, *The Consolation of Philosophy*, trans. R. H. Green (Indianapolis: Bobbs Merrill, 1962).

what he says pertains mostly to his physical well-being, all three spirits are represented. Love appears as a lord of terrible aspect, speaking many things, though Dante is able to understand only "Ego dominus tuus." In one arm, Love holds "la donna de la salute," apparently asleep, draped in a red cloth, and in the other a flaming heart: of this Love says, "Vide cor tuum." Beatrice then awakens, and Love forces her to eat Dante's heart, which she does fearfully. Love is happy a short time, but soon all is turned to the most bitter lament; weeping, Love ascends to heaven with Beatrice in his arms.

The interpretive challenges this vision poses are legion; by Dante's own account, none of his contemporaries understood the poem he composed about it, nor have we reached anything like a consensus today, despite Dante's assurance that its meaning is now manifest "a li più semplici." What does seem clear, however, is that Dante thinks his prose commentary on the genesis of the sonnet has provided information not in "A ciascun'alma presa e gentil core" that will make what he describes in it intelligible.[51] Some of this information consists of differences in details; in the poem, for instance, Beatrice sleeps covered by a cloth, while in the prose we learn that she was naked except for the red cloth that covered her. Just as important, Amore appears in a fiery cloud and departs toward heaven when he leaves. These additional features, as Robert Harrison argues, are crucial.[52] But without question the greatest difference between the two versions of Dante's vision is that in the prose we witness a dramatic rehearsal of what the spirits had said on the occasion of Beatrice's first appearance. The God of Love, who rules Dante's life and makes him able to think that in Beatrice he saw "li termini de la beatitudine," identifies himself from his fiery cloud by saying, "I am your Lord," words that recall those of the vital spirit: "Behold a god . . . who comes to rule over me." In revealing Dante's heart, Love says, "Look on your heart," a declaration that emphasizes the visual spirits and recalls their utterance, "Now your bliss has appeared." And the substance of the vision, that which Dante

---

51. I believe this in spite of the recent readings that have posited that the meaning, "lo verace guidicio," of Dante's dream is its meaninglessness, its inability, that is, to be interpreted univocally. In addition to Harrison and Menocal (see notes 52 and 66), see Gregory Stone, "Dante's Averroistic Hermeneutics: (On 'Meaning' in the *Vita Nuova*)," *Dante Studies* 112 (1994): 133–59.

52. Harrison offers perhaps the best reading of Dante's "maravigliosa visione," as well as a review of recent interpretations. See *The Body of Beatrice*, 17–30.

now speaks himself, in prose and poetry, has to do with the nourishing of love.[53]

Dante's dream consequently takes as its subject matter the network of analogous relations that constitute the process of sensible perception. Dante's flaming heart, the seat of the vital spirit, which says, "Behold a god," is like the God of Love who holds it as he stands in his "nebula di colore di fuoco." The periphrasis is significant; by saying "a cloud the color of fire" Dante in effect folds the spirit of vision into the "spirito de la vita," since color is what enables one to see.[54] Moreover, what we are enjoined to see, Dante's flaming heart, is linked to Beatrice, whose cloth is "sanguigno," a word that captures the redness of blood; at the same time, again through the mediation of sight, Beatrice's "drappo sanguigno" makes her like Love in his fiery cloud. Beatrice therefore is already related to Dante on the level of the vital spirit through their analogical resemblance to Love and on the level of the animal spirit through the likeness we see between her "drappo sanguigno" and his "core ardendo"; the experience is completed by reenacting the affinity between them on the level of the natural spirit. Love feeds Dante's heart to the nearly naked Beatrice, and she eats it fearfully ("dubitosamente" in the prose, "paventosa" in the sonnet); this action corresponds to Dante's fear on seeing Love ("una figura d'uno segnore di pauroso aspetto" in the prose, "cui essenza membrar mi dà orrore" in the sonnet), the first of many emotional seizures that will convulse his body. In this way, Beatrice, Dante, and Amore each preserves his or her own identity, yet together find the ground for union in the imagination's reconfiguration of Dante's faculties aroused by love. When in retrospect Dante says his dream is now clear to even the simplest souls, he is referring, I think, to just these analogous associations that the prose makes clear. The new life begins here, where it ought; Dante's education in love starts with a lesson in the aesthetic represen-

---

53. This is the obvious sense of the dream: it is the basis of many interpretations. As Bruno Nardi shows, the nourishing of love had been part of the poetic definition of Amore in Italian verse since Giacomo da Lentini. See "Filosofia dell'amore nei rimatori italiani del Duecento e in Dante," in *Dante e la cultura medievale*, 9–79. In "Amore e le visioni nella *Vita Nuova*," *Dante Studies* 92 (1974): 19–34, Margherita de Bonfils Templer reads Love in a manner similar to the way I read him here.

54. Colors prepare us to see: cf., for instance, Aquinas's analogy: "phantasms are preparations for the action of the intellect, as colors are for the act of sight." *On the Unity of the Intellect against the Averroists*, trans. Beatrice Zedler (Milwaukee: Marquette University Press, 1968), 4.105, 61.

tation of the informed vision, knowledge, and language of the natural spirit.[55]

In seeing the vision far less as a prophecy of Beatrice's death than as a representation of Dante in love, I agree, in a sense, with the response to his sonnet attributed to Cino da Pistoia (or, alternatively, Terino da Castelfiorentino).[56] Love feeds Dante's burning heart to his lady so that she may know it: "Naturalmente chere ogni amadore / di suo cor la sua donna far saccente" [It is a law of nature that every lover would have his lady know his heart]. But with the full context of the vision that the prose of the *Vita nuova* supplies, Love's weeping departure toward heaven certainly seems to refer not to the pain Beatrice will feel in love, as, let us say, Cino holds, but to Beatrice's death, as Cavalcanti intuited in his reply: Dante's lady was sinking toward death; Love feared this and so gave her his heart to eat—"nodrilla dello cor, di ciò temendo." Dante's vision, it is clear, is as much a retrospective as it is an inauguration. The double perspective that, as we saw, distinguishes memory here marks the imagination as well: the differentiated and interrupted qualities of memory, which are the epistemological foundation for the sense that events in the *Vita nuova*, though matters of record, are somehow unfinished and provisional, have become signs of the nature of the miracle they attempt to express.[57] For Beatrice, in her own way, is also differentiated and interrupted; the tension of Dante's vision is the tension of analogy, which is the hallmark of his aesthetic.

IV

Dante explicitly affiliates his vision with the natural spirit: the next chapter begins with the words "Da questa visione innanzi cominciò lo mio spirito naturale ad essere impedito ne la sua operazione"(*VN* 4.1) [From the time of this vision my natural spirit began to be impeded in its operation]. As a result Dante's physical appearance was transformed; he became frail and weak, to the extent that people who saw him said that he bore on his face so many of the signs ("insigne") of

---

55. This emphasis on vision at the beginning of the *Vita nuova* inaugurates a lifelong meditation by Dante on the power of imagination to make knowledge. See especially Mazzotta, "Imagination and Knowledge," in *Dante's Vision*, 116–34.

56. The text and translation of this poem and Cavalcanti's that follows are from *Dante's Lyric Poetry*. The physician Dante da Maiano also sent Dante a reply: see Mazzotta's trenchant remarks in "The Language of Poetry," 6–7 passim.

57. On these qualities of the *Vita nuova*, see Mazzotta, "The Language of Poetry," 3–14.

Love, he would never recover. But when they asked for whose sake Love had so ravaged him, he looked at them, smiled, and said nothing.

Dante then tells us that by chance people mistook another lady as the object of his affection. She happened to be sitting midpoint on the line of sight that connected Dante and Beatrice when they all were at a service to honor the Virgin Mary. When people noticed how the lady looked at Dante, they assumed she was the one who had so devastated his body ("distrugge la persona"). Dante decided to adopt this lady as a screen; he wrote a number of poems to her over the next few years, none of which, he tells us, he will record in the *Vita nuova,* except if they served as a pretext to praise Beatrice.

Eventually this lady left Florence; Dante felt he had to write something to express his sorrow. In "O voi che per la via d'Amor passate," however, we learn that Dante grieves not because the lady had departed but because with her departure he lost the means of expressing his love for Beatrice obliquely. After this, a friend of Beatrice dies; because he had seen her in Beatrice's company, Dante writes two poems lamenting her death.

The events of this section of the *Vita nuova* (chaps. 4–8) comprise a brief poetics of the impeded natural spirit. Dante first presents himself as a text: love's effects appear as signs that are written on his body. We soon realize, though, that these signs are not random but make Dante a somatic transcription of the vision of "A ciascun'alma presa." His eaten heart has been translated into the consumption that wastes his frame and marks his visage. But if, as before, sight and reason are the communal agencies that make the physical signs of love legible, what they mean remains mysterious. People see Dante; when they ask him why he is so altered, Amore, counseled by reason ("secondo lo consiglio de la ragione"), commands him to tell them he is in love. But the God of Love does not permit the people to know with whom; when they ask, Dante silently smiles at his interlocutors. Just as none of Dante's fraternity of poets guessed the true significance of his vision, access to the sense of what the people see is obstructed by the same body they have read. People see that Love has made Dante a sign, but the very act of seeing this impedes seeing what he means.

The screen lady is Dante's objective correlative. While she was in Florence Dante concealed his love for Beatrice by deflecting attention onto her person; in retrospect, however, the same body that prevented discovery is itself screened. From the moment she becomes Dante's "schermo de la veritade," she exists only in order for us to see past her. This fact is nowhere more evident than when she leaves Florence. Dante says he was discomfited not because she had gone but because his "beautiful defense" had failed him ("la bella difesa che m'era venuto meno").[58] The lady's very corporeality, once so substantive, has become adjectival; she is beautiful, but only to the extent that she is a defense. No sooner is her physical beauty acknowledged than it is dissolved by being entirely subordinated to the function she performed.

Like the lady herself, the poems Dante wrote to her are also reflexes of his own natural spirit; just as it was obstructed ("frequenter impeditus ero deinceps"), so they were meant, when they were written, to obstruct the discovery that Beatrice is his lady. Now, however, these texts have no place in the *Vita nuova* because the woman who was their referent no longer exists for Dante as an independent being. The very absence of the poems from the "libello" is a sign of how transparent she has become. Indeed, the single sonnet Dante does include about the screen lady, "O voi che per la via d'Amor passate," is about her parting. In its last stanza Dante summarizes the entire experience of the screen lady by transforming himself into a figure of allegory:

Sì che volendo far come coloro
che per vergogna celan lor mancanza,
di fuor mostro allegranza,
e dentro da lo core struggo e ploro.

[Therefore, wanting to act like those who hide their lack out of shame, I make a show of happiness outwardly, and within my heart I weep and am ravaged.]

In delineating its impediments, this poem of the natural spirit expresses the effects of Dante's discovery that the lady's true virtue lay not in her-

58. The full phrase Dante uses to describe his reaction to the lady's departure is significant: "per che io, quasi sbigottito de la bella difesa che m'era venuto meno, assai me ne disconfortai" [because I, as if bewildered by the fact that my beautiful defense had failed me, was greatly discomfited]. The "quasi," as de Robertis notes, tries retrospectively (and unsuccessfully in de Robertis's view), to suppress the distress that Dante's real affection for the screen lady caused when she left Florence. (See *Il libro della Vita nuova*, 50.) Nevertheless, as we shall see, Dante looks back at this phrase when he comes to realize that his poetry ought to praise Beatrice. The incident here shadowily prefigures that revelation; they are connected analogically, just as the natural and vital spirits are structured analogically.

self but in her going, that his "detti" about her are worthwhile not because they hid his love but because their cloakings were their revelation of it. The body, whether Dante's, the screen lady's, or the poem's, has become semiotic; in every case, when we look at it, we need to see the concealment it represents.

Why has Dante chosen so strange a way to satisfy the courtly demand that he keep his love for his lady secret? One reason, I think, is that he wants to establish an analogy between the natural spirit and the object it strives to comprehend, Beatrice's miraculous double nature. If she is angel and woman at once, the "spirito naturale" acts to make the body it nourishes an integument one must look through to see a deeper significance. While it is true that, as Dante says, "names are consequences of the things they name" [nomina sunt consequentia rerum (*VN* 13.4)], it is also true, as Boethius says, that things are known "according to the capacity of the knower." In keeping with this "ordo," the "spirito naturale" will seek to express how it is like Beatrice in a language natural to it. It will speak, therefore, of the accommodations that, in making the spirit resemble Beatrice, make it differ from her as well. It expresses these accommodations in terms of the dialectic of sight that sees its want of insight, drawing its vocabulary from the "spirito animale" and its "spiriti del viso," the next higher faculty of perception.[59] Hiding what is not present ("celan lor mancanza"), making joy the outward expression of inner torment; such doublings are all the natural spirit can manage in the presence of a creature at once woman and transcendent beatitude. They are the body's mode of representing Beatrice. We are asked to infer her nature from the way we have gained and have been prevented from gaining knowledge of her.

Similar considerations explain why the first lines of "O voi che per la via d'Amor passate" so clearly echo Jeremiah's lament: "O vos omnes qui transitis per viam, attendite et videte si est dolor sicut dolor meus." When these words became Christ's in the Passiontide liturgy, the sorrow that the faithful were asked to bear witness to was testimony that their God was also a man.[60] Dante includes this poem in the *Vita nuova* because the translation from *Lamentations* makes it "about" Beatrice; Jesus' two natures are the form of hers. Nor is it an accident that this is

---

59. I would also see this dialectic of sight that sees its want of insight as an analogy to the dialectics of memory I elaborated in the second section of this chapter.

60. On the use of this passage in the liturgy, see Foster and Boyde, *Dante's Lyric Poetry*, 2:40.

the first of the double sonnets in Dante's "libello." Far from being the record of a debt, then, Dante's way of disguising his feelings transforms a commonplace of Sicilian and Provençal poetry. The duality he has found in the utterances of the "spirito naturale" has become an analogy in a new poetics of existence.[61]

V

The death of Beatrice's friend serves as a fulcrum for this and the next section of the *Vita nuova;* it stands as an epitaph for what we might call the natural phase of Dante's love and marks the transition to the imaginative. The screen lady's departure suddenly becomes a sign of an absence that the death of Beatrice's friend makes absolute; the grief and lament that shook Dante's body when he lost his "bella difesa" reach a natural limit here. But if in the face of death the "spirito naturale" exhausts what it can say about love, Dante discovers in his woe a new motive for his poetry. "Piangete, amanti" and "Morte villana" eulogize the lady because she had been Beatrice's friend: unlike the verse to the screen lady, whose purpose had been to mask Dante's love for Beatrice, these poems are written to acknowledge her virtue. In the first sonnet, Dante commands lovers to weep because Love weeps. He then explains that Love weeps because he hears ladies weeping at the death of the "gentil core" who was their companion. This duplication of responses shows that the woman was indeed like Beatrice but only because the effects her death evokes are an analogue of the dual nature of the miracle who was her friend. The resemblance is what authorizes the appearance of Love "in forma vera" (10); Beatrice *is* the true form of Love. But the lady Love laments over is not a true form but a "lovely dead image" [la morta imagine avvenente (11)]. The body that once was so beautiful ("che . . . fu di sì gaia sembianza" [14]) dies.[62] The contrast does render oblique homage to Beatrice; we are, however, still within the realm of those "who draw nourishment from love" [chi d'amor . . . si notrica ("Morte villana," 9)]. Just as the lady's death is the palest foreshadowing of Beatrice's, we are far from the direct praise of

---

61. Foster and Boyde (*Dante's Lyric Poetry,* 2:42) note that the need for the lover to disguise his feelings was a topos in Sicily and Provence. They characterize Dante's use of it as evidence of his poetic debt.

62. On the valencies of "gaia sembianza," which can refer either to the lady's "gracious outward form" or her "charm," see Foster and Boyde, *Dante's Lyric Poetry,* 2:44–45.

"Donne ch'avete." The paired sonnets therefore are made a formal analogue to the "alieniloquium," the doublespeak of "O voi che per la via d'Amor passate." Nevertheless, though the form of the poems remains much what it was, through the agency of death, which removes the body from sight, Dante has found a new direction and purpose for his poetry.

For his own part, Dante clearly feels in himself an emptiness analogous to the screen lady's absence; to fill the void left by her departure, he falls back on the resources of his memory and imagination. At this point, however, it seems the "vis imaginativa" does not compose or invent so much as it repeats; it operates purely as the sense that stores intentions for further use. Consequently, the events that immediately follow the death of Beatrice's friend (in chaps. 9–11 of the *Vita nuova*) restage Dante's experience with the screen lady. Just as she has left Florence, so he rides toward the place she has gone to. When Dante is somewhere between Florence and his destination—when he is located, in other words, in a position analogous to the one the screen lady occupied between himself and Beatrice—Love, in tattered coverings, appears to him in his imagination. He says that he has come from the screen lady; since she will not return, Dante must choose another lady to mask his love and write to her as he had to the previous "donna," so that none will discern the simulated nature of his affection. Dante does so, only too well; the poems he wrote, none of which is recorded, caused people to say he was behaving so scurrilously, Beatrice denied him her greeting. Dante then explains the effects of her greeting; being deprived of it leaves him as if he were dead ("lo corpo mio. . . si movea come cosa grave inanimata").

Dante's movement, from the death of the lady and his departure from Florence to his own metaphorical death caused by the withdrawal of Beatrice's greeting, echoes his progress from the first vision of the eaten heart, with its intimations of death, through the adoption and loss of the screen lady. Even if we say the events, for all their similarity, are rehearsed in a different register—the focus has clearly shifted from the external senses to the mind—Dante's imagination still seems entangled in the cul-de-sac duplicities of repetition, which are the lure of nostalgia. At the end of "Cavalcando l'altr'ier," Love disappears when Dante "took from him so large a part" [presi di lui sì gran parte]. This union of the already similar—Dante and Love are clearly doubles in the sonnet—indicates that when Amor orders him to pay court to a new beauty ("servir novo piacere"), there is no change in the nature of the object of Dante's love. Clearly a reordering of the relationship between the imagination and love is needed; the crisis of the denied greeting brings about just such a reconfiguration.

The second vision of the *Vita nuova* recalls the first; now, however, when Love appears to Dante in his dream, he is dressed in white and announces he is Dante's lord by saying, "Fili mi, tempus est ut pretermictantur simulacra nostra" [My son, it is time to put aside our feignings]. Despite the familiarity this pronouncement presumes, however, a familiarity especially pointed when we compare it to the explicit naming, "Ego dominus tuus," of the first dream, Dante says he understood that the figure before him was the God of Love neither from what he said nor from his appearance but because he called him the same way he had many times previously in his sleep.

Allora mi parea che io lo conoscesse, però che mi chiamava così come assai fiate ne li miei sonni m'avea già chiamato. (12.4)

The emphasis Dante places on "chiamare" recalls the circumstances of Beatrice's first appearance ("la quale fu chiamata da molti Beatrice li quali non sapeano che si chiamare"); yet at this moment when Love will, we suspect, acquire deeper meaning and significance, Dante implies that he knows him because he addressed him as "Fili mi" [my son]. In this brief tableau of recognition, Dante hovers between old and new, alerting us that the form Love is about to reveal here will not abandon past "simulacra" so much as reform them.

As Dante gazes, Love begins to weep, much as the natural spirit had. When Dante asks why, Love responds in Latin, "I am like the center of a circle, from whom all points on the circumference are equidistant; you, however, are not so." Dante asks what Love means; Love responds in Italian that he should not inquire into what it is not useful for him to know. Love then instructs Dante to write "certe parole per rima" to Beatrice in which he speaks of the power Love has over him through her. He must not address Beatrice directly, however, for that would not be fitting; the words rather should be an intermediary ("Queste parole fa che siano quasi un mezzo").

That Love weeps and answers Dante's questions so cryptically certainly will seem in retrospect to presage Beatrice's death. The theological overtones of Love's definition surely look forward to the correspondence he will draw between himself and the Beatrice who is glorified in heaven.[63] But even more than in the first vision, which also foretold her death and beatification, Dante's dream pertains primarily to his relation to Love here and now. The natural spirit will still be impeded; tears and sighs will still bespeak the body's anguish. But Love proclaims a new order here: he installs himself at the center, and it is this new *ratio* of Love to Dante's faculties that every perception of his outer senses and every intention of the inner senses will now strive to express.

Indeed, Amore's trope of center and circumference is itself a perfect emblem for the quality and nature of Dante's love during this phase of his life. Even before Plato, geometry, with its figures and *archai*, was situated in the hierarchy of knowing between the material world and the pure abstraction of ideas. By means of its images we pass from the visible to the intelligible, from actual objects about which we have opinions to theorems and principles that account for the existence of those objects. As a science of images that understanding abstracts and controls, geometry in fact became so closely associated with the imagination, especially in Neoplatonic thought but generally throughout the Middle Ages, that the imagination could and did express its own nature in geometric terms.[64] Love's circle, therefore, circumscribes two worlds: it encompasses the linearity of the screen lady, making clear why Dante insisted on lines of sight, and it demarcates a limit, on the other side of which we find the mathematical metaphysics of Beatrice as a nine. In announcing a transition from the bodily to the imaginative, from a lower to a higher level of being, Love at the same time locates Dante betwixt and between, very much "quasi un mezzo."

This new order needs a different kind of language for its articulation. Dante recapitulates his vision in a "ballata," the first poem in the *Vita*

---

63. As we shall see, in chapter 24 of the *Vita nuova* Love equates himself with Beatrice precisely when he inspires the notion in Dante that Cavalcanti's "donna" is a John the Baptist to Beatrice's Christ. This episode has excited much interesting comment about the relationship between the poetry and prose of the *Vita nuova*; see especially Michelangelo Picone, "Strutture poetiche e strutture prosastiche nella *Vita nuova*," *Modern Language Notes* 92 (1977): 117–29.

64. On geometry in Neoplatonic thought, and especially in Proclus, see Trimpi, *Muses*, 39–40, 200–10. See as well, M. W. Bundy, *The Theory of Imagination in Classical and Mediaeval Thought* (Urbana: University of Illinois Press, 1928); Edgar de Bruyne, *Études d'esthé-tique médiévale*, (Bruges: De Tempel, 1946), 2:chap. 5. It is especially telling that Proclus chose to discuss the imagination as a faculty of knowledge in his *Commentary on Euclid's Elements*. Trimpi points out that Augustine also associated geometry with the imagination, *Muses*, 56 n.

nuova that is not a sonnet. More important than this formal marking, however, is the inner rationale of the new poetry, which Love speaks about at such length. When Love animates the imagination, the language it produces seems to take on a substance of its own. From the time of this vision until the revelation that culminates in "Donne ch'avete," Dante's poems will speak of Love's power over him. They become, in other words, surrogates for Dante himself; they are invested with agency and motion as if they had a body and will of their own: "Gentil ballata mia, quando ti piace, / movi in quel punto che tu n'aggie onore" [Noble ballata of mine, go when it pleases you, where you will have a good reception]. These poems incorporate, as it were, the natural spirit's urge to convert the body into a sign. As Dante increasingly sees that Beatrice embodies his beatitude, the imagination, whose phantasms can stand apart from the objects they were drawn from, substantiates itself here as the persuasions of rhetoric.

At the same time, because they are rhetorical, the poems are never more than a body of words; even though motion, according to Aristotle, implies a body, Dante will explain in chapter 25 of the *Vita nuova* that the movement he gives to Love is a poetic conceit. Dante nevertheless justifies the fiction; he says that so long as vernacular poets can explain their purpose in prose, they can claim the license that permitted their Latin counterparts to make inanimate things behave as if they were human. For all their increased self-referentiality, the poems of the imagination will remain simulacra; what corporeality they have is the corporeality of prosopopoeia. But because the inner senses comprehend intentions removed from the material world, because they grasp the abstraction of geometric figures, because their phantasms were the medium of dreams sent from above, the poems that are the product of their operations will not express the bodily impediments of the natural spirit so much as become palpable signs that point to the godlike reality of Beatrice.[65] Produced by the denial of her word of greeting, they too will be, in Dante's words, "quasi un mezzo."

VI

For many readers, the *Vita nuova* chronicles Dante's continuing reassessment of the history of vernacular love poetry. What I have

---

65. For the phantasm as the agency of dreams and the organ of divination, see Agamben, *Stanzas*, 94.

called the poetry of the natural spirit generally corresponds in manner and content to early Sicilian and Tuscan as well as French and Provençal love poems; the poetry of this period of the imagination shows the strong influence of Cavalcanti, who held, as we have seen, that love is an experience of the inner senses, "dove sta memoria."[66] Dante's battle of thoughts about love, which significantly turns out to be a debate about language, about whether names are consequences of things (chap. 13), recapitulates the concerns and the style of Dante's "primo amico." His anguish "quando la mia memoria movesse la fantasia ad imaginare quale Amore mi facea" (16.2) [when memory moved fantasy to depict what Love had done to me] is Cavalcantian; so too is the dramatic reappearance of the pneumatic spirits, especially those of sight, on the occasion of the wedding feast when the ladies mocked Dante (chap. 14). But as Giuseppe Mazzotta has said, Guido had moved relentlessly "to unsettle any possible bonds between poetic images and love, or love and the order of the rational soul."[67] Contrary to Cavalcanti, Dante will now claim that his aesthetic experience of Beatrice does participate in the suprasensible, even if only analogously, and that a poetry of praise that renders the experience can comprehend the transcendent.

The events that lead to the writing of "Donne ch'avete" occupy what de Robertis calls "the true center of the book."[68] By chance Dante found himself among ladies "che per la vista mia . . . avessero compreso lo secreto del mio cuore" [who knew the secret of my heart from my appearance]. He was called by one of them ("fui chiamato"), who asked, "To what end [A che fine] do you love your lady, since you cannot endure her presence?" Dante responds that the goal ("fine") of his love once was his lady's greeting, for bliss ("beatitudine") resided in it. Since this greeting has been denied him, however, Love has placed all his happiness "in quello che non mi puote venire meno" [in what cannot be taken from me [or fail me]]. When they hear this, the ladies speak and sigh, "just as sometimes we see rain fall mixed with beautiful

---

66. de Robertis's *Il Libro della Vita nuova* provided the impetus for seeing in Dante's book condensed versions of literary history. For a recent reading in this manner, see J. F. Took, *Dante, Lyric Poet and Philosopher* (Oxford: Clarendon, 1990), 1–60. For a far more theoretical interpretation, which recasts literary history in terms of Dante's increasingly sophisticated idea of poetics, see María Rosa Menocal, *Writing in Dante's Cult of Truth from Borges to Boccaccio* (Durham and London: Duke University Press, 1991), 12–50.

67. Mazzotta, *Dante's Vision*, 60.

68. de Robertis, *Il libro della Vita nuova*, 86.

snow." They ask Dante in what he finds happiness now; he answers: "in those words which praise his lady." To this the lady who had spoken to Dante before replies that if this is so, his poems seem to have been written with some other purpose. Dante withdraws in shame and resolves henceforth to make his words the consequence of his deeds by writing only in praise of Beatrice.

Dante then says that while he was walking along a path that followed a very clear stream, he thought about how he should sing Beatrice's praises. It occurred to him that no mode would be fitting except if he spoke to a group of noble ladies ("se io non parlasse a donne in seconda persona, e non ad ogni donna, ma solamente a coloro che sono gentili"). Then, as if moved of its own accord, his tongue uttered the words "Donne ch'avete intelletto d'amore." He remembered this line; after a few days' thought, Dante used it to begin a "canzone" in the new style of praise.

With the composition of "Donne ch'avete intelletto d'amore," which explicitly equates its praise of Beatrice and the intelligibility of love, we enter the province of the vital spirit, dominated by Amore, a stronger god who comes to rule it.[69] As we have seen, the vital spirit resides in the heart, which is the seat from which the soul operates all bodily functions, turning each sensation into movement. It is the place where the operations of the natural and animal spirits are coordinated. Love resides here throughout the *Vita nuova*, revealing his power in his corporeal and imaginative effects.

But the Love who presides over the heart is a god: for Dante, of course, his divinity is a metaphor, but one that speaks less to his power or status than to how we are equipped to perceive him.[70] Dante will soon tell us that love is not a corporeal but an intellectual substance. Like all such substances, he therefore is separated from matter and beyond its limitations; consequently, love cannot properly be comprehended by any faculty of the sensible soul. Rather we will know it by

---

69. Cf. J. A. Scott, "Dante's Use of the Word 'Intelletto,'" *Italica* 40 (1963): 215–24.

70. In light of the debate, which, as Nardi shows, stretches back to Plotinus, who asked whether Love is god, demon, or passion of the soul, it is something of a surprise that Dante retains the notion of Love as a god. Psychological explanations of Love's nature were favored by most Italian poets; certainly they are fundamental to the "stilnovisti." Yet Dante insists on Love's divinity not just to reconcile traditions but, I would maintain, because he takes that divinity to be a metaphor for the intellect. See Nardi, *Dante e la cultura medievale*, 9–79. Nardi is strangely silent about Love's divinity in the *Vita nuova*.

what is like it in us; only the intellect with its comprehension of that which is universal and immaterial is able to contemplate Love. Only the "verbum mentis" will be adequate to express Amore's status as a "sustanzia intelligente" (*VN* 25.1).

Despite these differences, however, the god would not take his place in the heart if he did not share some affinity with it—if, that is to say, the communal operations of the vital spirit, Dante's denomination now for all the activities of the sensitive soul, and the generic conceptualizations of the intellect were not analogies of one another. Indeed, Dante goes out of his way to suggest just such a relationship with a striking simile. When the women hear that he now finds all his bliss "in that which cannot be taken from me," they speak and sigh, "sì come talora vedemo cadere l'acqua mischiata di bella neve." Although rain and snow are the same substance, the description registers a change that borders on transformation. The praise of Beatrice clearly inaugurates a new chapter in Dante's love. It generates a heat that will retain the beauty of the snow but none of its coldness. And yet it is equally apparent that his love also remains what it was.

Accordingly, the account of the discovery of Dante's new manner of poetry revisits the virtues of the natural and sensitive spirits and transfigures them in the light of the intellect. The community of women who converse with Dante emblemize the rational operations of the inner senses. They know Dante's heart's secret from his appearance ("per la vista mia"), a phrase that captures how the imagination both depends on and sees beyond the corporeal effects of love. Similarly, when Dante says his bliss now resides "in quello che non mi puote venire meno," he recalls the loss of his screen lady as a defense, "la bella difesa che m'era venuto meno." Once again, however, the ladies see through the mask. Just as the inner senses can determine whether the images stored in the memory are true or false as images, the ladies at once perceive that Dante's poems do not accord with what he now identifies as their intention, the praise of Beatrice.

As we have seen, by the action of the spirits the inner senses collectively possess an intellectual aspect; they have the capacity to compose and divide and are capable of forming judgments about their materials. The insight of the ladies who are their surrogates forces Dante to recognize the inadequacy of his previous poems of the imagination, an inadequacy Dante immediately proceeds to dramatize. The words "Donne ch'avete intelletto d'amore" came to his mind while he was walking along a clear stream; the setting deliberately recalls Love's appearance to Dante as he rode along a path beside a "beautiful, flowing, most clear river" after the death of Beatrice's friend. This earlier epiphany marked the transition from the natural to the sensitive spirits of sight and imagination. Now, however, Love doesn't appear; there is no vision at all. Instead we hear how Dante, pondering the mode he should adopt in order to praise Beatrice (pondering, that is to say, how to make his words consequent to their subject), decides he must address noble women as a group ("in seconda persona"). A different order of intellective imagination is at work here, one to which even the judgments of the inner senses and the "spiriti" that enabled them are only a means ("quasi un mezzo"). To enable him to represent Beatrice in this new way, Dante will now call on a kind of knowing in which imagination and reason touch.

Like Cavalcanti, Dante learned from Albertus and Thomas that the intellect is joined to the sensitive soul as a whole specifically through the imagination. One of the acts of the intellect is to compare the universal idea it has abstracted with any individual instantiation of it—to consider an oak as a tree, for instance. To do this, the intellect needs to form a particular image of the idea of tree; it therefore enlists the imagination to make this image out of the phantasms available in the inner senses. When the intellect is in action, therefore, it communicates with the body by means of the imagination; for Albertus Magnus, insofar as the intellect is operating in the brain, it is indistinguishable from the fantasy.[71]

This is the type of knowing—imaginative intellection is not a bad name for it—that Dante will claim "Donne ch'avete" initiates. Dante's love is intellectual and sensible at once; from this "canzone" on, the joining of these two modes of being in him supports the analogy between his own nature and the miracle of Beatrice's, which the poetry of praise makes explicit: in her human beauty and divine perfection ("la bella neve" and "l'acqua") coincide. Certainly the newness of Dante's "dolce stil novo" derives in part from his conception of Beatrice; an equally significant innovation of the Vita nuova rests on two concomitant hypotheses. The first is that Dante's own development as man and

---

71. Albertus Magnus, De Anima 1.2.9, section 66, quoted in Shaw, Guido Cavalcanti's Theory of Love, 41. I have followed Shaw's explanation of this action of the speculative intellect in this paragraph. See also Hugh of St. Victor, De unione corporis et spiritus, PL 177.287–88, quoted in Agamben, Stanzas, 97.

poet is the history of his deepening understanding of the likeness he and his madonna bear to each other; the second is that in its full flowering, that similitude will enable the words that praise Beatrice to present a true image of beatitude itself.

The scope of Dante's analogies becomes especially apparent if we measure his new understanding of love against Cavalcanti's. The various hypostatizations of beauty in a poem like "Veggio negli occhi de la donna mia" make it an appropriate text to compare both to Dante's "Donne ch'avete" and to Cino's "Poi ch'i fu', Dante," the sonnet I discussed in the last chapter.[72] In his "ballata," Guido concentrates the phenomenology of love into three moments. The first is the actual sighting of his beloved; the second is the generation of her image in the internal senses.

> Cosa m'aven, quand'i' le son presente,
> ch'i'no la posso a lo 'ntelletto dire:
> veder mi par de la sua labbia uscire
> una sì bella donna . . .

(5–8)

[Something happens to me when I am in her presence that I am unable to express to the intellect; I seem to see issue from her countenance, a beautiful lady . . .]

From this "bella donna" there is born immediately another "donna" of new beauty, from whom it seems a star moves and says: "your salvation has appeared."

> ché 'mmantenente
> ne nasce un'altra di bellezza nova,
> da la qual par ch'una stella si mova
> e dica: "La salute tua è apparita."

(9–12)[73]

One would think this third elaboration of the woman, now figured as ideal beauty, emerges, as Picone says, from intellectual abstraction,

---

72. I quote Cavalcanti's poems from Contini, *Poeti del duecento,* vol. 2.

73. In line 9 I follow Marti and read "ché" for "che." See *Poeti del Dolce stil nuovo,* ed. Mario Marti (Florence: Le Monnier, 1969), 181–82.

especially in light of the statement—"La salute tua è apparita"—that her appearance has produced.[74] This, however, is not the case. Guido in fact seems to insist that the formation of this noumenal lady blocks rational comprehension: the mind, he says, cannot comprehend the image of the "bella donna" that the inner senses have abstracted *because* another lady of new beauty is born from her: "de la sua labbia uscire / una sì bella donna, che la mente / comprender no la può, *ché* 'mmantenente ne nasce un'altra" (7–9).[75] This "entità ideale," who, as Contini says, alone is fit to satisfy the lover, surely has her dwelling in the realm where beauty is a transcendental;[76] Marti, I think, is right to associate the metaphorical "stella si mova" with the star of the Magi and the voice that precedes her, seeming to sing her name "d'umiltà" (13–16), with John the Baptist.[77] But because the intellect, which is the image of God that joins humankind and the divine, has been circumvented, nothing finally connects this final beautiful woman with her intentional counterpart.[78] Yes, the lady of the sensible intellect and her celestial analogue are both "bell[e] donn[e]" (8 and 13); the one becomes beautiful when the imagination fashions her phantasm (condensed in the word *uscire*), the sublime beauty of the other is born ("nasce") out of the intention of the first. The poem strongly suggests these elements are analogous (an "analogia entis"), but in fact the physical and the sublime are juxtaposed rather than correlated. The lady whom Cavalcanti actually sees is a metonymy; we infer her entire aspect from her "labbia," which refers specifically to her face. The brilliant grace she evokes is given its perceptible form as a metaphor, the star that seems to move and speak his salvation. The beauty that excites love, as Robert Harrison says, "belongs to an independent order of reality that has no *substantial* links to the world of generation and decay, and no real similitude in the world of sub-

---

74. Michelangelo Picone, "Immagine e somiglianza: Dai Siciliani a Dante," *Versants* 12 (1987): 63–71. See also Marti's note in *Poeti del Dolce stil nuovo*, 182.

75. Similarly, Guido says that whenever his beloved is present, "Cosa m'aven, quand' i' le son presente, / ch'i' no la posso a lo 'ntelletto dire" (5–6). I take this to mean something more than Marti's gloss: "Che io non la posso esprimere in termini logici neanche a me stesso" [That I cannot express her in logical terms even to myself].

76. *Poeti del duecento*, 2:521.

77. Marti, *Poeti de Dolce stil nuovo*, 182.

78. For a brief but suggestive examination of the valency of "image" and "similitude" in early Italian poetry generally and in Cavalcanti and Dante in particular, see Picone, "Immagine e somiglianza," and the bibliography cited there.

stances."[79] Indeed, there is no link because there is no similitude; as Guido declares in "Donna me prega," Love is always unable to make an image that can establish a similarity between perfect beauty and an individual woman.

> Vèn da veduta forma che s'intende,
> che prende—nel possibile intelletto,
> come in subietto,—loco e dimoranza.
> In quella parte mai non ha possanza
> perché da qualitate non descende:
> resplende—in sé perpetüal effetto;
> non ha diletto—ma consideranza;
> sì che non pote largir simiglianza.

$$(21–28)$$

[[Love] comes from the seen form that is abstracted, which takes up place and dwelling in the possible intellect as in a substance. Love never has power in that part because it does not derive from quality [i.e., from physical causes]; it shines upon itself as a perpetual effect. It has no pleasure, but reflection, because it cannot project a kindred image.][80]

In "Veggio negli occhi" the analogy between the material and immaterial is one in which the "as" is missing.

As a response, "Donne ch'avete intelletto d'amore" and Dante's other poems of praise are not a refutation of Cavalcanti (whose explicit presence, one should note, is most pronounced in this section of the *Vita nuova*), so much as a qualification. For Dante the analogies that allow the phenomenal world to participate in the noumenal do make his poetry the kindred image, a true "simiglianza" of Beatrice, herself both sensible and ideal. Thus the "intento trattato," the formal treatment of the theme of "Donne ch'avete," begins, as Dante explains in his division of the "canzone," with how Beatrice is understood in heaven

---

79. Harrison, *The Body of Beatrice*, 87–88.

80. For the most part I follow Shaw, *Guido Cavalcanti's Theory of Love*, 37–49, although he insists that "in quella parte" of line 24 refers to the sensitive soul rather than the possible intellect. This has been challenged; for the purposes of my argument, however, it does not matter whether the sensitive soul or the possible intellect is intended. See as well Corti, *La felicità mentale*, 20–27; *The Poetry of Guido Cavalcanti*, ed. and trans. Lowry Nelson, Jr. (New York: Garland, 1986), 103–5; Harrison, *The Body of Beatrice*, 69–90.

("che di lei si comprende in cielo").[81] Dante approximates the instantaneous act of intellection on the part of creatures of light by reversing the
earthly order of understanding; the verbalization that is its end comes
first: "Angelo clama in divino intelletto / e dice." The angel's words,
however, do not arise, as ours do, from seeing Beatrice's body or its
image but as a response to her marvelous being that is light.

>   nel mondo si vede
>   maraviglia ne l'atto che procede
>   d'un'anima che 'nfin qua su risplende.

(16–18)

[in the world is seen a marvel in act which proceeds from a soul
which shines even here on high.[82]]

Light enables understanding; in a play of speculation that makes her
one with heaven's intelligences, Beatrice's light is reflected in the light
that is the angel's utterance in the divine intellect.[83]

The rest of the "canzone" treats "how Beatrice is known on earth." In
it the intellect joins with the senses to praise first "the nobility of her
soul, and the effective virtues that proceed from it," which are dis-
played as effects registered in the sensitive and nutritive souls. Dante
describes how wherever Beatrice goes Love freezes the thoughts in
every vile heart; should such a man look on her, he would either
become noble or die. And if a worthy man looks on her, he will grow so
humble, every offense will be forgotten. At the same time, however,
framing these "earthly" examples of her "virtù," are two statements

---

81. The division of this particular "canzone" has naturally attracted much attention.
See Robert Durling and Ronald Martinez, *Time and the Crystal* (Berkeley: University of
California Press, 1990), 53–70. For Durling and Martinez, the structure of the "canzone"
relies on the analogies that drive the Neoplatonic theory of the procession from unity to
multiplicity and the corresponding principle of return. For this reason, their reading is
quite similar to mine. I do not, however, think recourse to Neoplatonic emanationism is
necessary to explain the analogies of "Donne ch'avete"; the hierarchies of medieval
scholastic psychology, precisely the sort of thing that attracted Guinizzelli and Cavalcanti, furnished an equally effective set of analogies.

82. For the phrase "maraviglia ne l'atto," see Foster and Boyde, *Dante's Lyric Poetry*,
2:99. As they note, despite Michele Barbi's reservations, "atto" would seem to reflect the
scholastic sense of "actus": Beatrice is "a living miracle," a marvel actually realized on
earth.

83. Durling and Martinez specifically read Beatrice's light in terms of Neoplatonic
principles of procession and return in *Time and the Crystal*, 59–62.

that raise Beatrice to supernal heights. The stanza begins by saying, "My lady is desired in the highest heaven" [Madonna è disiata in sommo cielo]; it ends by disclosing that God has ordained even a greater grace for her than those Dante has already enumerated—no one who has spoken with her can come to an evil end.

> Ancor l'ha Dio per maggior grazia dato
> che non pò mal finir chi l'ha parlato.
>
> (41–42)

When we ponder the nobility of her soul, the homology of light that had made Beatrice one with the angels' understanding of her becomes an analogy that links heaven and earth: the counterpart of heaven's want of Beatrice is the numbness in the "cor villani" ("lor pensero agghiaccia e pere" [their thought freezes and perishes]) and the forgetting of offense in the "cor gentili." Like the kingdom of God, which shall be denied to those who would win it, Beatrice's virtues are felt on earth as the gains that result from losses.

Dante then treats the nobility of her body and the "bellezze" that attend it. He describes first those qualities of beauty that pertain to Beatrice's body generally, then those that pertain particularly to her eyes, which are the beginning of love, and to her mouth, which is the end of love. Those "bellezze che sono secondo tutta la persona" correspond to the communal understandings of the inner senses: Beatrice's color is pearl-like, "in a way that befits a lady, not to excess" [in forma quale / convene a donna aver, non for misura (47–48)]. Those that pertain specifically to her eyes and mouth correspond to the animal and vital spirits: "fiery spirits of love issue from her eyes," which reach the heart of anyone who sees her. Yet these too are linked to higher faculties of understanding. All beauty is known and tested by Beatrice's, and through her beauty itself is known: "per essempio di lei bièltà si prova" (50).[84] To those who regard her, Beatrice affords the palpable experience of perceiving beauty as a transcendental. Her every virtue reforms the body's existence so that it might conform to the mind's; she is presented as nothing less than the principle of aesthetic knowing.

---

84. Dante's line admits of both interpretations, as Foster and Boyde explain in *Dante's Lyric Poetry*, 102.

VII

For Dante, "Donne ch'avete" became the programmatic exemplification of the "sweet new style." In the accustomed manner of the *Vita
nuova*, however, he has indicated his ascension to this new poetic universe in ways that hark back to the old. The dialogue with the ladies in
chapter 18 began when Dante was called by one of them who was
known for her elegant speech ("fui chiamato da una di queste gentili
donne. La donna che m'avea chiamato era donna di molto leggiadro
parlare"). The repetition of "chiamare" invokes those earlier moments
when Dante was about to move to a nobler conception of love. Moreover, his statement that his bliss now rests "in quello che non mi puote
venire meno" recalls, as Singleton has pointed out, Mary's choice of the
good portion—that is, the life of contemplation—which cannot be
taken away from her ("quae non auferetur ab ea" [Luke 10.42]).[85] But
even this signal of transition to something new looks back, as we have
seen, to the loss of the screen lady. The locale of the "nove rime," as
Bonagiunta will call them in the *Purgatorio,* is not the rational soul:
Dante insists that the audience remains those "donne ch'avete intelletto
d'amore," ladies who are preeminently the spokeswomen of the inner
senses.

It is therefore important to note that in the *Vita nuova* at least, neither
ethics nor theology propels Dante's discovery of the new manner,
though ethics and theology certainly attend it. When Dante turns from
poetry about himself to more noble matter, as he says in chapter 17, he
does not move from a self-centered to a more selfless love out of moral
or religious conviction; rather the moral and the religious follow as consequences of his poetical development. To express Beatrice fully, he
comes to see that the knowledge of the imagination must be illumi-
nated by the light of the intellect; since intellection considers the
essence of its object in the absence of the body and sensation, Dante's
love will seek a poetry that can also pass beyond the flesh and its affec-
tions.

In the Middle Ages, two disciplines investigated the suprasensible:
metaphysics and theology. Dante's "stilo de la loda," his style of praise,
therefore undertakes to recast the psychology of love in the language of

---

85. Singleton, *Essay,* 153.

both: metaphysics predominates before the death of Beatrice's father and Dante's dream of her death, theology thereafter. In both cases, however, Dante insists that we acknowledge the analogical nature of his own discourse. Consider, for instance, "Amore e 'l cor gentil."

> Amore e 'l cor gentil sono una cosa,
> sì come il saggio in suo dittare pone,
> e così esser l'un sanza l'altro osa
> com'alma razional sanza ragione.
> Falli natura quand'è amorosa,
> Amor per sire e 'l cor per sua magione,
> dentro la qual dormendo si riposa
> tal volta poca e tal lunga stagione.
>
> (1–8)

[Love and the noble heart are the selfsame thing, just as the wise man states in his poem, and the one can be without the other as much as the rational soul can be without reason. Nature creates them when she is amorous, Love as lord and the heart as his domicile, within which he lies sleeping, sometimes a little and sometimes a long while.]

In the "divisione" of this famous sonnet, Dante says that love is a movement from potency to act. He tells us that the stanza I have quoted sets forth what kind of substance such a potentiality can exist in and how both are brought into being and "look after each other as form does matter" [come l'uno guarda l'altro come forma materia]. In the sestet that follows, he shows how this potentiality is realized in being, first in a man, then in a woman. By invoking the principles that explain how things come to be, Dante clearly has elevated what he calls his "ragionata cagione," his reasoned commentary on the genesis of love, to the level of an Aristotelian inquiry into the causes of things. But in the sonnet, potency and act are entirely absent; we read instead that love and the noble heart can no more exist without each other than the rational soul without reason, that Nature makes both love and the heart when she is amorous. Metaphysics exists in metaphors—Love is sire, the heart his house—both here and in the companion sonnet "Ne li occhi porta la mia donna Amore." These poems amount to a declaration not only that love is rational but that it can be imaged, provided we recognize both reason and the images are analogies of Beatrice's miraculous being.

The same is true of the events Dante recounts after his vision of Beatrice in death's shroud, a vision, I note in passing, that brings to a close all that was put in motion by the initial vision of the veiled Beatrice consuming Dante's flaming heart. In the wake of this "empty imagining" [vana imaginazione], Love appeared one day in Dante's imagination, where he says "bless the day that I took you captive." Dante then becomes aware that his friend Cavalcanti's lady, whose name was Giovanna but whose beauty led to her being called Primavera (Spring), was coming toward him, followed by Beatrice. Love interprets this procession: Giovanna has been called Primavera solely to indicate that like that other Giovanni, John the Baptist, she will come before ("prima verrà") Beatrice this day. Moreover, Love continues, "Anyone who considers the matter subtly would call Beatrice Amore, because she so greatly resembles me" [per molta simiglianza che ha meco]. After Dante records the sonnet he wrote for Guido about this remarkable advent, he interrupts the narrative of his "libello" with his excursus on love: Amore is an intellectual, not a corporeal, substance; poetic license permits Dante to lend him a body, movement, laughter. And with this digression into literary history, Love disappears as an actor from the *Vita nuova*.

Just as the denial of Beatrice's greeting, which had brought about a metaphorical death in Dante, was the occasion of a vision that marked his transition to a higher form of knowing—Love abandoned his "simulacra" so that he could image himself as center and circumference—so Love, appearing now in Dante's imagination after his "imaginar fallace" of Beatrice's death, appeals to the verities of theology to provide an ultimate series of analogies—all based on the affinity between knower and what is known—that make his perception the fullest image of her being. For Dante, as man and God are one in Christ, so woman and beatitude are one in Beatrice; as woman and beatitude are one in Beatrice, so mind and body join in Dante to sing her praise. It is just this play of relations that acknowledge difference as they establish similarity that Dante stresses in the sonnet to Guido: seeing the one marvelous lady follow the other, he says:

e sì come la mente mi ridice,
Amor mi disse: "Quell'è Primavera,
e quell'ha nome Amor, sì mi somiglia."

[And just as my memory retells it Love said to me: This one is Spring, and the other's name is Love, so much does she resemble me.]

Amor resides "dove sta memoria," as Cavalcanti held, but Love declares from there that the miracle that joins heaven and earth in Beatrice allows Dante to fashion metaphors from the language of theology and use them in poetry that issues from the conjunction of reason and sense.

Indeed, Love himself and Beatrice seem to stand in the same relation as remembered speech to its actual utterance. On the one hand, Dante tells us in chapter 25 in the *Vita nuova* that Love is a god, a "sustanzia intelligente"; on the other, Love raises his mansion in the sensitive soul only accidentally. It is important to note that nowhere does Dante imply that Love is simply a figure of speech. What is figurative is his corporeality, which Dante justifies by extending the license of poetic invention from Latin to vernacular poets. Dante hardly diminishes Love; rather he claims that the substantiation of imagination we saw after Love declared himself the center and circumference is now complete. Love's body and the poems of praise are one, even as Love's divinity and Beatrice's are the same.

These equations explain why Dante says he wrote "Tanto gentile" and "Vede perfettamente onne salute," the two sonnets in which "Beatrice's exaltation culminates and concludes,"[86] so that "not only those who could see her with their own eyes, but others as well might know whatever words could say of her" [acciò che non pur coloro che la poteano sensibilemente vedere, ma li altri sappiano di lei quello che le parole ne possono fare intendere]. No longer a "mezzo," a purely mediating agency, these poems have acquired a density almost corporeal in nature: they make Beatrice's virtues visible even to those not fortunate enough to have been in her presence.

We may say, therefore, that the poems of praise in general treat Beatrice from two perspectives, one the mirror of the other. Those grouped around "Amore e 'l cor gentil" contemplate Beatrice as metaphysical

---

86. The quotation is from de Robertis, *Il Libro*, 140. Dante makes the same point in introducing "Vede perfettamente onne salute": he wants to make manifest Beatrice's virtues "a chi ciò non vedea," that is, to those who had not seen her in the company of other ladies.

cause of love; in the technical terms of scholastic philosophy, she is represented as love's first perfection, she is love "in potentia." Those poems that follow "Io mi senti' svegliar" incorporate all love's real effects in Beatrice; not only is she the second perfection, from whom every actualization of love proceeds, she is Love's new soteriology, an incarnated greeting of salvation ("salute") come from heaven. Together the poems of praise constitute Beatrice as the body and soul of love.

VIII

To this point, Dante has compounded the aesthetics of the *Vita nuova* from the analogies that relate his poetry and Beatrice to the ways that the body and mind know. But the body dies. As Robert Harrison has said, Beatrice's death assassinates the lyric voice in the *Vita nuova;* the "canzone" "Sì lungiamente" is broken off, and Dante writes no poetry the following year.[87] The prose that comments on her death notoriously echoes this silence: Dante will not speak of it because it falls outside his book's purpose; and even if it had not, Dante says he lacks the language to deal with it as it deserves; moreover, to have done so would entail praising himself. This last reason, Harrison notes, should remind us that to this point "Dante has been the praiser of Beatrice. To disclose the *sentenzia* of Beatrice's death now would reverse the relationship of praiser and praised" (99), an act that hardly befits the announced intention of the book. But why would Dante's description of her "partita da noi" involve praise of himself? Since Dante has presented Beatrice alive as a miracle he can represent only by analogy to his own growing understanding of her, Beatrice's death leaves him with nothing for his knowing to be an analogy of. To treat her being gathered up in glory "under the banner of that blessed queen the Virgin Mary" is beyond Dante's intellect; to write poems in the current style about her earthly passing would be a narcissistic celebration of his own powers of

---

87. Harrison argues that Beatrice's death in fact marks and unveils the limitations of the lyric's power to incorporate into its all-inclusive present the phenomenality of experience. With its intense awareness of temporality, narrative battles to displace lyric narcissism in the concluding acts of the *Vita nuova* (*The Body of Beatrice*, 93–170). Although I disagree with some of his emphases—if we adopt Stillinger's equation that Dante is the prose and Beatrice the poetry, then I would say that narrative and lyric throughout the *Vita nuova* are more analogies than antagonists of one another—I am indebted to Harrison's reading.

description, since the woman who both sanctions their praise and is its object no longer exists.[88] "Reticent commentary" is Dante's only option.[89]

Instead of describing Beatrice's death, however, Dante tells us why the number nine loomed so large in her departure, why in fact Beatrice is a nine. The last vision *we* see of Beatrice, in other words, is, by Dante's own account, a vision of analogies: "questo numero fue ella medesima; per similitudine dico" [she herself was this number, by analogy I mean]. She is the abstraction of mathematics, a perfect number, the product of her own root; she is the metaphysical harmony among the nine spheres of heaven, which mediate their influences and affect the earth according to the relations they have to one another; she is a theological miracle, the unity of the Father, Son, and Holy Ghost.

In the wake of Beatrice's death, however, Dante, whose love for her finds its epitome in his realization of her capacity for similitude, has nothing but the history of how he came to this realization to console him. Without her, he can go no farther; his lone recourse, it seems, is to fall back on his own resources, just as he did when the screen lady departed and Beatrice's friend died. The rest of the *Vita nuova*, therefore, until its very end, reverses the trajectory of understanding that had governed Dante's development as Beatrice's lover. "Li occhi dolenti," the "cattivella canzone" [woeful song] that is the first poem of mourning Dante records in his "libello" (chap. 31), labors mightily to

---

88. Dante's comments here provide a retrospective explanation of why he positioned the poems about Beatrice's grief over her father's death between the metaphysical and theological poems of praise. "Voi che portate la sembianza umile" and "Se' tu colui," the two sonnets that precede the "nova fantasia" of Dante's "canzone," differ most from their earlier versions ("Onde venite voi così pensose" and "Voi, donne, che pietoso atto mostrate") in two respects. The first is that the emphasis has shifted from Dante himself to the ladies he addresses. The second is that in the poems Dante did include, the ladies have become the embodied signs of Beatrice's grief: "veggiovi tornar sì sfigurate, / che 'l cor mi triema di vederne tanto," ("Voi che portate," 13–14) [I see you return [from Beatrice] so disfigured that my heart trembles to see even only this]. These poems thus rehearse the period of the screen ladies and the impeded natural spirit, just as the "Donna pietosa," the "canzone" of the "vana imaginare," repeats the motifs of the period of the imagination. Once Dante admits, as he does in "Donna pietosa," that because Death has been with his lady, he so desires to die he has taken on Death's likeness ("ch'io ti somiglio in fede" [78]), Dante exhausts all he can say about death and Beatrice as analogies. On the two earlier versions of Dante's sonnets, see Foster and Boyde, *Dante's Lyric Poetry*, 2:111–12.

89. Reticent commentary is Durling and Martinez's felicitous phrase for Dante's practice at this point and elsewhere in the *Vita nuova*. See *Time and the Crystal*, 57 ff.

recall the Beatrice he had praised in the new style. The poems for Beatrice's brother and the anniversary sonnet (chaps. 32–34) recapitulate the indirection of the poems Dante wrote during the period when the imaginative spirits dominated his soul. The episode of the "donna gentile" (chaps. 35–39) physically repeats the experience of the screen lady. Only when Dante finally is able to break from her and rededicate himself to Beatrice (chaps. 40–42) does a miraculous vision appear to him, which is a prohemium to a new life.

IX

The period of silence that followed Beatrice's death ended when Dante wrote "Li occhi dolenti." He says his purpose was to give vent to his sorrow by speaking "of her for whom so much grief had destroyed my soul" (*VN* 31.1). The phrase reminds us of Cavalcanti; we therefore may be surprised to discover that the "canzone" rehearses the themes that dominated the poems of the vital, not the animal, spirit. Indeed, "Li occhi dolente" is the mirror image of "Donne ch'avete." Each poem begins with a "proemio" that specifies "donne gentili" for its audience. As we have seen, "Donne ch'avete" then treats of Beatrice in heaven, where an angel cries in the divine mind, at once in wonder at Beatrice and out of desire for her. "Li occhi dolente" announces "Ita n'è Beatrice in l'alto cielo, / nel reame ove li angeli hanno pace" [Beatrice has gone to the highest heaven, to the realm where the angels have peace], because her great humility

> passò li cieli con tanta vertute,
> che fé maravigliar l'etterno sire,
> sì che dolce disire
> lo giunse di chiamar tanta salute.
>
> (22–24)

[penetrated the heavens with such virtue that it made the eternal father marvel, so that sweet longing moved him to summon such blessedness to him.]

In "Donne ch'avete," Dante next discusses Beatrice's virtues on earth, how she makes perish the thought of every lowbred heart [cor villani] and causes each virtuous soul who sees her to forget every offense. In

"Li occhi dolenti," Dante contrasts those who do not weep when they speak of Beatrice's death and those who do. The first have stony hearts so evil and vile no kind spirit could penetrate it; indeed,

> Non è di cor villan sì alto ingegno,
> che possa imaginar di lei alquanto.
>
> (35–36)

[No base heart possesses sufficient wit to imagine her least quality.]

Those who in their thoughts do see what Beatrice was, and see that she was taken away, feel grief and the desire to sigh and die weeping. Finally, in "Donne ch'avete" Dante praises the noble beauty of Beatrice's entire person, and of her eyes and mouth in particular, on which no one can gaze fixedly. In "Li occhi dolenti," Dante says the grief, anguish, and sorrow he suffers are so great, no tongue can speak them.[90]

As pronounced as these parallels are, however, they do not obscure the chief difference between the "canzoni." Dante's inner states no longer serve as analogies of Beatrice's being; they have become objects of representation in their own right. Whereas in "Donne ch'avete" Dante had praised Beatrice's corporeal beauty, in "Li occhi dolenti" he describes the effects of her on him. These are located chiefly in his sensitive soul; after its praise of Beatrice, the poem effectively depicts how sensible pain and suffering make Dante waver in his attempt to sustain imaginative intellection of her.

> Dannomi angoscia li sospiri forte,
> quando 'l pensero ne la mente grave
> mi reca quella che m'ha 'l cor diviso:
> ⋯⋯⋯⋯⋯⋯⋯⋯⋯⋯⋯⋯⋯⋯
> E quando 'l maginar mi ven ben fiso,
> giugnemi tanta pena d'ogne parte,
> ch'io riscuoto per dolor ch'i' sento;
> ⋯⋯⋯⋯⋯⋯⋯⋯⋯⋯⋯⋯⋯⋯
> Poscia piangendo, sol nel mio lamento

---

90. These parallels, as well as others, have been noted; see, for example, Foster and Boyde, *Dante's Lyric Poetry*, 2:132. What has not been pointed out is how the praise of Beatrice, as I say below, is rendered from the perspective of the sensitive spirits.

chiamo Beatrice, e dico: "Or se' tu morta?"
e mentre ch'io la chiamo, me conforta.

(43–45, 49–51, 54–56)

[When dismal thought brings to mind the one who has split my
heart, harsh sighs cause me anguish . . . and when such imagining
takes strong hold of me, such pain wracks my every limb, I tremble
from the suffering I feel . . . [91] Then I weep alone and call to Beatrice
in my lament, and say "Are you really dead?" And while I call to her,
I am comforted.]

Half poem of praise and half personal lamentation, "Li occhi dolenti"
would embody Beatrice, would stand for her in the way "Tanto gentile"
and "Vede perfettamente" do stand as her surrogates. But Dante no
longer can maintain the analogy and give his poem her substance
because he knows Beatrice truly is dead; the praise throughout has been
rendered from the perspective of the sensitive spirits, which cannot sub-
stitute for her any more than imagination without intellection could
comprehend her. The transformative moment of their union that Dante
began to describe in "Sì lungiamente" has passed.[92] "Li occhi dolenti"
consequently initiates the descent through the hierarchies of knowing
that makes the part of the *Vita nuova* after Beatrice's death the reflection
of the part before it. The "canzoni" are "sisters" [sorelle], as Dante calls
them, not only to "Donne ch'avete" but to all those poems of the middle
period of imagination, in which Dante described the sometimes harsh
effects of his love for Beatrice obliquely, "quasi per mezzo."

The poems Dante wrote at the request of Beatrice's brother emphasize this obliquity. Either Manetto or Ricovero Portinari asked Dante to
compose something about a woman who had died but to disguise its
words so that it would seem that they were meant for some other lady.
Dante recognizes that his friend was actually referring to Beatrice; he

---

91. Though "'l maginar" can carry the sense of thought, without any sense of illusion,
as Foster and Boyde note (*Dante's Lyric Poetry*, 2:137), there is no reason to think Dante is
not referring to the faculty of imagination here.

92. Dante describes here how his long service has enabled Love to so empower his
spirits, they speak the name of Beatrice in all its meaning: "poi prende Amore in me tanta
vertute, / che fa li miei spiriti gir parlando, / ed escon for chiamando / la donna mia, per
darmi più salute." "Salute" here bears all its meanings; Dante's conceit looks back to and
completes his first encounter with Beatrice. On whether "spiriti" should be "sospiri," see
Foster and Boyde, *Dante's Lyric Poetry*, 2:131.

seized the opportunity to mask his own grief for her by constructing the sonnet "Venite a intender li sospiri miei" so that it would appear as if Dante had written it for his friend. After pondering the matter, however, Dante thought one sonnet too small a gift to give to someone who had been so closely related to Beatrice; he therefore wrote a "canzone," "Quantunque volte," in two stanzas, "the one truly for him and the other for myself, although both appear written for the same person" (*VN* 33.2).

In the poems themselves, Dante translates these indirections into sighs that speak and act as the sensitive spirits had done before. Their appeal is communal, just as sight and hearing had once appealed to the communal operations of the inner senses.

> E' si raccoglie ne li miei sospiri
> un sono di pietate,
> che va chiamando Morte tuttavia . . .
>
> ("Quantunque volte," 14–16)

[My sighs gather together into a pitiful sound that calls continually on Death . . .]

Dante still strives to invoke the glorious lady of his mind: the "canzone" ends by asserting that "when she died [or, literally, 'when she departed from our sight'] Beatrice's physical beauty was transformed into a great spiritual beauty, which spreads a light of love throughout heaven. This light greets the angels and moves their high, subtle intellects to wonder, so noble it is there."

> perché 'l piacere de la sua bieltate,
> partendo sé da la nostra veduta,
> divenne spirital bellezza grande,
> che per lo cielo spande
> luce d'amor, che li angeli saluta,
> e lo intelletto loro alto, sottile
> face maravigliar, sì v'è gentile.
>
> (20–26)

One way to measure the distance between "Li occhi dolenti" and "Quantunque volte" is to point out that in the latter work Dante's sighs precede and assume a certain priority over his description of Beatrice in glory; that description predominates in "Li occhi dolenti." Beatrice's presence is well on the way to becoming only Dante's memory of her.

Indeed, this period of Dante's life concludes on the anniversary of Beatrice's death. As he sat drawing an angel on some panels, Dante became aware that he was being watched by men of consequence in Florence. This public incident led him to write an anniversary poem that has two beginnings. They differ in the following way: in the first, Dante says that Beatrice was already in his memory; in the second, he tells when it was that she came into his memory. In fact every circumstance that attends either version of "Era venuta ne la mente mia" invokes memory; drawing on tablets, as Mary Carruthers documents, was a symbol for remembrance.[93] With its ontological breaks and temporal gaps, memory is a fit setting for a sonnet that passes in review all the levels of knowing that marked Dante's progress in love.

> Amor, che ne la mente la sentia,
> s'era svegliato nel destrutto core,
> e diceva a' sospiri: "Andate fore":
> per che ciascun dolente si partia.
>
> (5–8)

[Love, who felt Beatrice in my mind, was awakened in my ruined heart, and said to my sighs, "Go forth": so each left sorrowing.]

The sighs in turn look back to the "nobile intelletto" [noble intellect], which they address at the end of the poem. But Dante's heart is in ruins, and with Love issuing orders to his sighs from there, it was perhaps inevitable that the circle be completed and Dante pass from the communal consolations of remembrance to the personal involvements of physical infatuation.[94]

X

Dante first became aware that a "gentle lady, young and very beautiful" was gazing at him from a window while he was immersed in

---

93. Carruthers, *The Book of Memory*, 52.
94. See Harrison, *The Body of Beatrice*, 111–15.

thoughts of the past, thoughts so sorrowful they gave his face the appearance of terrible distress: "io fosse in parte ne la quale mi ricordava del passato tempo, molto stava pensoso, e con dolorosi pensamenti, tanto che mi faceano parere de fore una vista di terribile sbigottimento" (*VN* 35.1). The lady answers his anguish with compassion: "la quale . . . mi riguardava sì pietosamente, quanto a la vista, che tutta la pietà parea in lei accolta" [she looked at me so compassionately, it seemed from her appearance all pity was gathered in her]. This encounter set in motion Dante's notorious affair with the "donna gentile."[95]

Dante has marked very deftly the moment of transition from memory as an inner sense to the material domain of the natural spirits: just as his body, immediately before he saw the screen lady, had become legible because it bore the signs of love, so now sorrow has written its signs on his face, which the "donna gentile" reads and returns in the form of her solicitude.[96] As opposed to his love for Beatrice, however, which configured Dante's perceptions as analogies of the woman they strove to know, there is no difference here between the compassion of the "donna gentile" and the self-pity that impedes his spirit; "her face," as Robert Harrison has argued, "assumes an aspect of grief which literally doubles Dante's own grieving aspect" (116). From the start, and throughout their acquaintance, Dante never presents the lady as anything more than an extension of himself.

Indeed, the narcissism that lies at the root of this final stage in Dante's descent through the hierarchies of knowing in fact characterizes the essence of all that has happened to him after Beatrice's death. The affair with the "donna gentile" is merely the clearest indication that Dante's remembering Beatrice has actually been a slow forgetting of her; consolation all along has cloaked a growing self-absorption that finds its fullest realization here. From the time of her death, his life has been an illusion, an inverted mirror image of the progress of his devotion to Beatrice.

---

95. The affair is notorious, of course, because Dante radically reinterpreted it in the *Convivio*, where the "donna gentile" becomes Lady Philosophy. The transformation makes some sense if the "donna gentile" in some way epitomizes Dante's search for consolation following Beatrice's death. One might then say the descent through the hierarchies of knowledge that culminates in Dante's love for the "donna" in the *Vita nuova* was propaedeutic, a revealing of the wound, to adopt one of Philosophy's own metaphors, which the more sober, allegorical discourse of the *Convivio* could then cure.

96. This point is also made by Harrison, *The Body of Beatrice*, 115.

In light of this inversion, I would maintain that the events that follow Beatrice's death, even more than those prior to it, bear the stamp of Cavalcanti.[97] Guido's Averroism, especially in "Donna me prega," has long been debated.[98] Beyond the debate, however, lies a literary question that has not been discussed sufficiently: why would the idea that the intellect was a unity in and of itself, completely separated from the material world, appeal to a poet writing about love? One possible answer is that by embracing it, Cavalcanti could offer a radical response to the proposition the *Roman de la Rose* had made famous—"fin amor" is at heart a species of narcissism. As an Averroist, Cavalcanti could clasp narcissism to himself with a vengeance; he would insist that the entire process of love was completely sensible and self-contained, entirely divorced from the intellect. If there is an analogy between reason and the senses, Cavalcanti would hold that it is imaginary; indeed, the experiences that prove how far love is from the ideal are precisely those that convert "amor" into "morte." As a rejoinder to Sicilian-Tuscan poets, for whom love was sentiment, such a conception of passion is devastating, not only in itself but for the extraordinary transformations in the psychology of love it inspired.

With Beatrice's death, Dante seems almost explicitly to dramatize the premises of such thought. Beatrice now *is* an intellect wholly separated from the phenomenal world; by forgetting the living miracle she was, Dante in effect consigns her to the nonindividuated impersonality of the unified intellect. Moreover, as he comes to love the "donna gentile," Dante "lives through" both alternatives that Cavalcanti had

97. As if to signal that this phase of the *Vita nuova* is a direct meditation on Cavalcanti, Dante relates that he will not include his epistle "Quomodo sedet sola civitas," even though it bemoans the condition of Florence following Beatrice's death, because it is in Latin. Dante intends, however, that the *Vita nuova* should be entirely in the vernacular, an intention, he says, his "primo amico" fully endorses (*VN* 30.3).

98. See especially Bruno Nardi, "Noterella polemica sull' averroismo di Guido Cavalcanti," *Rassegna di filosofia* 3 (1954): 47–71; Corti, *La felicità mentale*, 3–37; Harrison, *The Body of Beatrice*, 75–81. Nardi was responding to Guido Favati, who argued that Cavalcanti was an Aristotelian; see Favati's response, "Guido Cavalcanti, Dino del Garbo e l'averroisimo di Bruno Nardi," *Filologia romanza* 2 (1955): 67–83. Other readings include Shaw, *Guido Cavalcanti's Theory of Love*, for whom the canzone reflects the doctrines of Albertus Magnus; there have been Thomistic readings as well. Agamben's comment is as follows (*Stanzas*, 107).

The so-called Averroism of Cavalcanti . . . consists in the fact that the phantasm (the phantastic pneuma), origin and subject of love, is precisely that in which, as in a mirror, the union *(copulatio)* of the individual with the unique and separate intellect is accomplished.

posited as the end of love: he already has "died," at least metaphorically, in his grief; now he falls in love with someone else.[99]

XI

The solipsism of Dante's love for the "donna gentile," however, threatens not only Beatrice's "otherness," as Harrison has said, but the dialectical nature of the *Vita nuova*. From its opening analogy of memory and book, Dante has challenged the narcissism of both the *Roman de la Rose* (let us accept, as Contini does, that Dante wrote *Il fiore*) and Cavalcanti's more subtle version, each of which ultimately makes desire, knowledge, and writing reflections of one another.[100] To the contrary, Dante's philosophy of the self has always recognized the differences as well as the similarities between his identity and that of the woman he loves. For this reason, Dante for the most part sidesteps the tendency toward abstract personification that a poetics that takes the love of Narcissus as its foundational event will almost inevitably embrace. His pneumatic spirits, for instance, seem far more "embodied" than Cavalcanti's because each looks back to the lower faculty that is its material

---

99. In this regard, Dante's extraordinary answer to Cino da Pistoia, "Io sono stato con Amore insieme / da la circulazion del sol mia nona," should be read as a late exercise in Cavalcantianism. Cino had asked Dante whether the soul, finding that it has not died ("poi se morte le perdona" [86a.5]), is at liberty to love another ("si può ben trasformar d'altra persona" [l.8]), since it is clear that the woman he has loved will never answer his soul's desires, and he feels that Love has again "entered through my window" [entrato, lasso, per la mia fenestra (11)]. Even though Dante responds by referring to himself as poet of the *Vita nuova*, he answers Cino's "quistione," which rehearses Cavalcanti's obsessions with perfect pitch, as if he were Guido. The man who urges reason and virtue against love, he says, raises his voice in a storm. Love abrogates free will; therefore we must love anew if Love has again entered our hearts. (For text and translation, see *Dante's Lyric Poetry*, 86a and 86). As Foster and Boyde note, Dante's poem was accompanied by an explanatory letter (*Epistle* III) that fixes the date of its composition: Dante gives voice to these sentiments, which contradict those of the *Vita nuova*, about a decade after he had written his "libello." Dante very well may have been reflecting on the "donna gentile," whom he also first saw at a window. In retrospect, the infatuation would seem to him completely Cavalcantian. As I argue in chapter 5, however, by the time Dante came to write the *Comedy*, he would classify these sentiments as a kind of Ovidianism. In his *Epistle*, Dante cites the Ovid of the *De Rerum Transformatione* as his authority for his explanation.

100. The question of whether Dante is the author of *Il fiore*, an early Italian translation of the *Roman de la Rose* into sonnets by ser Durante, has long been debated. For a full discussion, see the edition by Gianfranco Contini, *Il Fiore e Il Detto d'Amore* (Milan: Mondadori, 1984), lxxi–xcv. Following Contini, most scholars accept the poem's attribution to Dante. Even if he were not the author, however, it seems highly likely he knew the *Roman* when he wrote the *Vita nuova*.

base and forward to the higher faculty that is its form. They have been incorporated in a system of proportions that can coordinate the particularity of bodies and the universality of intellection because the operations of each result in language and all language moves to constitute itself as knowledge.

The remaining events of the *Vita nuova* therefore restore the multivocal qualities of analogical disposition; they bring the book to a formal conclusion by corresponding to the incidents that began it even as they reinterpret the very incidents they recall. Dante, for example, explicitly correlates the vision of Beatrice that precipitates his final rejection of the "donna gentile" and his first vision of her: one day, almost at the ninth hour, he was strongly seized in his imagination by a vision of Beatrice dressed "in those red garments [vestimenta sanguigne] she wore when she first appeared before my eyes" (*VN* 39.1). Just as Dante fell in love with the living Beatrice when he first saw her, so this moment of vision marks the true beginning of his love for Beatrice dead. The sonnet that recounts his rededication to her, "Lasso! per forza di molti sospiri," plots a condensed trajectory through the impeded natural spirit, the sensitive spirits of sight, and the vital spirits in the heart. Although everything still seems gloomy and full of self-pity—indeed, so great is Dante's grief, Love circles his eyes with the red crown of martyrs—nevertheless, for the first time since Beatrice died, Dante has become his beloved's similitude, not only in color, for his blood-red eyes match her red garments, but in condition: his martyrdom corresponds to her death.[101] So too has Love become an analogy of Beatrice; he is stunned into senselessness ("tramortisce") because the thoughts and sighs that cohabit with him in Dante's heart have Beatrice's name and many words about her death inscribed on them.

> Questi penseri, e li sospir ch'eo gitto,
> diventan ne lo cor sì angosciosi,
> ch'Amor vi tramortisce, sì lien dole;
> però ch'elli hanno in lor li dolorosi
> quel dolce nome di madonna scritto,
> e de la morte sua molte parole.
>
> (8–14)

---

101. Dante says his eyes are deep red, "uno colore purpureo," in the prose commentary (39.4). He describes them ringed with the crown of martyrs in the sonnet: " ch'Amore / li 'ncerchia di corona di martìri" (7–8).

[These thoughts and the sighs I send forth become so painful in the heart Love is stunned and senseless, so much anguish do they cause him; for that sweet name of my lady is written on those doleful thoughts and sighs, and many words about her death.]

Abject though Dante is, his mourning still is the bodily foundation on which he can reconstruct his love for Beatrice. He addresses pilgrims he sees passing through Florence, so that they might feel in their imagination the grief he feels in his heart. He sends the sonnet "Oltre la spera" to them, in which he describes the ascent of his sigh, given "new intelligence" [intelligenza nova] by Love, through the spheres to Beatrice, where it hears things Dante cannot understand. Finally, Dante again sees Beatrice in a miraculous vision of her in glory, which he will strive to find language for, when study and long practice in the craft of poetry shall have made him fit to write in a nobler way. The new love, we see, will ascend by seeking its analogies not from the mind but the spirit.

At the same time, however, Dante's vision of Beatrice in chapter 39 marks the end of both his love for the "donna gentile" and the influence of Cavalcanti. As at the beginning of the affair with the "donna gentile," so here Dante's every action conforms to Cavalcanti's ideas about love. He realizes that the lady cannot support the ideal of love reason demands: Dante introduces the "forte imaginazione" by saying "against this adversary of reason there arose one day . . . a vision." He therefore loves anew, even if once again it is Beatrice he loves. He also dies a metaphorical death; his eyes are ringed with the martyr's crown. At this point, however, even while Cavalcanti's opinions structure the events, they are submitted to ethical judgment. In the face of the deprivation of death, which Dante truly confronts only now when he denies his desire for the "donna gentile," he confronts as well the ultimate emptiness of Guido's thought, which has no place for the will to sacrifice its desires.

Clearly Dante has recaptured that sense of "betweenness" that occurs when endings are also beginnings. To love Beatrice now, Dante must repeat himself in a new way; he must seek a mode of writing that can translate his future experience by comprehending not so much the differences and similarities of intellect and the senses as those of the spirit and the flesh. The final chapter of the *Vita nuova* speaks to this quest: Dante hopes to write of Beatrice what has never been written of any other woman. Dante's final words open his "libello" to the future as much as they bring it to its conclusion; they correspond clearly to the "proemio" that begins the *Vita nuova* by granting it memory's closure. The book Dante has copied from the book of his memory preserves its integrity as an analogy throughout.

Dante found the mode of writing he sought in the *Divine Comedy*. When beauty was acknowledged a transcendental and became a metaphysical attribute of God, the compass of the aesthetic inscribed a larger circle; within its ambit now were all the relations that mediated between the everyday and the sublime, between flesh and soul, between time and eternity. By making poetry the discourse of the aesthetic, Dante was able to explore these relations, always preserving the differences between himself and his writing, his love for Beatrice and Beatrice herself, even as he established the ways in which they were alike. In this sense, the analogies of the *Vita nuova* are reducible to metaphor; what is real in the similarities Dante constructs is their likeness. But in the twenty-fourth canto of the *Purgatorio*, Dante revisits the "new style" of the *Vita nuova* and significantly revises it. In so doing, he reconceives the nature of aesthetics. Analogies become elements of existence; the idea of "like" is translated into the poetry of "is." No longer a form of knowledge between sensation and intellection that in some way images metaphysical verities, aesthetics is transformed, I argue in the next three chapters, into nothing less than Dante's discourse of being.

3

From the *Vita nuova* to the *Comedy*

In the twenty-fourth canto of the *Purgatorio*, Dante meets the Lucchese poet Bonagiunta Orbicciani on the sixth terrace, where gluttony is punished. When Bonagiunta asks if before him stands the man who brought forth the "new rhymes, beginning with *Donne ch'avete intelletto d'amore*," Dante's answer equates his identity as a poet with his existence as a human being.

> I' mi son un che, quando
> Amor mi spira, noto, e a quel modo
> ch'e' ditta dentro vo significando.
>
> (24.52–54)

[I am one who, when Love inspires me, takes note, and in the manner he dictates within goes signifying.]

On hearing this response, Bonagiunta suddenly sees the essential difference that set the practitioners of the "dolce stil novo" apart from poets like Guittone d'Arezzo, the Notary Giacomo da Lentini, and himself.[1] The knot ("il nodo") that he says kept him from participating in the new style was one that, at first sight, might be called a kind of scribal failure; unlike Dante's, Bonagiunta's pen did not closely follow Love's dictation.

> "Io veggio ben come le vostre penne
> di retro al dittator sen vanno strette,
> che de le nostre certo non avvenne;

---

1. Understandably, these remarks of Dante's have been endlessly commented on, usually in regard to the controversial question of whether they confirm the existence of a school of "stilnovisti." For a review of the positions, see Teodolinda Barolini, *Dante's Poets* (Princeton: Princeton University Press, 1983), 41, 86–123.

e qual più a gradire oltre si mette,
non vede più da l'uno a l'altro stilo";
e, quasi contentato, si tacette.

(58–63)

["Clearly I will see how your pens follow close after him who dictates, which certainly did not happen with ours; and he who sets
himself to seek further will see no other difference between the one
style and the other." And, as if satisfied, he was silent.]

The man who had attacked Guinizzelli, the father of the "nove rime,"
now realizes that he differed from him and from Dante only in the
ways they transcribed their responses to the modes of love; beyond
that, Bonagiunta sees nothing that distinguishes their poetic style from
his.

That Dante says nothing further seems an endorsement of Bonagiunta's declaration. Yet strictly speaking, the silence and complaisance
that complete the colloquy are not the Florentine's but the poet from
Lucca's: "e quasi contentato, si tacette." The slight narrative equivoca-
tion, "as if satisfied," has in fact become part of a large critical contro-
versy about the "dolce stil novo." While I disagree with those who see
in Dante's and Bonagiunta's remarks no reason to think that a school of
"stilnovisti" ever existed, others less skeptical do ask a pointed question when they wonder what it is Bonagiunta has grasped in his understanding of the "new style."[2] For there does appear to be more than a
tonal difference between what the two poets say. To Bonagiunta, it
would seem, the "stil novo" is still largely a literary matter, a manner of
writing. Dante, however, has emphatically defined his poetics here not
so much in terms of craft but as an act of identity and being: "I' mi son
un che . . ."[3]

---

2. Chief among critics who think Bonagiunta does not understand what Dante says is
Guido Favati, who entirely denies the existence of any school of "stilnovisti." See *Inchiesta sul Dolce Stil Nuovo* (Florence: Le Monnier, 1975). Among many others, however,
Gianfranco Contini and Mario Marti especially have convincingly established the existence both of the "stil novo" and of a school that practiced it. As I say below, I think
Bonagiunta understands the "stil novo" but that Dante is expounding a different poetics
here.

3. The grammatical construction of the phrase, with its use of the "so-called pleonastic
reflexive," has elicited much discussion. As Singleton says, the meaning amounts to "As for
myself, I am one who . . ." (*The Divine Comedy*, trans. Charles Singleton, *Purgatorio 2*,

Certainly the image Bonagiunta now uses to register his previous lack of insight, "nodo," does suggest new understanding. It was precisely the unknotting of the tongue, as Guglielmo Gorni has shown, that Dante had emphasized in his account of the genesis of "Donne ch'avete" in the *Vita nuova*.[4] Guinizzelli himself, in fact, had ironically signaled that it was the aesthetic joining of sensible and intellectual perception to spiritual love that set the "new rhymes" apart from the poetry that was written in the Sicilian or Tuscan manner when he cast his reply to Bonagiunta's parodic sonnet in the form of an analogy between human knowledge and natural will.[5] As soon as Bonagiunta

---

Commentary [Princeton: Princeton University Press, 1970–76], 569). R. L. Martinez notes that every word in the phrase means "I"; he argues Dante's formula intentionally recalls the Lord's "I am that I am" ("ego sum qui sum"); see "The Pilgrim's Answer and the Poetics of the Spirit," *Stanford Italian Review* 3 (1983): 37–63.

4. Guglielmo Gorni, *Il nodo della lingua e il verbo d'amore* (Florence: Olschki, 1981), 13–21 passim.

5. Guinizzelli's response in fact is an exemplification of his poetics: the analogies that order the sensible world and human understanding become the content of the poem (the text is from Contini, *Poeti del duecento*, 2.482–83).

Omo ch'è saggio non corre leggero,
ma a passo grada sì com' vol misura:
quand' ha pensato, riten su' pensero
infin a tanto che 'l ver l'asigura.
Foll' è chi crede sol veder lo vero
e non pensare che altri i pogna cura:
non se dev' omo tener troppo altero,
ma dé guardar so stato e sua natura.
Volan ausel' per air di straine guise
ed han diversi loro operamenti,
né tutti d'un volar né d'un ardire.
Dëo natura e 'l mondo in grado mise,
e fe' despari senni e intendimenti:
perzò ciò ch'omo pensa non dé dire.

[The wise man doesn't run without reflection but proceeds step by step as moderation requires. When he has pondered a matter, he keeps his thought to himself until truth verifies it. He is a fool who believes he alone sees the truth and does not think others seek it with care; a man ought not to think too well of himself but look after his own state and nature. The birds fly through the air in diverse ways, and differ in their manners; all do not fly as one, nor are all impelled by the same desire. God established degrees in nature and the world, and made different understandings and intents. Therefore a man ought not to say what he thinks.]

The implication is arch: although Bonagiunta and Guinizzelli are both poets and members of the same species, there nevertheless are hierarchies of being and intelligence

sees that the correlation between passion, reason, and "caritas," which he had thought problematic, was actually the spring from which the "stil novo" derived its sweetness, his language deploys the tropes of Dante's own discourse of Love. The metaphor of pens following dictation recalls Dante's earlier conceit that the *Vita nuova* was a book he copied from the book of his memory.[6] It is as if hearing Dante Bonagiunta has recognized the full implications of "Donne ch'avete intelletto d'amore" for the first time; his reply, in short, nicely exemplifies the "stil novo."[7]

The question remains, however, whether the words Dante speaks in the *Purgatorio* are entirely in the same mode. His response is less a declaration about literary stylistics than an aesthetic theory in which existence itself is configured as an analogy of being. Indeed, literariness now resides not in the production of a poem that claims to copy the workings of the appetitive and intellectual souls, as it did in the *Vita nuova*, but in the fact that Dante moves signifying through the world in embodied proportion to the inner articulations of Love's inspiration. As a consequence, Dante's reply to Bonagiunta substantially reforms the range and order of the aesthetics of the earlier "stil novo" in two ways: once on the level of style and again in its transformation into a discourse of being. In this chapter, I will discuss these literary and metaphysical renovations in turn. In the two chapters that follow, I will extend the scope of the argument to include heaven and hell; I hope to

that order creation. Because Bonagiunta fails to grasp that knowledge and the passions are correlate (Bonagiunta had addressed Guinizzelli as "Voi, ch'avete mutata la mainera / de li plagenti ditti de l'amore / de la forma dell'esser là dov'era, / per avansare ogn'altro trovatore"), Guinizzelli can admit the criticism but imply that it proceeds from Bonagiunta's own (lower) level of understanding. Guinizzelli's poem, in contrast, demonstrates a fuller vision of things by invoking the analogous structure of the world.

6. The philological problems of Bonagiunta's answer, especially his use of "le vostre penne" when he is speaking of Dante alone, have caused some critics (beginning with l'Anonimo Fiorentino) to take "penne" as "wings." By far the strongest arguments for such a reading have been put forth by Lino Pertile, "Il nodo di Bonagiunta, le penne di Dante, e il Dolce Stil Novo," *Lettere italiane* 46 (1994): 44–75. In this important article, Pertile convincingly relates Bonagiunta's "nodo" with the restraints in falconry; accepting "penne" as "ali" follows as a matter of course. (See also Pertile, "Dante's *Comedy* beyond the *Stilnovo*," *Lectura dantis* 13 [1993]: 63–68). Even if we read "penne" as "ali," however, the pen following dictation is implicit in Dante's metaphor of himself as scribe of the "dittator Amor."

7. A point reinforced by Martinez, who points to the internal affiliations of "nodo" to "noto" two lines before. See "The Pilgrim's Answer," 52; see also Gorni, *Il nodo della lingua*, 14–16. The practice of underscoring internal resonances was especially prized by Guinizzelli, Cavalcanti, and Dante.

show that the vision Dante delineates during his encounter with Bonagiunta is the linchpin in his exemplification of the state of souls after death.

I

Dante is accompanied by Forese Donati when he meets Bonagiunta; the fact that the two Florentine poets had engaged in a vituperative poetic correspondence, when added to Bonagiunta and Guinizzelli's own exchange of captious sonnets about the new manner of poetry, has led many to suspect, rightly I think, that Dante would reform the protocols of the "tenzone" here in Purgatory.[8] Given the nature of this place of reformation, however, where the old exists so that we can see it in the process of becoming new, I think it a simplification to view Dante's present interactions with Forese as an "antidote" to the "poison" that constituted their prior assays at defamation.[9] Sorrow for past indiscretions remains, but the motives that once produced conflict have been redirected. Former positions still linger, but as traces; what we notice is how the current condition of erstwhile adversaries has changed the desire to answer spite with spite into the desire to reconcile their differences with God.[10] Thus Dante tells Forese: "Se tu riduci a mente / qual fosti meco, e qual io teco fui, / ancor fia grave il memorar presente" (*Purg.* 23.115–17) [If you recall what you were to me and I was to you, the present memory will still be grievous].[11] In contrast to the *Vita nuova*, memory has not rewritten the "sentenzia" of their altercation here, for Dante wishes neither to efface nor to reinterpret their argu-

---

8. See, for instance, Teodolinda Barolini, *Dante's Poets*, 47–57, and the bibliography given there. As most readers, I accept the authenticity of Dante's "tenzone" with Forese, which occasionally has been doubted. On this question, see Mario Marti, "Rime realistiche (la tenzone e le petrose dantesche)," *Nuove letture dantesche* (Florence: Le Monnier, 1976), 8:209–30. More generally, John Ahern notes that the "tenzone" was one paradigm of poetic communication in "duecento" Italy. Rhetorically, the first poem of the *Vita nuova*, "A ciascun' alma presa," is a "tenzone." See "The New Life of the Book," 1–16.

9. The terms are Umberto Bosco's in *La Divina Commedia*, ed. Umberto Bosco and Giovanni Reggio , vol. 2, *Purgatorio* (Florence: Le Monnier, 1979), 392.

10. Another way to view these interactions between and among the poets is to see how a redirection of intention, which is the second perfection of a thing, can bring about realignment of its formal properties, which is its first perfection.

11. In a similar vein, Gaetano Savarese notes that with the phrase "il memorar presente" Dante does more than memorialize and repent past events; he also reveals the luminous, nostalgic aspects of his life in Florence before his exile. See "Una proposta per Forese: Il memorar presente," *Rassegna della letteratura italiana* 94 (1990): 5–20.

ment. Rather an alteration in Dante's and Forese's very existence has rendered it beside the point.[12] As Dante says when he hears the gluttonous sing the opening of Psalm 50:

Ed ecco piangere e cantar s'udìe
"Labïa mëa, Domine" per modo
tal, che diletto e doglia parturìe.

(*Purg.* 23.10–12)

[And lo, "Labia mea, Domine" was heard in tears and in song, in such a way that it gave birth to delight and sorrow.]

The repentant have become the psalm they weep and sing; mouths once opened to gorge now open to praise; their joy and sorrow modulate into the harmonies that express the being of souls no longer sinners but not yet blessed.

Such a song requires a new style. When Dante meets Bonagiunta, he therefore mingles past altercations with new understanding by interlacing Orbicciani's quarrel with Guinizzelli and his own with Donati. "Nodo," the very term that Bonagiunta now uses to acknowledge his failure to see why Guinizzelli changed the "mainera / de li plagenti ditti de l'amore," also recalls and rehabilitates the altercation between Forese and Dante.[13] Donati had said he saw Dante's father's soul bound among the tombs "by a knot, whose name I know not, whether it was Solomon's or some other sage's" [legato a nodo ch'i' non saccio 'l nome, / se fu di Salamone o d'altro saggio" (72a.9–10)]. Dante answers this imputation of avarice by damning Forese's gluttony.[14]

---

12. The presence of Dante's "tenzone" with Forese, or of reverse echoes of it, in cantos 23 and 24 of the *Purgatorio* has been debated ever since D'Ovidio. For a more recent study, see Piero Cudini, "La tenzone tra Dante e Forese e la *Commedia* (*Inf.* XXX; *Purg.* XXIII–XXIV)," *Giornale storico della letteratura italiana* 159 (1982): 1–25; and Barolini, *Dante's Poets,* 49–50. Most readers agree with Cudini that Dante deliberately recalls his "tenzone" in his encounter with Forese in the *Purgatorio.*

13. Here I follow the perceptive remarks of Giuseppe Mazzotta, *Dante, Poet of the Desert* (Princeton: Princeton University Press, 1979), 201–3; see further, Martinez, "The Pilgrim's Answer," 52–55. In light of the use of "nodo" in falconry, Pertile minimizes the effect of these intertextual echoes (see especially "Il nodo di Bonagiunta," 52–61). Bonagiunta's term rehearses the register of Sicilian-Tuscan poetry very neatly; Forese's presence, however, indicates that Dante thinks more is at stake here than the recreation of that style.

14. The association of the knot of Solomon with avarice is, as Foster and Boyde note, speculative: see *Dante's Lyric Poetry,* 2:248.

Ben ti faranno il nodo Salamone,
Bicci novello, e' petti de le starne,
ma peggio fia la lonza del castrone,
ché 'l cuoio farà vendetta de la carne.

(73.1–4)

[The knot of Solomon will be just the thing for you, young Bicci, and partridge breasts, but worse will be mutton loins, for the skin will take revenge for the flesh.]

As Foster and Boyde explain, Dante implies that the hide of the sheep Forese has gobbled up will be made into parchment on which his debts will be written. When Forese is unable to pay them, this document will be the instrument that causes him to be cast into prison.[15] In the *Purgatorio*, however, Dante's slur has become Forese's literal condition. Even before he sees the penitents, Virgil explains that the souls Dante hears chanting the *Miserere* are those who "perhaps go loosening the knot of their debt" [Ombre che vanno / forse di lor dover solvendo il nodo (*Purg.* 23.14–15)]. The shades Dante then does see are so wasted "that the skin took its shape from the bones" [che da l'ossa la pelle s'informava]. Unlike the Dante of the *Vita nuova*, however, on whose face Love had inscribed the signs of his ravaged condition ("Dicea d'Amore, però che io portava nel viso tante de le sue insigne, che questo non si potea ricovrire" [4.2]), Forese, Bonagiunta, and the other gluttons repay their debt to God by themselves becoming the parchment and the letters that record it.

Parean l'occhiaie anella sanza gemme:
chi nel viso de li uomini legge "omo"
ben avria quivi conosciuta l'emme.

(*Purg.* 23.30–32)

[Their eye sockets seemed rings without gems: he who reads man ("[h]omo") in the face of men would have clearly discerned the "M" there.]

Writing here is not a system of representational markings that bear a likeness to the images that are inscribed in the "libro de la memoria"; it

---

15. *Dante's Lyric Poetry*, 2:249.

is an element of being per se. Instead of singling him out as a specific individual in a certain condition, Forese's "M" is part of the visible form of his intelligible species, humanity, "omo." By "bye[ynge] it on [his] flessh so deere," as Chaucer's Pardoner would say, Forese exists, like Dante in his response to Bonagiunta, as a "modo di dire." "Strive not with the dry scab that discolors my skin [pelle]," Forese begs, "nor with my lack of flesh [difetto di carne]" (*Purg.* 23.49–51); his lips opened not to abuse but by love, Forese goes signifying his willing submission of "cuoio" and "carne" to the just vendetta of God.

This linking of changes in the inner constitution and outward expression of Forese's being explains why Dante dwells on the process by which he recognizes him.

Mai non l'avrei riconosciuto al viso;
ma ne la voce sua mi fu palese
ciò che l'aspetto in sé avea conquiso.
Questa favilla tutta mi raccese
mia conoscenza a la cangiata labbia,
e ravvisai la faccia di Forese.

(*Purg.* 23.43–48)

[I would never have recognized him by his countenance (or face), but in his voice was apparent that which his appearance had obliterated in itself. This spark rekindled all my knowledge of the changed features [literally face] and I recognized the face of Forese.]

Dante must reconstruct Forese's face as an echo of his voice because the man he knew cannot be seen here. Though Donati's "viso," his "aspetto," his "labbia," all of which are equivalents of "faccia," are directly before him, neither Dante's eyes nor his imagination can extract an image of his friend, less because of a failure of material form ("difetto di carne") than because the figure he gazes at has become more a rational abstraction than a particular human being. Forese is what the intellect's phantasm of the body would look like if it could kick a stone; the "flesh and bones" Dante confronts is a "verbum mentis." The face Dante finally recognizes from the "voce" he hears is this "idea of corporeal man" returned to physical features memory has supplied. This is a new order of existence, one that the perceptual apparatus of the *Vita nuova*, with its emphasis on memory's "ontological gaps and temporal breaks," cannot express. Understanding these hitherto unheard of discourses of body and soul calls for a new kind of "vulgari eloquentia."[16]

Equally unexpected intertextual accommodations also inhere in Dante's words to Bonagiunta. Like Forese, himself now an "emme," the poet from Lucca, as we have seen, had held it a "gran dissimigliansa" for the Bolognese Guinizzelli to make his "canzone" by violently extracting it from authoritative texts ("*traier* canson per forsa di *scrittura*" [my emphasis]).[17] His question to Dante seems to repeat the charge: "ma dì s'i' veggio qui colui che fore / *trasse* le nove rime." Once Bonagiunta hears Dante's answer, the words he is given to express his new understanding exhibit a new "dissimigliansa"; the old emulation that caused Bonagiunta to highlight his difference from Guinizzelli becomes his insight that the manner in which each followed Love's informing dictation was the only difference between their styles.[18] Indeed, Bonagiunta had attacked Guinizzelli for having changed the manner of love poetry in a phrase that ironically joins the vocabularies of sentiment and scholasticism: "ch'avete mutata la mainera / de li plagenti ditti de l'amore / de la forma dell'esser là dov'era"; Dante's declaration does the same but in a way perhaps only one whose "forma dell'esser" Love has altered the way Bonagiunta's has been could understand. Thus it is fitting that the same Bonagiunta who complained that Guinizzelli was so obscure, no one could explain his intellectual subtleties, now hears from the poet of the "canson" "Donne ch'avete intelletto d'amore" words that instantly undo the knot ("nodo") of his own perplexity. The very hastiness with which Bonagiunta questions Dante and gives voice to his newfound understanding, which Guinizzelli had chastised as foolhardiness ("Omo ch'è saggio non corre leggero"), seems to recall the moment of inspiration when the first words of "Donne ch'avete" flashed into Dante's mind.[19]

---

16. These discourses culminate in Statius's disquisition on the generation of the soul's aerial body in canto 25 of the *Purgatorio*, which I discuss in detail in chapter 5.

17. Pertile, "Il nodo di Bonagiunta," 62–64 also makes this point.

18. Bonagiunta's conviction that nothing other than what Dante has said separates his style from that of the stilnovists ("e qual più a gradire oltre si mette") itself seems an echo of Guinizzelli's response to him: "Dëo natura e 'l mondo in grado mise." For the superiority of the reading "gradire" to "riguardare," see Petrocchi's note, ad loc., in *La Divina Commedia secondo l'antica vulgata*, ed. G. Petrocchi, 4 vols., Società Dantesca Italiana (Milan: Mondadori, 1966–67).

19. To comment again on Guinizzelli's reply: the first line is remarkably adroit. It manages to answer Bonagiunta's every charge. It makes rhetoric inseparable from philosophy, all the while implying that Bonagiunta knows neither. "Omo ch' è saggio"

By knotting voices so that their words provide agreeable answers to other voices' arguments, Dante in effect creates a new poetic mode, one with both a new formal and a new intentional perfection. The object of this new "stil novo" is nothing less than a reordering of literary history. The motives that engendered the discord of the "tenzone," indeed, that set the new style against the old, have been resolved in a concordat of harmony and proportion.[20] Emotions and passions that, when prosecuted as ends in themselves, once produced dyspeptic or scandalous poems, here have been depersonalized; verbal "vendetta" yields to the silence that follows the reconciliation that comes when injuries are referred to love of God.[21] Bonagiunta disappears from the *Comedy* in a simile that Dante could have drawn from Guinizzelli's acerbic reply to him.

Come li augei che vernan lungo 'l Nilo,
alcuna volta in aere fanno schiera,
poi volan più a fretta e vanno in filo,
così tutta la gente che lì era.

(*Purg.* 24.64–67)

[As the birds that winter along the Nile sometimes group in the air, then fly in greater haste and go in file, so all the people who were there.]

seems to confirm Guinizzelli as an adept of the philosophy for which Bologna's university made it famous, but "non corre leggero" inevitably recalls Geoffrey of Vinsauf's first words of advice to the poet: "if anyone sets out to build a house, his rash hand does not rush into action" [Si quis habet fundare domum, non currit ad actum / Impetuosa manus]. Guinizzelli in fact suggests his poetry is of a different species from Bonagiunta's: he has shifted the grounds of poetry from "plagenti ditti de l'amore" to ethics, since the precept that the wise man does not hurry itself comes from the *Nicomachean Ethics*.

20. We see how saturated with the atmosphere of the "tenzone" this moment of poetic self-definition is if we accept, as I think we should, Robert Hollander's arguments that Dante's words to Bonagiunta recall "Qua' son le cose vostre ch'io vi tolgo," Cino da Pistoia's counterblast to Guido Cavalcanti, who it seems had called Cino a "vil ladro." See "Dante and Cino da Pistoia," *Dante Studies* 110 (1992): 201–31. See also Gorni, *Il nodo della lingua*, 135–37. It is also appropriate to note Contini's opinion that Cavalcanti had lowlifes such as Forese in mind when he wrote "I' vegno 'l giorno a te 'nfinite volte," a poem many see as part of the "tenzone" that led to Dante's break with his "primo amico." See *Un'idea di Dante* (Turin: Einaudi, 1970), 151.

21. A number of readers have commented on how the impersonality of Dante's self-definition as poet recapitulates the moment of transit in the *Vita nuova* from the personal to the universal that attends, indeed allows, the writing of "Donne ch'avete intelletto d'amore." See, for example, Barolini, *Dante's Poets*, 85 ff. I argue that the *Comedy* in fact records a far more radical transition from the earlier poetry.

In his sonnet, Guido reminded Bonagiunta that God established degrees in nature and the world and different capacities of understanding in people ("Dëo natura e 'l mondo in grado mise, / e fe' despari senni e intendimenti").

> Volan ausel' per air di straine guise
> ed han diversi loro operamenti,
> né tutti d'un volar né d'un ardire.

(9–11)

[The birds fly through the air in diverse ways, and differ in their doings; all do not fly as one, nor are they all impelled by the same desire.]

Through Dante's words, Bonagiunta is now of one "senno e intendimento" with Guido, even as all of them, through the obvious recall of the simile to the "stornei," the "gru," and the "colombe" of the canto of Paolo and Francesca, hold themselves in conflict with the stilnovism she espouses. Dante does not make amends for the "tenzoni" he revisits here—his with Forese, Bonagiunta's with Guinizzelli, his with himself—so much as he emends them by coordinating all three so that they speak to the idea or essence of poetry; as he goes signifying "in that mode" [a quel modo] that Love, joining all things, dictates inwardly, Dante rewrites literary history in the style of the aesthetics of existence.

II

Instead of calling attention to the disagreements that separated Dante from others who spoke of love, therefore, the poetry of the *Comedy* subsumes them. Its style, for this very reason, is a new style, which differs from the "stil novo"; Dante's definition of poetic selfhood is his explanation of its formal constitution. Thus when we compare Dante's description of his practice here with the opening of the *Vita nuova*, the book that inaugurated his career as a stilnovist, the alterations are notable. Gone is memory as the exemplary text; the past now exists as the process of its transformation into the present tense of being—"il memorar presente," as Dante puts it. Gone as well is the explicit presence of a book, either as copy or as translation; in place of an invitation to consider difference as a rhetorical function of continuity, Dante now posits a homology that equates writing and bodily existence. This homology is itself an analogy; its unities are ultimately based on those of the Incarnation and Trinity. In response to the Love that is consubstantial with the Father and the Son, Dante as person becomes indistinguishable from Dante as text: when Love breathes, he takes note and goes signifying. Unlike the *Vita nuova*, where Dante's various conditions while in love seemed effects of the inner "spiriti" that caused them, neither pneumatology nor a science of intellection can account for these similitudes. Knowing and being have become reflexes of Love; they are constituted and structured by it, joined as one through it, as body is to soul, in a way that only a theologized poetry can represent.[22]

Certainly the Love that has authored Dante's responses in the *Comedy* has changed from what it was in the *Vita nuova*. No longer an accident in a substance, a transient resident in the heart where it ruled the vital spirit, Love stands here as the source of Dante's essential being. It breathes ("spira") and speaks ("ditta") with originary, animating force—both words look to the creation of the world by the Word that became flesh. Ultimately, as Mazzotta has said, Amor's breathing ("spira") takes for its model the procession of love in the godhead, which is called spiration and which has as its analogue in corporeal beings the "movement and urging of the will of the lover towards the beloved."[23]

In this sense, when Dante acts and reacts in concert with Love, he becomes Love's body. Indeed, when he says "I go" ("vo"), Dante is insisting on his bodily existence, since to move from place to place by one's own power ("localmente mobile per sé"), as he himself had noted about the personified Love in the *Vita nuova* (25.2), requires a body.[24] In

---

22. Even though I will stress the metaphysical implications of Dante's definition, I certainly agree with critics who have read it in theological terms. In addition to Mazzotta and Martinez, see Luigi Derla, " 'I' mi son un, che quando / Amor mi spira, noto . . .': su *Purg.* xxiv, 49–61," *Aevum* 58 (1984): 274–76; Robert Hollander, "Dante 'Theologus-Poeta,' " in *Studies in Dante* (Ravenna: Longo, 1980), 39–89.

23. St. Thomas Aquinas, *Summa Theologica* 1a.36.1, quoted and discussed in detail by Mazzotta, *Dante, Poet of the Desert*: 202–10.

24. In their commentary on "Tanto gentile," Foster and Boyde (*Dante's Lyric Poetry* 2:125) note that the construction "va dicendo" in the line "un spirto . . . va dicendo a l'anima: Sospira" means "says," not "goes saying." Although in early Italian the periphrastic form often did not carry its original sense of continued action, Dante's use of "vo significando" in these lines in *Purgatory* does seem to me, as I argue below, to give full force to his bodily movement forward.

this earlier work, as we have seen, Love inscribed its signs on Dante's body; now, however, Dante is not a sign but an incarnation of love. Whereas before the actual vocalization of "Donne ch'avete" and "Tanto gentile" was what made their style "dolce," at least on a rhetorical reading, now it is Dante's "going signifying" that by analogy lends his physical movement the sweetness of recitation.[25] Exemplar or copy is an entirely inadequate metaphor to convey such ratios of being as man or poet. When Love dictates within, the word is made incarnate, and Dante himself becomes its aesthetic expression.

If Love and Dante are conjunct as a cause is to its effect, however, the action that has joined them is the notice he takes of Love's inspiration. With its recall to Augustine's "notitia," which with "mens" and "amor" make the mind like the Trinity, "noto" refers directly to the act of discursive intellection. Like Amor, the mind for Dante is rooted in God; ultimately intellection, with its production of the word that expresses the universal, corresponds to the first procession in the divinity, which is "by way of the intellect, and . . . is the procession of the word."[26] As Wisdom, the Son is the Word that Love made flesh: these identities provide the pattern that gives the analogy between Dante and Amor its structure. Just as Love's breath becomes a kind of dictation, so the abstractions of intellection end with the production of the word that signifies the concept. And just as the intellect returns to the phantasms to beget the propositions of knowledge, so Dante himself moves as a word, going signifying the poem of (his) life.

But by subordinating intellection to Love, instead of making it the faculty Love approximates only by analogy, Dante allows the human capacity to know to transcend the function it played in the "stil novo." Substituting for the dialectics of book and memory of the *Vita nuova*, "noto" here marks epistemology as a form of being rooted in the correspondence between the inner word that Love inspires and the mind's word for the universal concept. In the new style of the *Comedy*, "noto" denotes the intelligence that establishes Love as the principle, the rea-

---

25. Dante himself equates sweetness with the actual vocalization of certain combinations of sounds in the *De Vulgari Eloquentia* (2.7.5), where he speaks of "smooth-haired" and "shaggy" words. The early commentators, it is interesting to note, held that the difference between Dante's kind of poetry and Bonagiunta's was precisely that Dante's was informed by far greater rhetorical knowledge.

26. In advancing this suggestion I am offering a reading that complements Mazzotta's discussion (see note 22) of Love's breathing in terms of the procession of love in the godhead.

son why, undemonstrable in itself, that accounts for the effects it has produced.[27]

Indeed, the very way Dante answers Bonagiunta's question suggests that as much as Love transforms both the "stil novo" and earlier Italian verse, so it will also reconfigure the discourse of the mind. Dante knew from the opening of the second book of the *Posterior Analytics* (2.1.89b24–35) that of the four questions one can ask, two ("whether something is" and "whether something is this or that") are empirical and can be answered by observation or experiment.[28] But when one asks "what something is" or "why something is this or that," one is seeking a cause, "the reason why." Bonagiunta's inquiry clearly is a request for factual information: "Ma dì s'i' veggio qui colui che fore / trasse le nove rime . . ." Dante's reply, however, shows that he has reformulated the question; he answers as if Bonagiunta had asked, "What makes you, the man I see before me, the poet you are?"

This shift of focus from the sensible to the metaphysical by itself recapitulates the difference Dante saw between his poetry and Bonagiunta's. As Bernard Lonergan says, one grasps the cause of something not through "ocular vision" but through "insight into the sensible data."[29] The example Aristotle gives to illustrate this point is famous (*Post. An.* 2.2.90a15–17): a man on the moon during an eclipse would not have to ask what an eclipse was. The answer would be obvious, since he would see the earth cutting between the sun and himself. Because the sensible data had assumed a suitable order, the man would at once pass beyond observation and understand the cause and the universal, the idea of an eclipse itself.

For Aristotle, however, knowing a cause was only the first act of understanding; the second act was expression of this insight in a scientific syllogism (*Post. An.* 1.2.71b9 ff.). In questions that inquire after the reason why, what is being sought, as Aristotle explains in the *Metaphysics* (Z.17.1041b.4 ff.), is the formal cause, which in general is that which makes matter to be a thing. The formal cause stands as the middle term of a syllogism: it provides the insight into the sensible data, which constitutes the first term or subject of the syllogism, and causes

---

27. For a fine discussion of first principles in this technical sense in Aristotle, see Trimpi, *Muses,* 47–48.

28. Here I am following Bernard Lonergan's analysis of this passage; see *Verbum: Word and Idea in Aquinas* (South Bend, Ind.: University of Notre Dame Press, 1967), 12–14.

29. Lonergan, *Verbum,* 14.

the real presence of the predicate, which is the concept whose genesis was sought, in the subject.

To the extent that Dante's definition of himself resembles a syllogism ("Amor . . . noto . . . vo significando"), we can say that he posits his "noto," his act of understanding, as the formal cause, the reason why his poems are the kind of poems they are. Such an answer would be very appropriate for Bonagiunta, who, as we have seen, had criticized Guinizzelli for having changed the essential form of poetry ("la forma dell' esser là dov'era"). And in fact Bonagiunta frames his new knowledge of Dante's poetry largely in formal terms.

But Dante's reply speaks to more than the kind of poetry he composes. It defines what he is and in so doing explodes the neat progress of the syllogism. As Lonergan points out, form asks about the matter; intellection, Dante suggests, explains why he is the kind of poet who writes "nove rime." But because the formal cause is not the whole of understanding, it alone cannot comprehend what Dante is as a complete being. The man who begins a definition with "I' mi son un" is not only speaking of his essence or quiddity; he is telling why he has that combination of form and matter that makes him what he is. Dante, we see, does not merely stress his bodily existence; Love's inspiration has compounded it into his poetic being in the same way his flesh and soul are compounded in him as a human being. Insofar as his body is real, though, it is sensible and so should correspond to the first term of the syllogism. Yet Dante's "going signifying" is properly a predicate as well, since it is that union of intellect and will with the flesh that makes him a human being in the image of the Love that breathes in him. For Love's breath, by virtue of its etymology and its form as a reflexive verb, "mi spira," is also tactile and spiritual at once.[30]

By presenting himself simultaneously as man and poet, Dante exceeds the capacity of the scientific syllogism to define what he is. The categories and methods of investigation that the philosopher would rely on to determine Dante's substance are incapable of explaining the equivalences he says make him susceptible to the promptings of Love. As a person of the Trinity, however, Amor is complete in itself, the instantaneous generation and expression of love. The union of body and soul, while establishing a likeness, does not make Dante identical with the Love that inspires him. Dante underwrites both the likeness

---

30. Lonergan, *Verbum*, 15–16.

and the difference in this relationship by making his intellect the metaphorical scribe of Love's word: he takes note when Love inspires him and goes signifying in the mode that Love had already dictated within. Although this profession of his subsidiary position itself has theological parallels, Dante's disavowal that he is the primary agent in the creation of his own poetry has other effects as well.[31] For one thing, it makes Dante's understanding end in love; for another, it makes his love an act of understanding.

As I noted earlier, the product of intellection, according to Aquinas, was the inner word that expresses the universal.[32] Here, however, the word I am claiming Dante's noting will have produced, though derivative, is less a copy than an analogy of the word Love had dictated, whose effect is comparable to the illumination that enables human beings to see first truths.[33] Or, to put it in terms Dante had used just a few cantos prior to his meeting Bonagiunta, Love has become one with the "prime notizie" (*Purg.* 18.55–56), those "first cognitions" that reason uses as premises in a syllogism to determine whether a proposition is true or false. This, I would submit, is what Dante signifies when he goes signifying "in that mode" in which Love had dictated—that intellection is a function of love.

Yet in relation to his going, which is consequent to Dante's taking note, understanding remains a formal cause. Dante goes signifying the way he does because he has taken note. As a result, though Dante's movement signifies his love, from this point of view it remains an expression of a form of intellection. It corresponds to the process of reflection wherein the mind returns to sensible data after the universal has been extracted from them and articulates its knowledge of individual things in a proposition. To return again to Virgil's discourse on love at the center of the *Comedy*, intellection has become one of the "primi appetibili" (*Purg.* 18.57), those first objects of desire that are the end for

---

31. Compare Yves of Chartres's declaration that "He alone speaks of that subject [i.e., Love as charity] worthily who composes his words according to the dictates of his heart"; noted by Mario Casella, *Studi danteschi* 18 (1934): 108. On the attribution to Yves (the work, *Tractatus de gradibus charitatis,* had been thought to be by Richard of St. Victor), see Martinez, "The Pilgrim's Answer," 52. For further scriptural citations, and a reading of God's dictation as inspiration, see Mazzotta, *Dante, Poet of the Desert:* 206–9.

32. As Lonergan says, "grasping the universal is the production of the inner word that expresses that insight." *Verbum,* 14.

33. As Nardi explains, the idea that divine light illuminates the human intellect is Neoplatonic, not Aristotelian; it was an idea Dante subscribed to throughout his life. See Nardi, *Dante e la cultura medievale,* 149–66.

the sake of which the will moves to obtain any object we perceive as good. Dante now makes intellect and love cause to the other's effect.

These correspondences, converging and diverging at once, all arise from the formal determinations by which Dante has united his nature as person and poet. Reason would have to protest: by elevating to essence qualities that depend on his craft as writer, Dante has confounded substance and accident. Perhaps a poet may fancy himself possessed of two souls; no one else should. But against the logician, who sees only contradiction, Dante sets forth the harmonies that are born from the interplay of likeness and difference he creates between himself and Jesus, the Word he believed was God and man, joined to his Father by Love, and in whose image he was made.

The analogy of intellect and scribe, which gives Dante's self-definition its shape and direction, therefore takes an accepted paradigm of perception, a program of philosophical analysis and synthesis, and makes from it a complete curriculum, if you will, for a new kind of poetry, which only a school of one ever completed. Because human beings are composites of flesh and soul, Aristotle held that we acquire knowledge by proceeding from what is more apprehensible to our senses but less intelligible with respect to its own nature, to what is more intelligible with respect to its own nature but less apprehensible to the senses. Analysis technically is the process of using the objects and experiences clearer to us because they are sensed to progress upward to things, such as causes or principles, that are more intelligible in an absolute sense (*Meta.* 5.11.5; 7.4.2–3). Once grasped, as Wesley Trimpi says, "these principles may be used as starting points for a deductive synthesis" that then proceeds downward to sensible data and provides an explanation for their being what they are. Full intellection, as Trimpi stresses, is the negotiation between analysis and synthesis.

> the inherent intelligibility of first principles clarifies our apprehension of those things perceived by our senses. The apprehensibility of sensory objects, in turn, embodies and expresses the luminosity of the intellective principles in the order, intensity, and clarity of our perceptions. In this reciprocation we experience the greatest degree of consciousness.[34]

---

34. Trimpi, *Muses*, 88.

Dante's reply to Bonagiunta establishes Love as the first principle of being and of poetry through the sensible induction of analysis: "quando Amor mi spira." And Bonagiunta's immediate comprehension of this reply shows that, once Dante takes note, Love does indeed initiate a deductive synthesis that makes the sensible objects that are its effects—both the poet and his poems—more apprehensible. But neither the philosopher nor the theologian can trace the trajectories of this ascent and descent of Love without considering the form of Dante's "terzina" as well as its content.[35] The elements of Dante's poetic being, "Amor, noto, vo significando," are so arranged to suggest that reason's syllogism comes closer to the truth when it is comprehended by an aesthetics of analogy.

The three lines Dante delivers on the sixth terrace of Purgatory are nothing less than a concentrated treatise on the cognitive conditions of literary representation per se. And it is fitting that they should be so: all the machinery in the *Vita nuova* that led to the writing of "Donne ch'avete intelletto d'amore" and its enshrinement of the intellect finds its essential gloss here. In response to Bonagiunta, who questions with the eyes of his senses, Dante unveils the verities only aesthetic vision can comprehend. These verities are the proportions that join flesh and mind to the Incarnation that transcends both; they are the verities that make Dante who he is.

---

35. On the importance of "terza rima," see John Freccero, "The Significance of *Terza Rima*," in *Dante: The Poetics of Conversion,* ed. Rachel Jacoff (Cambridge, Mass.: Harvard University Press, 1986), 258–71.

4

The Aesthetics of Eternity:
Forese, Cacciaguida, and the
Style of Fatherhood

Dante's meeting with Forese and Bonagiunta is a nodal event in the *Comedy*, one of those places where the entire poem seems concentrated in a few cantos. In the last chapter, I proposed that Dante reconfigured himself as a poet in the company of a man who was his friend in life and foe in verse because the proportions that constitute Forese's new manner of existence are beyond the reach of the *Vita nuova*'s spirits and phantasms. To grasp shades such as these, each of whom is human being and intelligible species at once, Dante had to construct a new aesthetics. I now want to extend this argument: my thesis is that the ratios that establish Dante's poetic identity in Purgatory are a key point of reference in his overall exemplification of the state of souls after death. As with the penitents, neither the senses nor reason alone can fathom the damned in hell, who are matter without animating form, and the redeemed in heaven, who are pure form awaiting the regenerated body of the Resurrection. Dante therefore fashions an aesthetics for each region of the afterlife according to the nature of the souls in it. Even though as a consequence these aesthetics differ, each is formed by analogy to the way Love has made Dante the poet he is.

I

Dante rehearses his journey a number of times during the *Comedy*: nowhere is he more forthcoming than in his explanation to Forese of how it happens that he veils the sun.

"Se tu riduci a mente
qual fosti meco, e qual io teco fui,

ancor fia grave il memorar presente.
Di quella vita mi volse costui
che mi va innanzi, l'altr'ier, quando tonda
vi si mostrò la suora di colui,"
e 'l sol mostrai; "costui per la profonda
notte menato m'ha d'i veri morti
con questa vera carne che 'l seconda.
Indi m'han tratto sù li suoi conforti,
salendo e rigirando la montagna
che drizza voi che 'l mondo fece torti.
Tanto dice di farmi sua compagna
che io sarò là dove fia Beatrice;
quivi convien che sanza lui rimagna.
Virgilio è questi . . .

(*Purg.* 23.115–30)

["If you bring back to mind what you have been with me and what I
have been with you, the present memory will still be grievous. From
that life he who goes before me turned me the other day, when the
sister of him," and I pointed to the sun, "showed full to you. He it is
who has led me through the profound night of the truly dead, in this
true flesh which follows him. From there his counsels have drawn
me up, ascending and circling this mountain, which makes you
straight whom the world made crooked. So long he says he will bear
me company until I will be there where Beatrice shall be: there I must
remain without him. Virgil he is . . .]

By itself the length of Dante's answer suggests that his meeting with
Forese occupies a crucial position in the larger architecture of the poem.
But why? Why does Dante so implicate Donati in his poetic enterprise?
One reason surely lies in their "tenzone," to which we must return
again. In response to Dante's highly offensive innuendos concerning
his wife, Forese reports that he undertook a journey eerily similar to the
one the pilgrim has just described to him in Purgatory. "The other
night" [L'altra notte], Forese says, unable to sleep because of the cough
that plagued him since he was too poor to afford the clothes that would
keep him warm, he set off with the first rays of light to look for money.
What he found instead was Dante's father among the tombs [fosse],
bound by a knot whose name he does not know. Since Alighiero had

been dead at least a decade, Forese immediately crossed himself, facing toward the sun ("Allora mi segna' verso 'l levante"); the shade then prayed that Donati release him for love of his son. Forese could not see how and so turned back and returned home ("compie' mi' vïaggio" [literally, "completed my journey"]).[1] Dante's previous scorning of Forese's poverty has provided Donati the opportunity to retort that he at least seeks money for the legitimate reason that he is poor; how different the motives that moved Dante's father, who shamefully clings to his florins long after they could do him any good. Forese's dramatization of this imputation of avarice is caustic: he pictures Alighiero, who was a money changer, as a spirit still tied to the earth because even in death he continues to share Forese's desire for "be' fiorin coniati d'oro rosso" [lovely florins struck from red gold].[2] Had Forese had some of

---

1. The full text of Forese's sonnet (72a in *Dante's Lyric Poetry*) is as follows.

L'altra notte mi venne una gran tosse,
perch'i' non avea che tener a dosso;
ma incontanente che fu dì, fui mosso
per gir a guadagnar ove che fosse.
Udite la fortuna ove m'addosse:
ch'i' credetti trovar perle in un bosso
e be' fiorin coniati d'oro rosso;
ed i' trovai Alaghier tra le fosse,
legato a nodo ch'i' non saccio 'l nome,
se fu di Salamone o d'altro saggio.
Allora mi segna' verso 'l levante:
e que' mi disse: 'Per amor di Dante,
scio'mi.' Ed i' non potti veder come:
tornai a dietro, e compie' mi' vïaggio.

2. In a later sonnet, Forese pictures Alighiero changing money (74a: see note 4). In the "tenzone," Dante generally uses money and the ill-usage of women to insult Forese's lineage and manliness. At the start he pictures Nella coughing and cold from lack of clothing and her husband's neglect ("per difetto ch'ella sente al nido") [from the lack she feels in the nest (72)]. Later he doubts Forese's legitmacy, says his gluttony has driven him to become a thief, and again implies he neglects his wife in bed (74). Donati's slurs are similar, though less vicious: they are founded chiefly on the conceit that Dante has inherited his father's grubbing spirit. Dante, he says, takes others to task for their poverty but solicits an inordinate amount of charity for himself, either from institutions for the poor or from his stepsister and stepbrother (73a). Forese matches Dante's charge of want of manhood by calling him a coward for failing to revenge an offense done to his father. As we shall see, in the *Comedy* Dante converts each of these slanders, either into a more righteous "tenzone" or into an occasion that celebrates the reordering of Christian love in Dante's new style. For a recent reading of the "tenzone," which places it within its literary context and assesses the give-and-take between the poets, see Antonio Stäuble, "La tenzone di Dante con Forese Donati," *Letture classensi* 24 (1995): 151–70. See also Eugenio

those florins, he then intimates in a parting irony, perhaps he could have charitably offered a few of them "per amor di Dante" to help secure Alighiero's release.[3]

On the slopes of Purgatory Dante charts his own homeward "viaggio" for Forese. This journey "l'altr'ier" also began with Dante looking toward the rising sun;[4] on the sixth terrace he points to the planet whose rays the morning before had given him hope when he abandoned "la verace via."[5] Dante's passage has taken him through the "fosse" of Hell and up the mountain that, with the aid of prayers from loved ones, loosens the knots that bind souls to the world. Dante even looks beyond to the completion of his earthly transit and his reunion with Beatrice. Clearly this itinerary radically differs in letter and in spirit from the one Forese had imagined. But Dante deliberately evokes Donati's otherworldly encounter not only to atone for having invited its vilifications. He revisits it and the derogations of his response so that he might make good the traducing of fathers that propelled both. By emending the very idea that had been a primary weapon of discord and contumely in the "tenzone," Dante is able to beget in its place a genealogy for his new definition of poetic selfhood.

Throughout his recitation to Forese, Dante stresses that Virgil has guided each step he has taken: it was Virgil who turned him from his earthly entanglements, Virgil who conducted him through the Inferno, Virgil who led him up Purgatory. From the start of the *Comedy*, of

---

Chiarini, "Tenzone con Forese" in *Enciclopedia dantesca* 5 (Rome: Istituto dell'Enciclopedia Italiana, 1976): 562–63; and Fredi Chiappelli's ironic reading of the entire exchange, "Proposta d'interpretazione per la tenzone di Dante con Forese," *Giornale storico della letteratura italiana* 142 (1965): 321–50.

3. The situation strongly resembles that of Chaucer's "Pardoner's Tale"; see my "Preaching and Avarice in the Pardoner's Tale," *Mediaevalia* 2 (1976): 77–99.

4. As Foster and Boyde note, "L'altra notte" is a "nice variant on the common 'narrative' opening 'L'altr'ier'" (*Dante's Lyric Poetry* 2:247). More to the point, as we shall soon see, Forese uses the phrase "l'altr'ieri" when he taxes Dante with cowardice in the final sonnet of the "tenzone" (74a.4). Donati implies that Dante's faintheartedness is a fit inheritence from his money changing father.

5. Dante's periphrasis for the moon, "quando tonda vi si mostrò la suora di colui, e 'l sol mostrai," signals the preoccupation with relations that forms the thematic matrix in these cantos. Forese's wife, Nella, and his sister Piccarda are explicitly named; his brother Corso appears as the "guiltiest" of those wicked Florentines whom the tail of the beast drags down to Hell. I doubt I am alone in hearing an allusion to Gemma Donati, a distant relation of Forese, in Dante's description of Forese's eyes, which seemed an "anella sanza gemme." As we shall see, these familial relations are transformed when Dante meets his "true" father, Cacciaguida.

course, Virgil has been preeminently a textual presence: he is the source from whom Dante drew the "bello stilo che m'ha fatto onore" [fair style that has done me honor (*Inf.* 1.87)]. Just prior to anatomizing himself as a vernacular writer, Dante seems to suggest that Virgilian eloquence, now implicated equally in the contestatory poetics of the "tenzone" and the deepest logic of the "dolce stil novo," is an essential part of his identity.

Virgil, however, is not the only Latin poet who witnesses the conversation that loosens Bonagiunta's knot; Statius is there as well. In the previous cantos Statius had described how he had been converted to Christianity by reading Virgil allegorically. In his case, spiritual meaning was so strong it altered not only the literal sense but the actual letter of Virgil's poem.[6] Although Polydorus in the *Aeneid* had denounced humankind's greed, saying, "To what do you not drive the appetite of mortals, O cursed hunger of gold," Statius was saved from the sin of avarice by hearing otherwise: "O why do you not rule, o sacred hunger of gold, the appetites of mortals?" [Per che non reggi tu, o sacra fame / de l'oro, l'appetito de' mortali? (*Purg.* 22.39–40)]. The new words Statius vocalizes as Virgil's text, which force the reader to understand gold as something more than metal, epitomize Dante's new style of salvation; at the same time the tropes of hunger and appetite link this moment of conversion to Dante's self-definition on the terrace of the gluttons.

In these cantos of the *Purgatorio*, Dante configures his rewriting of Virgil, which constitutes the greatest of all "tenzoni" in the *Comedy*, as a meditation on the ratios that simultaneously bond and separate fathers and sons. The moneygrubbing aspersions Forese had cast at Alighiero, as well as the repeated taunts of illegitimacy and thievery Dante had flung at Forese and his father, Simone, become the backdrop against which Dante reformulates the relation of Latin to vernacular poetry. The same ratios also explain why Forese enters the poem in a manner that recalls Brunetto Latini, author of the French *Tresor*, whose "cara e buona imagine paterna" (*Inf.* 15.83) Dante honors and damns in the circle of the sodomites. Both shades see Dante before he sees them: "Qual maraviglia!" Brunetto exclaims; "Qual grazia m'è questa," says Forese. The difference in the expressions is telling, as is the difference in the way Dante recognizes each of them. Even though Brunetto's baked

---

6. Here I am following Mazzotta, *Dante, Poet of the Desert,* 221–24.

and scorched features have wasted his face almost as much as Forese's fast has altered his, Dante knows Brunetto by sight but Forese only by his "voce"; by means of these separate acts of perception, Dante appears retrospectively to repudiate whatever allegiance he seemed to give to his former master's voice. In similar fashion, Dante stresses Virgil's importance as guide of his journey to both men but names him only to Forese. Finally, Donati's exit from the poem, as Singleton notes, again recalls Brunetto's.

> Qual esce alcuna volta di gualoppo
> lo cavalier di schiera che cavalchi,
> e va per farsi onor del primo intoppo,
> tal si partì da noi con maggior valchi;
> e io rimasi in via con esso i due
> che fuor del mondo sì gran marescalchi.
>
> (*Purg.* 24.94–99)

[As a horseman sometimes issues forth from a troop that is riding and goes to win the honor of the first encounter, so he parted from us with great strides, and I remained on the way with those two who were such great marshals of the world.]

By associating Forese with Brunetto, Dante establishes a "post hoc" "tenzone" with his mentor that, because he is in hell, is irreparable. In every instance, Forese supplants Brunetto. When Latini joins his troop, he appears the winner of the "palio" at the Lenten games at Verona only because he runs ahead of a different group that threatens to overtake him; in relation to the one he must rejoin, he is dead last (*Inf.* 15.121–24). Donati by contrast can go forth to win the honor of the first encounter. The simile is not simply a gallant riposte to Forese's jeer that Dante is a coward who inherited his faintheartedness from his money changing father.[7]

> Ben so che fosti figliuol d'Alaghieri,
> ed accorgomen pur a la vendetta

---

7. The trope of Forese going forth to gain the honor of the first encounter may be the amends Dante offers for having fired the first salvo in the "tenzone." Unless other poems have not survived, Dante's "Chi udisse tossir la malfatata / moglie di Bicci vocato Forese" certainly seems to initiate the exchange.

che facesti di lui sì bella e netta
de l'aguglin ched e' cambiò l'altr'ieri.

(74a.1–4)

[I know you're Alighieri's son all right—I can tell that by the fine clean vengeance you took on his behalf for the money he exchanged the other day.]

By recalling the mockeries of this final sonnet in their exchange, Dante shows how death has entirely altered both the nature and the rules of engagement. If Brunetto would teach "come l'uom s'etterna" [how man makes himself eternal] in his *Tesoro*, Dante finds a better text in Forese, for though his eyes are indeed like rings without gems ("anella senza gemme"), Dante reads in them the genetic form of all mankind. If in the *Tesoretto* Brunetto contrasts Nature's order to Florence's ruin, which he traces to the conflict between the Guelfs and Ghibellines and the defeat at Montaperti, Forese's denunciation of the unnatural ways of Florence's women and his own brother Corso speaks to more fundamental causes of civic ruin.[8] Latini's fatherhood survives not in himself but as an image in Dante's mind; Forese survives in the revised text of his altercation, whose "voci" translate the contentious defamation of fathers and birthright into the inner contest every penitent must wage to disown himself if he is to authenticate the true paternity of his soul.[9]

Virgil and Statius in turn stand as godfathers to this baptizing of blood and breeding, since their poems were pattern and model of the antagonisms that had produced the "tenzone." Dante designates them "great marshals of the world" because they are the authors of the

---

8. As we shall see, Forese's animadversions will be taken up by Cacciaguida, who, in accordance with the privilege of the blessed, reverses the misogyny of Forese's outburst without actually canceling it. On the *Tesoretto*, see, among others, Elio Costa, "Il *Tesoretto* di Brunetto Latini e la tradizione allegorica medievale," in *Dante e le forme dell'allegoresi,* ed. Michelangelo Picone (Ravenna: Longo, 1987), 43–58; Francesco Mazzoni, "Brunetto Latini," in *Enciclopedia dantesca* (Rome: Istituto dell'Enciclopedia Italiana, 1976), 3: 579–88; more generally, see André Pézard, *Dante sous la pluie de feu (Enfer XV)* (Paris: J. Vrin, 1950); Julia Holloway, *Twice Told Tales: Brunetto Latini and Dante Alighieri* (New York: Peter Lang, 1993); John Najemy, "Brunetto Latini's 'Politica,'" *Dante Studies* 112 (1994): 33–51.

9. It is significant that in canto 16 of the *Purgatorio*, Marco Lombardo pictures the new made soul issuing from God's hand as a child ("a guisa di fanciulla") that proceeding from its happy creator, turns eagerly to whatever delights it.

Aeneid and *Thebaid*, the great epics of civil war prompted by misdi-
rected love. They, like Dante, are what they wrote. And they, like
Forese, go signifying "sub specie aeternitatis" through what Dante
writes. Great though Virgil may be, by himself he remains marshal of
this world alone; as Statius says, he was the man who traveled through
the night lighting the way for others by holding the lantern behind him.
When Virgil vanishes in the Garden of Eden, Dante beweeps his loss
until Beatrice sharply rebukes him. As John Freccero has argued, in a
series of allusions to Dido and Marcellus in the *Aeneid* and Orpheus in
the *Georgics*, Dante underscores the failures of his sweetest father, "Virgilio dolcissimo padre," as poet of love and empire in the face of
death.[10] It is not Virgil but Dante's Virgil whose "modo di dire" truly
incarnates the light of the understanding soul: "per che non reggi tu, o
sacra fame / de l'oro, l'appetito de' mortali." Only the Christian Statius
can convert Polydorus's curse, uttered from the limbs of the tree he has
become, into an exhortation to follow the example of Jesus, who turned
the tree of death into the tree that satisfies all hunger. Transfigured into
allegories of the internal civil war that makes the soul a citizen of "that
Rome where Christ is Roman" (*Purg.* 32.102), this Virgil and this Statius
father forth the poetics of conversion that redeems Dante and Forese's
"altercatio" and indicts the translation of Brunetto's *Tresor* into the
Tesoro as a forgery.

Dante recognizes that such a dialectic, in which transgression is not
just necessary for reconciliation but indistinguishable from it, so pro-
foundly reconceptualizes both patrimony and literary history that our
understanding of earthly categories such as masculine and feminine, or
father and mother tongue, needs to be re-formed as well. Statius had
characterized Virgil's poetic influence in maternal rather than paternal
terms: the *Aeneid* was "mother and nurse to him in poetry" [mamma /
fummi, e fummi nutrice, poetando (*Purg.* 21.97–98)]. Since Latin was
the vernacular of both poets, the trope can account for itself. But at the
moment of Beatrice's advent, Dante turns to Virgil like "the little child
who runs to his mother" [il fantolin corre a la mamma] and says precisely what Dido said to her sister Anna but not in her language:
"conosco i segni de l'antica fiamma" [I know the tokens of the ancient

---

10. See John Freccero, "Manfred's Wounds and the Poetics of the *Purgatorio*," in *Dante: The Poetics of Conversion*, ed. Rachel Jacoff (Cambridge, Mass: Harvard University Press, 1986), 195–208.

flame (*Purg.* 30.44, 49)].[11] These words, which mark his disappearance, do not embody Virgil but the "bello stilo" Dante took from him. Exalted and humble, the line enacts its own "contrapasso," affirming Dante's filial devotion to his "dolcissimo patre" (*Purg.* 30.50) and denying Virgil's sufficiency to be even his Anchises at the same time. Italian in form, Latin in content, the selfsame utterance bespeaks a tragedy of passion that led to death and the bittersweet joy of a love that died and is now renewed. The line captures the transformation of Virgil into Beatrice; as such it demonstrates how the poet whose name is its sign, and Statius, whose conversion reveals the beauty of its style, stand as the true progenitors of Guinizzelli, "il padre / mio e de li altri miei miglior che mai / rime d'amor usar dolci e leggiadre" [the father of me and of others my betters who ever used sweet and gracious rhymes of love (*Purg.* 26.97–99)] and of Arnaut, the Provençal master whom Guido calls "the better craftsman of the mother-tongue."[12] Artistic rivalry and social contest have become, as it were, the trace elements of history in the spiritual "tenzone" that forms the renovated soul; in the *Purgatorio*, Dante's poetry transposes mother tongue and father tongue alike into a new language of love, whose style delineates the aesthetics of being.[13]

---

11. As many have pointed out, the infernal counterpart of this moment of poetic self-awareness occurs when Dante describes his descent to the bottom of Hell: "non è impresa da pigliare a gabbo / discriver fondo a tutto l'universo, / né da lingua che chiami mamma o babbo" (*Inf.* 32.7–9 [to describe the bottom of the whole universe is not an enterprise to be taken up in sport, nor for a tongue that cries momma and daddy]. To cite only two studies that inform my reading here: Zygmunt Barański, "Significar *per verba*: Notes on Dante and Plurilingualism," *Italianist* 6 (1986): 5–18, for whom the layering of various linguistic registers and literary genres in these passages reveals Dante's understanding of his poem as a comedy; Robert Hollander, "Babytalk in Dante's *Commedia*," in *Studies in Dante* (Ravenna: Longo, 1980), 115–29, who, as I, relates these passages to Cacciaguida.

12. Virgil's "bello stilo" and Beatrice are homologous; I note in passing that if this claim is persuasive, it offers a solution to one of the most famous cruxes of the *Comedy*. In canto 10 *Inferno*, Dante points to Virgil as he says to Guido Cavalcanti's *father* (in light of the theme of paternity I am tracing, the fact that Dante is speaking to Cavalcante dei Cavalcanti is significant): "He who waits yonder is leading me through here," "forse cui Guido vostro ebbe a disdegno" (62–63). Does "cui" mean "whom" or "to whom," both of which are possible? The first option would mean Guido held Virgil in disdain, the second Beatrice. Dante, I would argue, would disdain anyone who argued there was a difference.

13. On the tensions in Dante between mother tongue and father tongue, see Kevin Brownlee, "Why the Angels Speak Italian: Dante as Vernacular *Poeta* in *Paradiso* XXV," *Poetics Today* 5 (1984): 597–610. From the perspective of the set of concerns I have introduced, the interplay of tongues in the *Purgatorio* is resolved by Cacciaguida, who says

II

Dante achieves the mystical union of words with the Word in the *Paradiso;* he appropriately foregrounds its intelligible and supraintelligible effects when he meets the spirit he unequivocally declares is his father. "Voi siete il padre mio," Dante says to Cacciaguida after his great-great-grandfather has identified himself as Dante's "root."

> Dal "voi" che prima a Roma s'offerie,
> in che la sua famiglia men persevra,
> ricominciaron le parole mie;
> onde Beatrice, ch'era un poca scevra,
> ridendo, parve quella che tossio
> al primo fallo scritto di Ginevra.
> Io cominciai: "Voi siete il padre mio . . ."
>
> (*Par.* 16.10–16)

[With that *You* which was first used in Rome and in which her family least perseveres, my words began again; at which Beatrice, who was a little withdrawn, smiled and seemed like her who coughed at the first fault that is written of Guinevere. I began, "You are my father . . ."]

In a place where Father and Son are one, however, paternity is undetermined by birth or descent; human institutions can in fact do little more than present a distorted image of a condition that is outside time and beyond understanding. Dante is incapable of acknowledging more than mortal faculties can comprehend; he can therefore only imply the kind of kinship he claims with Cacciaguida by emphasizing that the blessed spirit he addresses is less his forebear than his father-to-be. Dante's "voi" conveys this the best way it can by asking us to consider the difference between the two calendars it invokes: the eternal menology of unchanging familial honor in Christ, which is Cacciaguida's, and history's chronicle of the decline of generations, the calendar by

---

that in the Florence of old, wives would tend the cradle and "spoke that speech which first delights fathers and mothers" [usava l'idïoma / che prima i padri e le madri trastulla" (*Par.* 15.122–23)]. "Padri" and "madri," in contrast to the less dignified forms "mamma" and "babbo," serve to establish a set of relations between and among the four languages of the Cacciaguida cantos, which I discuss in the next section.

which Dante still reckons his years and relations. Were Dante to assign a tense to the self-legitimation and affirmation of identity we hear in his "voi," it would have to be the future; from an earthbound perspective, however, the "you" he utters is a disavowal of past fathers. "Voi siete il padre mio," not Brunetto Latini, whom Dante identifes with a cry whose astonishment belies its respect: "Siete voi qui, ser Brunetto" (*Inf.* 15.30). Cacciaguida is the "sweetest father," not Virgil, whose absence is felt in the sigh that echoes in Dante's commentary on the form of "you" he uses.[14] In his "voi" we measure the distance between "our scanty nobility of blood" [O poca nostra nobiltà di sangue], whose "mantle soon shrinks" [Ben se' tu manto che tosto raccorce (*Par.* 16.1, 7)], and the succession Dante will rejoice in, which was not determined by his earthly nativity but by the heavenly chrism of Beatrice's mediation.

Dante's sign for the incommensurability between entering into God's patrimony and inheriting one's worldly portion is the disproportion of comparing Beatrice's agency to that of the Lady of Malehaut. The latter's cough, of course, could not prevent the disunion of husband and wife, the quarrels between friends, and the unjointing of kingdoms that were the consequences of Gallehault's pandering. In Malehaut Dante locates the beginning of every dissension of blood and station; in Beatrice's deference to Cacciaguida he celebrates their transcendence. This incommensurability, which, as the inverse of proportion, is one of the means whereby Dante constructs the aesthetics of paradise, accounts for why there are so many reminiscences of his "tenzone" with Forese in these lines. By comparing "our scanty nobility" to a "mantle that soon shrinks," Dante evokes his disparaging picture of

---

14. Dante's trope for decline, the "famiglia" that has given up the noble usages of the Roman past, has a political dimension that again joins Brunetto and Virgil and sets them in contrast to Cacciaguida. Florence was commonly referred to as "parva Roma" by contemporary historians, including Brunetto in his *Tresor.* (See Nicolai Rubenstein, "The Beginning of Political Thought in Florence," *Journal of the Warburg and Cortauld Institutes* 5 [1942]: 198–227.) On Brunetto's political vision, see especially Najemy, "Brunetto Latini's 'Politica,' " 33–51. Dante's "voi" transfigures the fallen course of Florentine history it embodies, a history Cacciaguida will chart in this and the next canto. See Jeffrey Schnapp, *The Transfiguration of History at the Center of Dante's Paradise* (Princeton: Princeton University Press, 1986), especially 36–69, and his fine examination of the intertextual dynamics between Dante and Virgil in "Sì pïa l'ombra d'Anchise si porse": *Paradiso* 15.25," in *The Poetry of Allusion: Virgil and Ovid in Dante's "Commedia,"* ed. Rachel Jacoff and Jeffrey Schnapp (Stanford: Stanford University Press, 1991): 145–56.

Nella Donati, cold in mid-August because her bedclothes are too short ("merzé del copertoio c'ha cortonese" [72.8]). Coupling Beatrice's smile to Malehaut's cough recalls Nella's coughing in the same sonnet ("Chi udisse tossir la malfatata / moglie di Bicci vocato Forese" [72.1–2]); the association allows Dante to redeem the sexual innuendos and hints of illegitimacy he had floated throughout the exchange by shamelessly using Nella and Forese's mother ("Monna Tessa," whose name echoes faintly in Malehaut's cough), to defame him.[15] By means of these allusions Dante joins the "tenzone" and the "stil novo" together; they are stylistic memorials to the petty pride and self-promoting passion that could drive both. Even as Francesca condemned book and author of the romance of Lancelot as Galeottos, Dante once and for all leaves these bequests from his literary heritage behind him in the name of and for the love of Beatrice.

Cacciaguida is the patrimony that has always stood in their place; he is the essential father from whom Dante learns his past and his future—everything, in short, that defines who he is.

One is not surprised, then, that in the lines that preface Cacciaguida's advent, poetics and aesthetics are conjoined in imitation of the Word that is the Father who is the Son.

Benigna volontade in che si liqua
sempre l'amor che drittamente spira,
come cupidità fa ne la iniqua,
silenzio puose a quella dolce lira,
e fece quïetar le sante corde
che la destra del cielo allenta e tira.

(*Par.* 15.1–6)

[Gracious will, wherein right-breathing love always resolves itself, as cupidity does into grudging will, imposed silence on that sweet lyre and quieted the holy strings which the right hand of heaven slackens and draws tight.]

---

15. These are good amends, a belated gallantry to a woman he wronged. Yet even in heaven Dante cannot completely rein in his antifeminism: like Forese before him, when Cacciaguida speaks of Florence, his trope for its decline is the fall of a chaste and sober woman into dissipated profligacy.

Dante recalls not only his explanation of his poetic selfhood to Bona-giunta but Brunetto Latini as well.[16] He rehearses with perfect pitch the *Tesoretto*'s analysis of cupidity as the root of all corruption in Florence and the world—a theme that Cacciaguida, with an understanding that far surpasses Brunetto's Natura's, will soon make the subject of his own sermon to his descendant. Indeed, Dante underscores the finality of his repudiation of his former teacher, even as he recuperates the truth of his teaching; when the "dolce lira" grows still, Dante fills the quiet space that follows with a moral that shuts the door on his "tenzone" with Brunetto.

> Bene è che sanza termine si doglia
> chi, per amor di cosa che non duri
> etternalmente, quello amor si spoglia.

(Par. 15.10–12)

[Right it is that he should grieve without end who, for the love of what does not endure forever, robs himself of that love.]

In Paradise, however, all renunciations are analogies, earthly shadows of the tongue struck dumb because it cannot describe realities transfig-ured beyond human speech.[17] Counterbalancing Dante's relegation of Brunetto to the silence of allusion is the silence that God's love inspires the blessed to impose on themselves. This silence of the souls in the heaven of Mars, however, which is the expression of their goodwill, produces the language of the *Comedy*; prompted by same "Amor" that

---

16. The connections between *Inferno* 15 and the Cacciaguida cantos were recognized by Dante's earliest commentators. For more recent studies, see, for instance, Thomas Werge, "Dante's Tesoro: *Inferno* XV," *Romance Notes* 7 (1965–66): 203–6; Peter Armour, "Brunetto, the Stoic Pessimist," *Dante Studies* 112 (1994): 12–14. I agree entirely with Jef-frey Schnapp: "As for Brunetto's vision of Florentine history, I take it for granted that it is essential to the capsule history of Florence presented by Cacciaguida" (*The Transfigura-tion of History*, 236). I think it is essential as well to the language that presents that history.

17. Commentators have noted how in these cantos Dante stresses the conflict between the necessity of communicating what he sees and the impossibility of doing so. These are readings I obviously agree with and have been influenced by. See especially André Pézard, "Volgare e latino nella Commedia," *Letture classensi* 2 (1966–67): 95–111; Dino Cervigni, "I canti di Cacciaguida: Significato della storia e poetica della lingua," in *Dante Alighieri 1985, in memoriam Hermann Gmelin*, ed. R. Baum and W. Hirdt (Tübingen: Stauf-fenburg, 1985): 129–40; Schnapp, *The Transfiguration of History*; Claire Honess, "Express-ing the Inexpressible: The Theme of Communication in the Heaven of Mars," *Lectura Dantis* 14 (1994): 42–60; Hollander, "Babytalk in Dante's *Commedia*," 15–29.

inspires Dante's poetry, it now elicits Dante's righteous prayers (7–9), "that speech," as he had put it, "which is one in all" [quella favella / ch'è una in tutti (*Par.* 14.88–89)]. Clearly Dante encourages us to think his poem is continuous with the fullness of God's word, which, according to Augustine (*Confessions* 11.7), is said all at once and silently; just as clearly, he knows the two are not the same.[18] The *Comedy* is related to the Word only analogously, in the way that an utterance is related to the silence that completes its meaning, or in the way that time is to eternity (Dante is inspired *when* Love breathes in him, "quando Amor mi spira"; Love *directly* breathes in the saved, "l'amor che drittamente spira"). Dante therefore introduces a series of discontinuities to suggest this distance, whose literary analogue is the distance that separates Brunetto (and all other practitioners of what we might call the "stil vecchio") from Dante. When Cacciaguida departs from the cross, his movement is compared to a shooting star that sometimes ("ad ora ad or") draws the eye as it moves across the still and cloudless evening sky ("per li seren tranquilli e puri").

> e pare stella che tramuti loco,
> se non che da la parte ond' e' s'accende
> nulla sen perde, ed esso dura poco.
>
> (*Par.* 15.13–18)

[And it seems a star that changes place, save that from where it shines [literally, is kindled] no star is lost, and it lasts but short while.]

Dante learned his physics of meteors from Albertus Magnus, but here he recalls Phaethon, who in the *Metamorphoses* falls

---

18. Beatrice endorses this continuity in specifically literary terms: "rimossa ogne menzogna / tutta tua visïon fa manifesta" (*Par.* 17.127–28). On the one hand, the lies that have been removed from the *Comedy* validate it as something more than poetic fiction, a "bella menzogna" whose letter covers a deeper truth. On the other hand, the removal points to an inherent lack of perfection; as a species of absence, it marks Dante's discourse as only analogous to the silence that God's love inspires the "sweet lyre" of blessed souls to impose on themselves. The differences between the two, of course, are productive; they not only generate Dante's poetry but are their subject matter. They are what enables Teodolinda Barolini to present her "de-theologized" reading of the *Comedy*. See *The Undivine Comedy* (Princeton: Princeton University Press, 1992); especially pertinent are her comments on the Cacciaguida cantos, 137–40.

ut interdum de caelo stella sereno,
etsi non cecedit, potuit cecidisse videri.

(2.321–22)

[As sometimes a star from the clear heavens, even though it has not fallen, can seem to have fallen.]

Phaethon is Ovid's archetypal story about the relation between paternity, perception, and identity: despite the Sun's acknowledgment that Phaethon is his son, his child's mortality proves that he is not his father's child.[19] The death of the son, which again serves as a metaphor of Dante's falling-out with Brunetto, here is made a sign of Dante's union with his true father, who will unfold his descendant's fate in the fallen world.[20] Phaethon's tragedy is then coupled to Anchises's greeting of Aeneas in the underworld (*Par.* 15.25–27), the pagan paradise, the house of the past in which father can teach son enough of the future to found Rome but not enough to foresee its fall or his own permanent exile in Limbo. When Cacciaguida inclines toward Dante with Anchises's affection, the poet's banishment from Florence becomes the shadow-bearing preface of his welcome into the City of God. In these gaps and disjunctions Dante transmogrifies all the "tenzoni" that have become part of his poetic identity. The quarrel between Ovid and Virgil and between himself and both of them (which I discuss in the next chapter); the quarrel between Latin and vernacular poetry; the quarrels within the vernacular itself—Brunetto, Forese, Bonagiunta: all now echo in the language Dante writes here, a language that itself is an echo of the divine silence that elicits it.

---

19. For further elaboration, see my "Ovid's *Metamorphoses* and the Politics of Interpretation," *Classical Journal* 84 (1989): 222–31. By alluding to the tale, Dante reinforces the connection between his meeting Cacciaguida and his prior meeting with Forese and Bonagiunta: both are "about" fatherhood, identity, and poetry. Prior to encountering Forese, Dante had also alluded to Ovid by comparing the gluttons' penance to Erysichthon; see William Stephany, "Erysichthon and the Poetics of the Spirit," in *The Poetry of Allusion,* ed. Rachel Jacoff and Jeffrey Schnapp (Stanford: Stanford University Press, 1991), 173–80.

20. Dante of course returns to the story of Phaethon and Helios precisely when Beatrice encourages the pilgrim to ask Cacciaguida to illuminate the prophecies of his exile (*Par.*17:1–12). On Dante's use of Ovid's story, see Kevin Brownlee, "Phaeton's Fall and Dante's Ascent," *Dante Studies* 102 (1984): 135–44, and Jeffrey Schnapp, "Dante's Ovidian Self-Correction in *Paradiso* 17," in *The Poetry of Allusion,* ed. Rachel Jacoff and Jeffrey Schnapp (Stanford: Stanford University Press, 1991), 214–23.

The celestial harmony of love and "benigna volontade" that expresses itself as the silence of heaven's lyre: metaphors such as these are the articulations of an aesthetics of the metaphysical, which is the only medium that permits humankind to grasp paradise with sense and mind. As if to emphasize this point, Dante draws our attention to the epistemology of his recognition of Cacciaguida. Unlike Brunetto, Dante does not know him by sight. Departing like a shooting star, yet never leaving the cross of the Church Militant, Cacciaguida moves toward Dante, a gem [gemma] who shines like "fire behind alabaster" (*Par.* 15.22, 24). Since the radiance of any of the beatified surpasses memory's capacity to retain its image, Dante cannot offer a mimetic representation of his ancestor. Instead he depicts a variation in intensity of light; as a condescension to his senses, Cacciaguida's fire shines more lambently than the alabaster souls he is among.[21] Cacciaguida's difference is the textual marking from which we must infer the superabundant unity of his being; it is the paradisial inversion of the infernal irony that separates the image of Brunetto Dante venerates from the scorched body he damns.

Nor does Dante know his ancestor from his voice, or even from what he says, as he did Forese. Unable to fathom words Cacciaguida adds to his greeting, Dante can only look at Beatrice, whose smile so amazes his eyes, he thinks he has touched the limit of his beatitude. When he turns back, Cacciaguida speaks again.

Indi, a udire e a veder giocondo,
giunse lo spirto al suo principio cose,
ch'io non lo 'ntesi, sì parlò profondo;
né per elezïon mi si nascose,
ma per necessità, ché 'l suo concetto
al segno d'i mortal si soprapuose.

(*Par.* 15.37–42)

---

21. As Thomas Aquinas had just explained, all the souls of any circle are invested with a brilliance that equals their ardor, which in turn matches their vision of God (*Par.* 14.37–60). Aquinas's comments are part of his explanation of how the resurrected body will increase the happiness of the blessed. They form a final gloss on Statius's discourse on the generation of the soul's aerial body in 25 *Purgatorio*, which I discuss in detail in the next chapter. In this way, Dante makes Aquinas's comments one more element in the nodal cluster of cantos that elaborate the *Comedy*'s poetics, whose center is Dante's encounter with Forese and Bonagiunta.

[Then, a joy to hearing and to sight, the spirit added to his first words things I did not comprehend, so deep was his speech; nor did he conceal himself from me by choice, but of necessity, for his conception was set above the mark of mortals.]

Though sight and sound had combined to reveal in Forese the universal that humankind brings to its form, the pleasure Dante felt in recognizing him still was coordinated to knowing. Here, however, intellection has become the reflex of aesthetic knowing. "Elezion" and "concetto"; choice and concept are precisely the conclusions that the discursive operations of free will and reason arrive at. Their nonpresence here makes them analogies to the sensible play of music and light that produces Dante's delight, a delight that in turn is the mark of the language beyond comprehension that Cacciaguida speaks. Beyond the analogies that allow Aquinas in some measure to know God, Dante's ratios of blindness to insight provide human experience of his Word, an experience that is aesthetic.[22] Thus it is fitting that "when the bow of [Cacciaguida's] ardent affection was so relaxed that his speech descended toward the mark of our intellect," the next thing Dante says he did understand was a prayer of thanksgiving to the Word that is beyond understanding, three persons yet one.

> Benedetto sia tu . . . trino e uno,
> che nel mio seme se' tanto cortese!
>
> (*Par.* 15.43–48)

[Blessed be Thou, Three and One, who show such favor to my seed.]

Here is the quintessence of Cacciaguida: he is the Trinity in Dante's life, the masculine form of that principle of conjuncture whose feminine aspect is Beatrice, that has made Dante the singular being he is. Cacciaguida is the progenitor, the creator of Dante's line, who stands for the Father whose mystical body is the Son in whom all the children of redemption are confederated by love. Cacciaguida is that love as well:

---

22. It is appropriate to note here that Aquinas associates God with beauty through the Son: "species autem sive pulchritudo habet similitudinem cum propriis Filii" (*S.T.* 1a.39.8); quoted in Kenelm Foster, *The Two Dantes and Other Studies* (London: Darton, 1977), 140. By centering both in Christ, Dante makes the poetics of his *Comedy* one with its aesthetics.

the heaven of Mars, from which he greets his offspring, was the heaven of the Holy Spirit, the love breathed between Father and Son that makes them three and one. This love is the blood that makes Cacciaguida Dante's father; it is the same love whose dictation determined his identity as a poet. And this love is the Word that, before anything else, makes Cacciaguida the only begetter of Dante's style.

With the affection that inclined Anchises toward his son in Elysium, Cacciaguida thus speaks these words when he addresses Dante for the first time.

> O sanguis meus, o superinfusa
> gratïa Deï, sicut tibi cui
> bis unquam celi ianüa reclusa?
>
> (Par. 15.25–30)

[O my blood, o grace of God infused from above and beyond measure! To whom as to you was ever the gate of heaven opened twice?]

This Latin, enseamed by love into the pattern of Italian "terza rima," is not a quotation or even a recall from Virgil. It is the source of the Roman poet's legacy to Dante. In it father and mother tongue talk at once. In it classical rhetoric ("O sanguis meus") is married by anaphora to the totally different vocabulary of Christian salvation ("o superinfusa gratïa Deï"). Cacciaguida's Latin, of which Virgil's is a historical echo, is the true origin of the "bello stilo" that has done Dante honor. His language is the form that the verbal reifications of Hell and the synaesthesia of Purgatory's "visibile parlare" copy in their very different ways.[23] As "living topaz ingemmed in this precious jewel" [vivo topazio / che questa gioia prezïosa ingemmi (Par. 15.85–86)], Cacciaguida subsumes Brunetto's Tesoro and Forese's "anella sanza gemme." As soldier of Christ, Crusader of the Church Militant, Cacciaguida undercuts the illusions of Brunetto's athleticism and estab-

---

23. Critics have noted the different languages Cacciaguida speaks in his cantos. I agree with Hollander that there are four different kinds of discourses: Cacciaguida's Latin, the language Dante cannot comprehend, his Florentine dialect, and the language in which Dante reports what Cacciaguida says. See Hollander, "Babytalk in Dante's Commedia," 125–27; see also Honess, "Expressing the Inexpressible," for a recent and full review of positions. I am obviously less concerned with establishing the differing provenances for each discourse than with the aesthetical metaphysics that subsumes them all.

lishes himself as the perfection of courage that Forese's chivalric riding forth can match only in simile.[24] In Cacciaguida Dante finds the "fons et origo" of his style. In Cacciaguida Dante discovers the aesthetics that enables him to express the heart and marrow of who he is.

---

24. As "miles Christi," Cacciaguida is as well Dante's final answer to the charges of cowardice Forese had brought against Dante and his father in the "tenzone." Not by chance does Cacciaguida recall Dante's memorial to Brunetto Latini when he indicates he was born in the sesto of Porta San Piero by designating it as "the last ward the runner reaches in your annual games" (*Par.* 16. 41–42).

Ovid, the Transformation of Metamorphosis, and the Aesthetics of Hell

Dante's encounter with Cacciaguida in Paradise represents one pole of the spiritual physics that governs the aesthetics of the afterlife. For the other, we must turn to the thieves in Hell, who undergo a horrific series of Ovid-like metamorphoses in which men are changed into snakes or unidentifiable amalgams of matter. Since theft violates particular justice, which is a dynamic process that coordinates relations, Dante makes metamorphosis and the lack of relation it creates between the forms that are changed the proper punishment for Vanni Fucci and his fellow sinners. Ovidian metamorphosis, however, can only image the mutations they experience because Dante's brigands have suffered a transformation even before they are changed into the nonhuman conglomerations they become. For every sinner in Hell has undergone a deformation, a disordering movement away from form, which unbalances the vital relationship between body and soul that had made him or her human. As Aristotle says, particular justice is only part of a more general kind of justice that is complete excellence.[1] In the *Inferno*, this global justice is the final cause of Hell ("Giustizia mosse il mio alto fattore" [*Inf.* 3.4]) and the principle of retribution that establishes the balance between the punishment and crime of those in it. This general justice, I shall argue, also effects a metamorphosis, a metamorphosis of unbecoming that makes each of the damned a perverse parody of the being God had originally created.

More precisely, even though we learn from Statius in the *Purgatorio* that the damned retain the rational soul, it no longer functions as the

---

1. *Nicomachean Ethics* V.1.30 (1129b): particular justice bears the same relation to complete justice as the part to the whole. All quotations are from *The Complete Works of Aristotle*, ed. Jonathan Barnes, 2 vols. (Princeton: Princeton University Press, 1984).

form of the body since it has ceased to be the determining element that distinguishes the being that it is in as human. Indeed, as the particular transformations of Agnello and Buoso will make clear, the substantial form of all the damned has become less the intellectual soul than the shape of their matter, from which the intellect can no longer abstract any intelligible form. As their increasing corporeality suggests, the sinners throughout Hell are being transformed into creatures of ever greater density but no inner depth since they lack an animating essence whose powers persist despite outer change.[2]

In other words, because Dante relates metamorphosis to justice, which is of two kinds, transformation in the *Inferno* also has two forms, one comprehensive and the other specific, each of which needs to be understood in relation to the other. To register the effects of infernal metamorphosis in its common aspect as a failure of form, we shall have to refer to its specific action on the thieves; and to determine its specific relation to theft, we must understand it in its general operation as a process of unbecoming. Dante in effect signals this network of relations by explicitly linking the changings of the thieves to Statius's description in canto 25 of the *Purgatorio* of how all human beings are born. That canto corresponds more than in number alone to the metamorphoses cantos of the *Inferno.*

To give metamorphosis such ethical, philosophical, and theological dimensions, however, clearly would put it beyond the reach of Ovid, for whom change alters nothing but the external frame. Indeed, to Dante transformation in the *Metamorphoses* could never be more than rhetoric, a device Ovid used to locate the meaning of his text exclusively in its surface. Dante therefore engages his Roman forebear in a poetic "tenzone."

Taccia di Cadmo e d'Aretusa Ovidio,
ché se quello in serpente e quella in fonte
converte poetando, io non lo 'nvidio;
ché due nature mai a fronte a fronte

---

2. The damned in effect can engage only in the meaningless transformations of chaos ("Nulli sua forma manebat / obstabatque aliis aliud," Ovid says of the elements in primal matter [No element kept its form, and each was at odds with the others (*Met.* 1.17–18)]. All quotations are from *P. Ovidii Nasonis Metamorphoses,* ed. W. S. Anderson (Leipzig: Teubner, 1977). All translations, unless otherwise indicated, are mine.

non trasmutò sì ch'amendue le forme
a cambiar lor matera fosser pronte.

(Inf. 25.97–102)

[Let Ovid be silent about Cadmus and Arethusa, for if he poetically
converts the one into a serpent and the other into a fountain, I do not
envy him, for two natures front to front he never so transmuted that
both forms were ready to exchange their matter.]

This "silencing," though, is less a boast than a gloss on what Dante
means when he says that Ovid "converts in his poet's manner" [con-
verte poetando]. The Italian poet's metamorphoses out-Ovid Ovid's
because they at once establish the limits of outward change and point
to substantive transformations beyond the power of any pagan writer
to imagine. In the last analysis, Dante will show that for a Christian
poet, only a Christian poetics could adequately describe "in noua . . .
mutatas . . . formas corpora" [forms changed into new bodies (*Met.*
1–2)]. Thus, in the long simile that opens canto 24, Dante steals Ovid's
idea of metamorphosis not only to transform it into a figure for allegory but also to announce his opposition to the common medieval
tendency—a tendency he shared in the *Convivio*—to allegorize Ovid.[3]
In short, Dante organizes the changes that afflict the lost souls in Hell
so that they delineate an antiaesthetics of being. But to see why and
how Dante manages these revisions, which as in the *Purgatorio* and
Paradiso are both metaphysical and stylistic, we must first take into
account the general metamorphosis of unbecoming in the damned,
which itself is underwritten by Statius's description of the creation of
life in humans.

---

3. The school of Orleans is, of course, the notable exception to the tendency to read
Ovid allegorically. There is a large literature about the medieval traditions of Ovidian
commentary, but see especially the work of Fausto Ghisalberti, "Arnolfo d'Orléans: Un
cultore di Ovidio nel secolo xii," Reale Istituto Lombardo di Scienze e Lettere (Milan),
Memorie 246, no. 4 (1932): 157–234; "L' 'Ovidius Moralizatus' di Pierre Bersuire," Studi
Romanzi 23 (1933): 5–136; "Giovanni del Virgilio espositore delle 'Metamorfosi,'" Il Gior-
nale Dantesco 34, n.s., 4 (1933): 3–110; and Paule Demats, Fabula (Geneva: Droz, 1973). For
Ovid as ethical poet, see Judson Allen, The Ethical Poetic of the Later Middle Ages (Toronto:
University of Toronto Press, 1982): 9–10 passim.

I

Statius explains the natural generation of the body and the vegetative and sensitive souls in it by describing a series of purifying digestions. These digestions, which, as Bruno Nardi says, were themselves understood to be transformations, constitute the medieval elaboration of Aristotle's account of how food is converted into the substance of the body it nourishes.[4] The discussion is technical; simplifying it somewhat, Statius says that after the third digestion, perfect blood, which "is left like food taken from the table" [si rimane / quasi alimento che di mensa leve (*Purg.* 25.38–39)], comes to the heart, where it receives its informing power ("virtute informativa") to nourish bodily organs. A superfluity of blood is left over from this banquet in the members; after two further digestions it becomes semen capable of generating a new organism. When joined with the mother's blood in the uterus, which serves as the passive matter of reproduction, this semen becomes the active principle or form of generation.[5] It produces first the vegetative soul and then the sensitive soul; both then form the bodily organs appropriate to their powers. After the child has thus been fully formed in the embryo, God breathes into it the intellectual soul, which draws into itself what it finds active in the vegetative and sensitive and so becomes "one single soul, which lives and feels and circles on itself" [un alma sola, / che vive e sente e sé in sé rigira (*Purg.* 25.74–75)]. This soul, Dante says in the *Convivio* (3.6.12), is the possible intellect, which is the form of the body; it is full of power since "it potentially absorbs into itself all the universal forms, according as they are in its producer." This is the soul whose qualities establish the likeness between human beings and their creator.

After death, Statius says that the intellectual soul separates itself from the body and drops to one of two rivers: the Tiber if the spirit is destined for Purgatory or the Acheron if it is destined for Hell. Once there, the soul informs and shapes the surrounding air into bodily organs for the soul's powers. In this way, the damned gain a perceptible shape and think and feel and move.

---

4. Bruno Nardi, *Studi di filosofia medievale* (Rome: Edizioni di storia e letterature, 1960), 46–58, provides the definitive commentary on Statius's lines. Nardi says, "According to the Aristotelian idea, food is not converted into the substance of the nourished body until after a series of transformations or *digestions* ('trasformazioni o *digestioni*'), by means of which it leaves off being *dissimilar* ('cessa di essere *dissimile*') and is rendered perfectly assimilable" (47).

5. The terms "matter and form" derive from Aquinas, *S.T.* I.118.1 ad 4 (see Nardi, *Studi di filosofia medievale*, 49).

To have died the second death, however, must cause a catastrophic disruption in the relation of body and soul. As the form of the body, the intellectual soul is that which actualizes matter and gives it existence by realizing its potential: "forma dat esse," in the words of the scholastic tag. But because the souls in Hell have turned to evil, they have moved toward privation and nonbeing; as Aquinas says, evil is neither an existent nor a good (*S.T.* I.48.1.sc).[6] The damned, therefore, will retain the intellectual soul, which on the shore of the Acheron shapes for itself a body of air, wherewith the "perduta gente" suffer their own lack. But once they have crossed the river, the rational soul must also somehow lose its substantive principle, its power to be that intrinsic and unifying form that makes human beings what they are. The souls have now lost forever "the good of the intellect" [c'hanno perduto il ben de l'intelletto (*Inf.* 3.18)], who is God, the author of the soul by which the child becomes like the creator who perfects it. The "evil seed of Adam" [il mal seme d'Adamo (*Inf.* 3.115)], in other words, have no part in the analogies that once allowed them to participate in the aesthetics of being.

This movement away from existence in the damned, which I am arguing is a loss on the part of the intellectual soul of its essential "virtute informativa," takes the form of a metamorphosis of unbecoming. Augustine had said that evil cannot utterly devour good (*Enchiridion* 12); Aquinas agreed and commented that insofar as this good is the ability to be actual, evil can diminish it but never entirely take it away. Evil effects this "diminutio" by lessening matter's readiness to receive the form that perfects it. For the living soul, this form, from one point of view, is its readiness to receive grace. Though sin be piled on sin, Aquinas says the readiness would remain, for it follows from the soul's very nature (*S.T.* I.48.4). Charles Singleton has shown that in the *Purgatorio*, Dante's journey to Beatrice and the sanctifying grace she embodies is a "motus ad formam" that is itself a double transformation. For any movement toward grace is a movement toward justice, and "justification," as Thomas says, "implies a transmutation [transmutationem] from the state of injustice to the . . . state of justice."[7] Such a change in turn implies, as John Freccero has said, the corruption of the old form

---

6. Unless otherwise noted, all quotations and translations from Aquinas are from the Blackfriars edition of St. Thomas Aquinas, *Summa theologiae* (London and New York: McGraw-Hill, 1964).

7. *S.T.* I–II.113.1, quoted in Charles Singleton, *Dante Studies 2: Journey to Beatrice* (Cambridge, Mass: Harvard University Press, 1967), 60.

before the new one can take its place.[8] The souls in the *Inferno,* however, have lost all possibility of grace. Sin has made them irreversibly dissimilar from the highest good ("Solo il peccato è quel che la disfranca / e falla dissimìle al sommo bene" [*Par.* 7.79–80]), which is the grace whereby human beings are made complete. The only "place" where the effects of such a disenfranchisement could be registered is in the intellectual soul, given by God as an act of grace but now essentially alien to itself, because the souls it is in have deformed themselves. Dante therefore images the dead souls' irrevocable turn to evil as a parody of the process of justification. Instead of becoming "angelic butterflies," they undergo what we must call a "motus a forma," which transforms them into matter invested with a form unable to actualize it as something human.[9]

Dante most clearly conveys these general consequences of damnation in the metamorphoses of the thieves. It is no accident that the fiery serpent (Francesco Guercio de' Cavalcanti) that attacks Buoso moves toward his belly and transfixes him in "quella parte onde prima è preso / nostro alimento" [in that part where our nourishment is first taken (*Inf.* 25.85–86)]. But what horrifies Dante most about each of the transformations he witnesses is not that men have turned into something else but that one cannot tell what they have become because they no longer have the formal distinctions that could identify them as men or beasts. Agnello's transformation is precisely one of unbecoming due to the failure of form.

> Ellera abbarbicata mai non fue
> ad alber sì, come l'orribil fiera
> per l'altrui membra avviticchiò le sue.
> Poi s'appiccar, come di calda cera
> fossero stati, e mischiar lor colore,
> né l'un né l'altro già parea quel ch'era:
> come procede innanzi da l'ardore,

---

8. John Freccero, "The Sign of Satan," in *Dante: The Poetics of Conversion,* ed. Rachel Jacoff (Cambridge, Mass.: 1986), 173.

9. At the beginning of active purgation in the *Purgatory,* the spiritual generation of saved souls that Dante imagines as both a metamorphosis and a movement toward form particularly recalls the metamorphoses of the thieves: "non v'accorgete voi che noi siam vermi / nati a formar l'angelica farfalla, / che vola a la giustizia sanza schermi?" (*Purg.* 10.124–26) [Are you not aware that we are worms, born to form the angelic butterfly that flies to justice without defenses?]. The damned, having denied their birthright, in some form all undergo transformation into "vermi."

per lo papiro suso, un color bruno
che non è nero ancora e 'l bianco more.

(25.58–66)

[Ivy was never so rooted to a tree as the horrible beast envined its members about the other's. Then they stuck together, as if they had been hot wax, and mixed their colors; neither the one nor the other then seemed what it was before, even as before the flame a dark color moves across the paper, which is not yet black, and the white dies away.]

As Buoso and Puccio both say to this creature, "See, you are already neither two nor one" [Vedi che già non se' né due né uno]; and Dante elaborates:

Già eran li due capi un divenuti,
quando n'apparver due figure miste
in una faccia, ov'eran due perduti.
. . . .
due e nessun l'imagine perversa
parea . . .

(25:69–72, 77–78)

[The two heads had already become one when we saw two shapes mixed in one face, where the two were lost . . . the perverse image seemed two and neither.]

The image is perverse because it makes visible the dissolution of that unity of soul Statius insisted on when he argued against Averroes that the intellectual soul is one with the sensitive and vegetative. Agnello's metamorphosis exactly reverses what happens when the Prime Mover breathes "spirito novo" into the creature nature has made. Rather than making "un' alma sola, che vive e sente e sé in sé rigira," his intellectual soul oversees the disintegration of what it found active in the sensitive and vegetative souls.[10]

---

10. The similarity of Agnello's transformation to that of Hermaphroditus and Salmacis in the *Metamorphoses* has long been noted. With its allusions to Aristophanes's famous account of hermaphroditism in Plato's *Symposium,* Ovid's tale is particularly concerned with exploding notions of identity based on gender. Dante's recall of it here establishes the classical base that he will transform when mother and father tongue merge in

Aquinas's comment on the unity of the intellectual soul is particularly relevant.

> In man the sensitive soul, the intellectual soul, and the nutritive soul are numerically one soul. This can be easily explained if we consider the differences of species and forms. For we observe that the species and forms of things differ from one another, as the perfect and the imperfect; as in the order of things, the animate are more perfect than the inanimate . . . For this reason Aristotle compares the species of things to numbers, which differ in species by the addition or subtraction of unity. And he compares the various souls to the species of figures, one of which contains another; as a pentagon contains and exceeds a tetragon . . . so neither is Socrates a man by one soul and animal by another; but by one and the same soul he is both animal and man.[11]

Integrity of form is precisely what Agnello's transformation denies him; indeed, Dante specifically recalls his metamorphosis when Statius seeks to explain how the intellectual soul confers that absolute unity that makes a man human.

> E perché meno ammiri la parola,
> guarda il calor del sol che si fa vino,
> giunto a l'omor che de la vite cola.
>
> (*Purg.* 25.76–78)

[And that you may marvel less at my words, look at the sun's heat, which is made wine when combined with the juice that flows from the vine.]

Dante's verb for the entwining of the beast's members with Agnello's is "avviticchiò"; its root is "vite," the vine that appears as a metaphor, itself a metamorphosis, for how the intellectual soul makes "un alma sola." "Alma," in the union of its Latinate meanings of "fruitful,"

---

the language of Cacciaguida. On Ovid's story, see my "Ovid and the Problem of Gender," *Mediaevalia* 13 (1987): 20–25.

11. *S.T.* I.76.3. The passage is quoted by Singleton in his note to the line, and I follow his translation, which is closer to Thomas than the one given in the Blackfriars edition. See *The Divine Comedy: Purgatorio 2: Commentary*, 611–13.

"food-giving," and "kind," is the perfect word for the soul God gives.[12] Indeed, the wine that is likened to it is itself a product of sun's heat and vine's juice, a substance that is comprised of both but is neither. Agnello, by contrast, is a disjointed, unformed thing that can no longer be identified as a substance: "né l'un né l'altro già parea quel ch'era." In him the soul Statius speaks of has clearly lost its unifying power.

"Due capi un divenuti, due figure miste in una faccia"; as Paratore says, numbers oscillate so often with the qualities of the natures involved in the transformations they become a leitmotiv in these cantos. Dante clearly thinks the thieves cannot be considered forms in whom the different souls are unified as figures that contain one another. In the order of things, they have been reduced, from perfect to less perfect, from man to beast; they have devolved into species of things, which Aristotle had compared to numbers.[13] Instead of being differentiated by the addition or subtraction of unity, however, these figures are now distinguished by quantity, the "forma corporeitatis" by which matter individuates a creature. Indeed, matter that has an exigency for the quantitative determination it receives in the union with form, "materia insignata quantitate," became for Thomas what it was for Aristotle, the principle of individuation.[14] Quantity, however, does not distinguish Agnello as a particular person; rather it becomes a sign of the dissolution of the unified soul that made him human. Dante in fact quotes Aristotle's comparison of souls to figures in the *Convivio* (4.7.14–15), precisely at the end of a passage in which he says that were the rational soul subtracted from men they would be dead as men. Even if they still moved about on earth, they would possess nothing more than a sensitive soul; they would be able to feel but would be indistinguishable from beasts, who also have this power. So if one were to ask, "Come è morto e va?" Dante would answer "è morto [uomo] e

12. Indeed, "alma" sets in even greater ironic contrast the "figs" [fiche] Vanni Fucci aims at God at the beginning of 25 *Inferno*, which, in conjunction with the snakes that prevent him from speaking further, recall the Fall and the transformations it brought about, not only in the serpent but in Adam and Eve, and in the world, as well. The full implications of Dante's imagery, however, are revealed, as we shall see, in cantos 24–25 of the *Paradiso*.

13. Ettore Paratore, *Tradizione e struttura in Dante* (Florence: Sansoni, 1968), 273.

14. See *S.T.* I.85.1 ad 2. See also Copleston, *A History of Philosophy*, 46. For matter as the principle of individuation in Dante, see Daniele Mattalia, *Il Canto XXV dell' Inferno* (Florence: Le Monnier, 1962); and Paratore, *Tradizione*, 273 ff. For another reading of the damned in terms of their loss of identity, see Harold Skulsky, *Metamorphosis: The Mind in Exile* (Cambridge, Mass.: Harvard University Press, 1981), 114–20.

rimaso bestia" (4.7.10–14). Vanni ("Va-nni") Fucci thus speaks for all his fellow sinners when he says, "Vita bestial mi piacque e non umana, / sì come a mul ch'i' fui; son Vanni Fucci / bestia" [A bestial life, not human, pleased me, mule that I was. I am Vanni Fucci, beast (*Inf.* 24.124–26)].[15]

Now theft, according to Aquinas, violates particular justice, which regulates the relation of one person to another and therefore takes as its subject the "due coordination of one person with another."[16] As a consequence, justice requires that all acts of restoration be duly proportionate with the nature of the person to whom something unjust was done. Justice therefore establishes a mean that is "a certain proportion" that matches and equalizes "the external work to an external man" (*S.T.* II–II.58.10). Yet in the extraordinary transformation of Francesco and Buoso, who change from snake to man and man to snake *in concert with* each other, we see that the thieves are not coordinated as one person to another but as men to not-men. This violent transgression of nature and proportion entirely estranges them from justice. What can they and the things they become exchange that is commensurate?

But the radical disordering of the relation between body and soul that precedes the thieves' metamorphoses and makes them possible is not unique to them. It becomes the fundamental condition of all the souls in Hell, because all the damned are unjust. In its widest sense, justice unites the virtues; as Aristotle says, when the brave man does not desert his post, and the temperate man refrains from adultery, and the good-tempered man does not strike someone else, each is acting justly. Justice, therefore, is the actual exercise of complete excellence, both with reference to a man himself and in his relation to others (*Ethics* V 1 [1129b–1130a]). Of all the sinners, the thieves most obviously transgress what Cicero called the communal aspects of justice.

For, as Plato has admirably expressed it, we are not born for ourselves alone, but our country claims a share of our being, and our friends a share . . . and as men, too, are born for the sake of men, that

---

15. Compare: "vivere ne l'uomo è ragione usare, ragione usare è l'essere de l'uomo, e così da quello uso partire è partire da essere" (4.7.10–12) [In humans, to live is to use reason, to use reason is the essence of being human, and thus to depart from that use is to depart from that being]. Cf. *Conv.* 2.7.3.

16. "Secundum eas [i.e., man's external deeds and things] unus homo alteri coordinatur" (*S.T.* II.5.8).

they may be able mutually to help one another; in this direction we ought to follow Nature as our guide, to contribute to the general good by an interchange of acts of kindness, by giving and receiving . . . and thus cement human society more closely together, man to man [in hoc naturam debemus ducem sequi, communes utilitates in medium aufferre mutatione officiorum, dando accipiendo . . . devincere hominum inter homines societatem].[17]

But prior to these relations with others, which Cicero describes as "mutationes" and whose violation Dante punishes by metamorphosis, there is a sense in which justice effects the constitution of a man by establishing the proper bond between the souls within him. For Aristotle this justice consists of

> the ratios in which the part of the soul that has reason stands to the irrational part; and it is with a view to these parts that people also think a man can be unjust to himself, viz. because these parts are liable to suffer something contrary to their desires; there is therefore thought to be a mutual justice between them as between ruler and ruled (*Ethics* V 11 [1138b6]).

Precisely because they have had the just relation between the rational and irrational parts of the soul disrupted, a relation that expresses itself as an analogy, the damned as a species are disordered as human beings. To represent the nature of such a condition, Dante, like Cicero, follows nature: the metamorphoses Statius says account for the generation of men are coordinated with and gloss the metamorphosis that brings about their unmaking. Because every sinner has dealt unjustly either with himself or with others, they have all been robbed of the capacity to be just to themselves. They all are matter in which form has failed. They all are the paper over which the dark color of combustion moves, not yet black but whose whiteness dies away. These are the proportions from which Dante constructs the aesthetics of Hell.

In fact, it is precisely the souls' materiality that allows both the particular metamorphoses of the thieves and the unforming of the damned in general. Aristotle had said in the *Physics* (I,7) that substantial change occurs only in bodies: primal matter, with its potential to receive form,

---

17. *De officiis* 1.7.22. The text and translation are from Cicero, *De officiis*, ed. and trans. W. Miller, Loeb Classical Library (Cambridge, Mass.: Harvard University Press, 1928).

must stand as the substratum of all change and make it possible. But the transformations of the thieves really bespeak less an alteration of body than of form. As Dante later says, to distinguish his metamorphoses from Ovid's:

> ché due nature mai a fronte a fronte
> non trasmutò sì ch'amendue le forme
> a cambiar lor matera fosser pronte.
>
> (*Inf.* 25.100–102)

[For never did he so transform two natures front to front that both forms were ready to exchange their matter.]

Clearly in such creatures the intellectual soul, which was made by God, has lost the virtue by which those who possess it can be said to be in his image. Indeed, with the impairment of the intellectual soul, the corporeality of *any* shade in the *Inferno* will bear witness to the extent it has exhausted its potentiality for the form that should realize it. The very degree the damned have become material—"vermo," as Dante says, "in cui formazion falla" [a worm in whom full form is wanting (*Purg.* 10.129)]—indicates the degree each sinner has turned to nonbeing. This is a metamorphosis whose endpoint is Satan, the "evil worm" [vermo reo (*Inf.* 34.108)] who is the principle of materiality: "'l punto / al qual si traggon d'ogne parte i pesi" [the point to which all weights are drawn from every part (*Inf.* 34.110–11)]. As Aquinas says, even in death each soul still strives to realize the full potential of its species, since all things participate in the process of entelechy by nature, and the damned continue to obey the natural impulses of the soul (*S.T.* I.64.4).[18] The souls' tangibility as a result increases throughout the *Inferno:* the bulk of their corporeality is an index of the extent to which the damned have turned to evil.[19]

18. Here Aquinas argues that the damned cannot want good actually, yet their wills are still naturally inclined toward good.

19. From a different perspective, John Freccero has concluded that the souls' bodies are fictive; the damned are there in Hell only as a reified irony or through the irony of reification. In one sense, all Freccero says is a presupposition of my argument here, but I would maintain that the souls' corporeality is real, in the same way that evil is real. The mode of representing the privative reality of nonexistence, however, would, as Freccero holds, necessarily be ironic. See "Infernal Irony: The Gates of Hell," in *Dante: The Poetics of Conversion*, ed. Rachel Jacoff (Cambridge, Mass.: Harvard University Press, 1986), 93–109. In "Dante's Prologue Scene" (in *Dante: The Poetics of Conversion*, 1–28), Freccero

In order to judge fully the psychic effects of damnation, however, we must return to Statius's disquisition one last time. He says that in the creature newly separated from the body, the powers of the intellectual soul, "memory, intellect, and will in act" [memoria, intelligenza e volontade in atto (*Purg.* 25.83–84)], are keener than they were before. But in every soul whom Minos has judged, these faculties are essentially deficient in that none can achieve its end.

The damned certainly can remember, but the purpose of memory everywhere in Hell has been said to be to revive a soul's fame. The transformation of Buoso and Francesco, each turned to smoke ("fummavan forte, e 'l fummo si scontrava" [*Inf.* 25.93]), pointedly recalls Virgil's words to Dante on entering the bolgia of the thieves: he must cast off sloth because it prevents one from gaining fame.

> sanza la qual chi sua vita consuma,
> cotal vestigio in terra di sé lascia,
> qual fummo in aere e in acqua la schiuma.
>
> (*Inf.* 24.49–51)

[without which he who consumes his life leaves such trace of himself on earth as smoke in air or foam on water.]

Virgil continues by telling Dante to rise and conquer his panting with the soul ("l'animo") that wins every battle if it does not sink down with its heavy body ("se col suo grave corpo non s'accascia"); he then urges Dante to remember the journey he will make through Purgatory ("Più lunga scala convien che si saglia"). By creating this network of reminiscences and foreshadowings, Dante is able to suggest that the general metamorphosis of unbecoming in the damned is the context of the thieves' transformations.

But the memory that Statius is referring to specifically is not the ability to recall particular past events and retain images of things gained through the body's senses, which is the kind of memory humans share

---

points out that matter in essence is a metaphor in the *Inferno*. I would not deny this; but in the prologue scene, the matter is there as matter as well. As Albert Wingell says in "The Forested Mountaintop in Augustine and Dante," *Dante Studies* 99 (1981): 11, even for Augustine the "regio dissimilitudinis," in which Freccero locates the prologue scene, had an ontological aspect as primal matter besides its moral aspect as vice. But in Hell proper, insofar as the damned are concerned, matter is "there" as the souls' corporeality, joined, however, to a form unable to realize its potential as a member of the human species.

with beasts and which therefore is lodged in the sensitive soul. Rather it is intellectual memory, which with intelligence and will is one mind, according to Augustine: "memoria, intelligentia et voluntas sunt una mens."[20] This sort of memory serves as the "treasure-house or place of conservation for thoughts" [thesaurus vel locus conservativus specierum (*S.T.* I.79.7.sc)]. By using "species" in a technical sense, Thomas signals that memory is inseparably joined to understanding. Consequently, if, as I have argued, the rational soul in the damned has lost its force as unifying form, Dante's "intelligenza" is an act they should no longer be able to participate in fully.

In a sense, understanding itself is a metamorphosis because, as we have seen, a process of conversion ("se convertendo ad phantasmata") is an integral part of intellection, and conversion, as Dante alerts us ("converte poetando"), is a kind of transformation. Intellectual memory undergirds this process by allowing the mind to think about the forms it has abstracted whenever it wants to ("cum volerit" [*S.T.* I–I.79.6]); in this way, will is also made one with knowing by bringing thought into full activity ("volontade in atto").

From what Farinata tells Dante in canto 10 of the *Inferno*, intellection must be essentially faulty in the damned since in the bad light ("mala luce") of Hell they cannot see things that are happening or are about to happen on earth: "Quando s'appressano o son, tutto è vano / nostro intelletto" (*Inf.* 10.103–4). If the sinners have, as it seems, lost contact with what actually is, they cannot entirely realize the process of knowing it, because intellection, for both Dante and Thomas, is an act, and something must be in order for it to be an act. Aquinas, however, goes on to say that separated souls comprehend natural things through the species they receive under the influence of divine light; they understand, in other words, without the mediation of the senses or phantasms, since these belong to the bodies they no longer have. But it is natural for the human soul to gain its knowledge "se convertendo ad phantasmata." Therefore, the knowledge separated souls have of things is general and confused (*S.T.* I.89.3).[21] Dante's separated souls,

---

20. *De Trinitate*, 10.11 (*PL* 42.983), quoted and commented on by Thomas in *S.T.* I.79.6.sc. Thomas's comments here are especially pertinent since Statius's insistence that the intellectual soul after death retains virtually the human powers of the vegetative and sensitive soul comes directly from this section of the *Summa* (I.77.8).

21. For the connection of this to *Inferno* 10, 99 ff., see E. G. Parodi's review of G. Surra, *Studi di Dante: La conoscenza del futuro e del presente nei dannati danteschi*, 1911, in *Bulletino della Società Dantesca Italiana* NS 19 (1912): 169–83.

however, do have aerial bodies; his shades presumably can turn their intellects to the phantasms they continue to form. But the fact that the damned depend on God's light for their knowledge, and that this light is insufficient to illuminate anything actually occurring on earth, suggests that in them the faculties by which they know have become as confused as the knowledge itself. Because the intellectual soul, which is the general name for these faculties, is defective, no "verbum mentis" has been articulated; consequently, the damned gain sense knowledge, but there is nothing that that knowledge can refer itself to as an analogy, nor can their minds return to the things they see armed with the concepts that explain what they are. Thomas's expression for the turning of the intellect to the images, "se convertere ad phantasmata," implies that he saw intellection as a real metamorphosis, a substantial change of the material and sensible to the nonmaterial and rational. The short-circuiting of understanding Farinata describes bespeaks a metamorphosis completely contrary in nature and effect in the souls of the reprobate.

Moreover, as unsure as understanding is in the damned, it is also evident that Dante's perception of them must be equally problematic. For human knowledge does proceed by the soul's "conversio ad phantasmata." Certainly when Dante looks at the changings of the thieves, his rational powers cannot extract an essential form that would identify what he sees as human beings. Subtending Buoso's and Agnello's transformations, however, is the previous impairing of their intellectual soul, which is the form by virtue of which any entity is truly human. The damned have no perfect form, no fully realized intelligible species that the intellect can extract. As a consequence, there must also be a radical gap in understanding them, which corresponds to the radical emptiness of their being.[22] Any comprehension of them must pattern itself after Dante's understanding of Satan. When Virgil points him out, Dante says in a famous simile that he did not die nor yet remain alive, so the reader should not ask how frozen or faint he became, for he does not write it, since all words would fail. This is far more than a

---

22. Dante signals this gap in understanding by noting that the first voice he hears in the "bolgia" of the thieves "was ill-suited for forming words" [una voce uscì de l'altro fosso / a parole formar disconvenevole]. He tries to see who has been making these sounds but can not. He therefore tells Virgil to go on, since "not only do I hear without understanding, but I look down and make out nothing" (*Inf.* 24.65–66, 74–75). As we have seen, Dante again takes up this relation of sight and sound to understanding when he meets both Forese and Cacciaguida.

topos of inexpressibility; it is an exercise in nonintelligibility, made all the more forceful by Dante's enjoining the reader, if he has any wit, to think what he became, deprived of both life and death.[23]

Because the damned lack the perfection they should have, they are fundamentally defective not only in their being but also in their voluntary actions, which follow from yet are one with the act of intellection. In rational creatures still living, such a defection from nature takes two forms. A creature suffers evil in his being if he loses a form required for his integrity, such as when he is blind (*S.T.* I.48.5). This evil Aquinas calls pain ("poenam"). The second and graver kind of evil is a fault ("culpa"); this evil occurs when the will acts unjustly by disregarding its rule and measure and thus causes a withdrawal in activity (*S.T.*I.49.1 ad 3).[24] For the dead in Hell, culpable evil that affects voluntary actions and diminishes actuality becomes one with penal evil that results from the privation of form ("privatio formae" [*S.T.*I.49.1]).

This metamorphosis in which moral and ontological realities have been merged is itself, of course, a parody of the Incarnation, wherein two natures, God and man, are said to have united in one flesh. Dante, however, would regard the form of metamorphosis as falling less under the aspect of the Incarnation than the Resurrection. Dante makes the damned what they are, after all, by means of his unparalleled invention of their regenerated bodies of compressed air after death. That this act aims to be a sort of embryonic resurrection of the flesh seems clear; that the thieves' metamorphoses directly parody it we see when Vanni Fucci is incinerated; his ashes immediately "drew together

---

23. For a reading of this simile as the expression of a double mutation, the simultaneous corruption of an old form and generation of a new one, see Freccero, "The Sign of Satan," 174. From another point of view, one could argue that we do gain positive knowledge of each sin the damned have committed, not from the sinners themselves but from the good they are bound to, which is to say from the justice of their punishments. As Aquinas says, the equality that justice requires must be between diverse beings capable of acting for themselves ("necesse est quod aequalitas ista quam requirit justitia sit diversorum agere potentium" [*S.T.* II–II .8.2]). But the souls in perdition have lost not only their ability to do anything for themselves but also the capacity to be diverse as human beings, as opposed to numbers. They have nothing to bring to that act of commensuration with another that defines justice. The sinners therefore participate in making intelligible the nature of their sin and the equity of their punishment only in the shadowiest of ways, by making apparent that justice in the *Inferno* is entirely other to those it orders and gives a place; we can understand infernal justice only insofar as we realize that it starts, ends, and takes its whole measure from the virtue that corresponds to each sin.

24. On this article, see Jacques Maritain, *St. Thomas and the Problem of Evil,* The Aquinas Lecture, 1942 (Milwaukee: Marquette University Press, 1942), 20–46.

by their own power and resumed his former shape." Dante stresses the speed of this change, which he compares to the death and rebirth of the phoenix, to remind us that Paul had said all souls will be changed ("immutabimur") in a moment, in the twinkling of an eye, when they put on their flesh again at the last trumpet (1 Cor. 15.51).[25] Dante speaks often of the Resurrection in the *Comedy* but nowhere more deeply than in cantos 24–25 of the *Paradiso,* which correspond numerically to the cantos I have been discussing in the *Inferno* and *Purgatorio.* Peter, James, and John, the three apostles who were present at the Transfiguration, question Dante on faith, hope, and charity; not surprisingly the subject of the examination they set is less these virtues per se than their seamless relation to the Resurrection that perfects them. Dante signals the connection between his divine audit and Statius's account of the body's generation in nature by the simile that opens canto 24.

O sodalizio eletto a la gran cena
del benedetto Agnello, il qual vi ciba
sì, che la vostra voglia è sempre piena,
se per grazia di Dio questi preliba
di quel che cade de la vostra mensa,
prima che morte tempo li prescriba,
ponete mente a l'affezione immensa
e roratelo alquanto: voi bevete
sempre del fonte onde vien quel ch'ei pensa.

[O fellowship chosen to the great feast of the blessed lamb, who feeds you so that your desire is forever filled, if this man by the grace of God foretastes some of what falls from your table before death prescribes his time, consider his immense longing and bedew him somewhat: you drink forever from the fountain whence comes what he thinks.]

The images not only recall those Statius used to describe the body's digestions—the perfect blood, which is never drunk ("non si beve") by the thirsty veins but is left like food taken from the table, and so forth—

---

25. On the ironic implications of Paul's statement, which Dante renders as the speed with which the transformations of the thieves take place, see D. L. Derby-Chapin's reading of the allusion to Io, "Io and the Negative Apotheosis of Vanni Fucci," *Dante Studies* 89 (1971): 19–31.

but also describe the union of the mystical body, "sodalizio eletto," in terms of the substance that nourishes it and gives it its form, the "benedetto Agnello."[26] This Lamb in turn both establishes the link to the cantos of the thieves by recalling the metamorphosis of Agnello's matter[27] and stands as the direct fulfillment, as we shall soon see, of the opening pastoral simile of canto 24 of the *Inferno*. The point I want to make now, however, is that Dante figures his meeting with the apostles as an examination because faith is the precondition for intellectual understanding; indeed, to Aquinas it is its form. Every act of cognition contains two things, a material object, which is what is known materially, and a formal aspect, whereby it is known. But since the object of faith is the First Truth, which is the means by which any truth is known, faith must underwrite all understanding of things seen in relation to God. Faith, therefore, "is a virtue that perfects the intellect" (*S.T.* II–II.1.3.sc; II–II.4.2 and 5).[28]

These cantos are the form of Statius's earlier discussion on the generation of life: because faith is the necessary base on which all syllogisms rest, Dante describes it as substance (*Par.* 24.70–78) and sees the trinitarian God as its form ("la forma . . . del pronto creder mio" [*Par.* 24.128]).

> e credo in tre persone etterne, e queste
> credo una essenza sì una e sì trina,
> che soffera congiunto 'sono' ed 'este.'
>
> (*Par.* 24.139–41)

[And I believe in three eternal persons, and these I believe one essence, so one and so threefold, that it allows "are" and "is" to be joined.]

---

26. Compare *Par.* 25.24: when Peter is joined by James, who examines Dante on faith, the apostles rejoice, "laudando il cibo che là sù li prande" [praising the food which feeds them there above]. Dante also discusses the Resurrection, as we have seen, in canto 14 of the *Paradiso*. Though it is Aquinas who speaks there, what he says is prelude to the appearance of Cacciaguida and links him to the matrix of ideas I am discussing here.

27. A point noted in James Chiampi, "The Fate of Writing: The Punishment of the Thieves in the *Inferno*," *Dante Studies* 102 (1984): 51–60, perhaps the most suggestive of all the recent articles on these cantos.

28. See also *S.T.* II–II.8.8, in which Thomas argues that among the fruits of the Holy Spirit, faith responds to the gift of understanding.

The three that are one recalls how Statius said the intellectual soul made one soul of itself and the sensitive and vegetative powers. The vine that joins with the sun's heat to produce wine has its origin here: Peter's faith, Dante says, "sowed the good plant that once was a vine [vite] and now has become a thorn" (*Par.* 24.110–11). The Trinity also defines how the faithless sinners in Hell, their intellectual soul disabled, have been reduced to random numbers lacking a principle of unity. Not one is "un alma sola"; all are perverse miscegenations of matter, man and beast-shape "envined" [avviticchiò] within and about each other. How fitting, then, that at the summit of paradise, one final metamorphosis attends Dante's access to his final vision of his three-personed God.

> Non perché più ch'un semplice sembiante
> fosse nel vivo lume ch'io mirava,
> che tal è sempre qual s'era davante;
> ma per la vista che s'avvalorava
> in me guardando, una sola parvenza,
> mutandom'io, a me si travagliava.
>
> (*Par.* 33.109–11)

[Not because more than one simple semblance was in the living light I was gazing in, which ever is such as it was before; but through my sight, which was strengthening in me as I looked, one sole appearance, as I changed, was altering itself to me.]

The dual nature of Christ as God and man, the single simplicity of the Trinity, such "metaformations" as these, beyond the power of human reason to understand or words to express, indeed, beyond the power of justice to compass, Dante figures in this ultimate transformation. Even as he became as like God as possible, whose rest he can only describe in terms of change, "che tal è sempre qual s'era davante," so in Hell the thieves never become anything but what they already have been as they degenerate from men to snakes or snakes to men.[29]

When he determined the status of souls in Hell, Dante thus synthesized scientific traditions of anthropology and pneumatology, derived

---

29. On the final vision as a metamorphosis, see Paul Priest, "Looking Back from the Vision: Trinitarian Structure and Poetry in the *Commedia*," *Dante Studies* 91 (1973): 114.

largely from Aristotle, with the biblical and theological idea that the damned are indeed dead souls because they have died the second death. Metamorphosis, as we have seen, underwrites every element of that synthesis: it not only informs the constitution of the damned and how we understand them but is an instrument in the general distribution of divine justice throughout the *Comedy*. Little wonder then that Dante would feel the necessity to distinguish his transformations, even in their purely rhetorical aspect as descriptions of change, from those of Ovid. For Ovidian metamorphosis, with its even exchange of forms, might appear to be an analogue of justice and so a fitting mechanism for the "contrapasso."[30] Indeed, by making the other one change into part of oneself, metamorphosis would seem to internalize justice's outward exchange with another. But in Ovid metamorphosis is a trope that enables him to locate the meaning of his text exclusively in its surface. Since the essential character of any creature does not alter with the alteration of its external shape, both the original and the new figure would have exactly the same identity if it were determined by that inner being. As Apollo makes clear when he redefines the laurel, however, Daphne the tree is not the same as Daphne the nymph; a substantive difference does accompany every transformation.[31] The meaning of this difference must therefore reside in the disparity between the altered outer forms rather than in a change in the soul they cover. Nonetheless, precisely because the inner nature does retain its identity, all attempts to fix the significance of any change by referring solely to either the old or the new form, or to the difference between them, will be fruitless. Daphne is something more than a tree or a nymph. As much as the things they transform, Ovid's metamorphoses throw our understanding of them into flux.

Such a radically rhetorical conception of metamorphosis could never capture the nature of the deformations the sinners in Hell experience. At most Ovidian transformation can vaguely suggest infernal "un-justice," the *lack* of relation between the retribution and the sinner who does not change at all because of it. To represent the real deprivations

---

30. See Kenneth Gross, "Infernal Metamorphoses: An Interpretation of Dante's Counterpass," *MLN* 100 (1985): 42–69. Gross finds a number of parallels between Ovidian metamorphosis and the "contrapasso." Both, for instance, are at once a kind of death and a kind of survival, a perverse form of stasis and a grotesque sort of self-realization (52).

31. I have outlined both the political and the linguistic implications of Daphne's metamorphosis in particular in two articles, "Ovid and the Politics of Interpretation," *Classical Journal* 84(1989): 222–31; and "Ovid and the Problem of Gender," 9–28.

of evil, Dante had to rely on a different theory of metamorphosis, one that in large part stems from Augustine's elaboration of the Neoplatonic notion that sin is a perverse imitation of a soul's conversion to God.[32] In the second book of the *Confessions*, to cite the classic instance, Augustine asks what it was he loved when he stole some pears for no discernible reason. Everything we do, Augustine tells us, imitates God, either perversely, when we sin, or virtuously, when we act as we ought. Because his theft was gratuitous, Augustine says his crime parodied not one particular aspect of God but the free act of love by which he created the universe. The nature of his deed accounts for the form Augustine gives his fall; as his Edenic sin, he had to set it in an orchard that doubles as a garden. It accounts as well for why he frames the answer to his question in terms that reflect a loss of knowledge. Augustine tells us the only thing he is sure of is that it was not beauty ("species") he loved, for there was no beauty in the theft, not even the faulty and shadowy comeliness ("defectiva species et umbratica") that sin usually dresses itself in. All the vices, he continues, are in fact imitations of virtues that exist preeminently in God.

> For pride imitates high-spiritedness, whereas you alone are God, highest over all. And what does ambition seek but honors and glory, whereas you alone are to be honored above all things, and glorious forever . . . Idleness pretends to desire quietness, but what stable rest is there beside the Lord? Luxury wants to be called plenty and abundance; you however are fullness and inexhaustible bountifulness of incorruptible sweetness . . . (2.6)[33]

In other words, vice depends on metamorphosis; it exists only to the extent that it seems to transform itself into its corresponding virtue by wearing the outward form of that virtue: "effusio liberalitatis obtendit umbram" [extravagance covers itself with the shadow of liberality]. Once this surface beauty (which Augustine nicely captures with the word "species," since it means both beauty and an appearance, or pre-

---

32. A number of critics have made this point; most recently, see Gross, "Infernal Metamorphoses," 45 ff.

33. All quotations are from Augustine, *Confessionum libri tredecim*, ed. P. Knöll, *Corpus scriptoroum ecclesiasticorum latinorum* (Prague, Vienna, Leipzig: Geroldi, 1896). I have altered the translation of R. S. Pine-Coffin to make it more literal (St. Augustine, *Confessions* [New York: Penguin, 1961]).

tense) has been assumed, vice could make the will turn to it. When he stole the pears, however, Augustine was not drawn by some vileness masquerading as a virtue; he did not take them for any quality they possessed or in order to exchange them for something else. Rather, because he stole them for the sheer sake of committing the theft, Augustine feels he participated in the purest form of evil. As a consequence, he brought about a metamorphosis of unbecoming in himself. By willfully wandering from God, he says, "I made myself a region of want" [factus sum mihi regio egestatis]. Although Augustine was the agent of this transformation, the deponent construction "factus sum mihi" captures how he now is something less than he was before. In imitation of the sin he was imitating, Augustine became a fallen world of lack and need; he knows he has thrown himself out of the Garden of Eden, but, having eaten from his own tree of knowledge, he cannot understand why he did it.

Augustine analyzes virtue and vice in terms of beauty because he feels the perversions of the mind that turns away from God, and of the will that turns toward a created object, locate the sinner in a "region of lack." This region, material yet not sensible, able to be occupied yet impossible to understand, is compounded out of the undoing of the proportions that fit an object to the organs that apprehend it and its image to the intellect that abstracts its essence. It is the negative image of the "regio dissimilitudinis," the space Augustine will later inhabit before his conversion, when he knows the truth but still cannot make the act of will he needs to commit himself to it.

> And I found I was far from you in a place where everything differed from you [in regione dissimilitudinis], as though I could hear your voice from above: "I am the food of full-grown men; grow and you shall eat of me. But you shall not change me into your own substance [me in te mutabis] as you do with the food of your body, but you shall be changed into me [tu mutaberis in me].[34]

Augustine can imitate the nature of the metamorphoses that beget these places only in aesthetic terms.

Because he subscribed to such a theory of mimesis, Dante presents the damned suffering their punishments as a metamorphosis of loss. In

---

34. Augustine, *Confessionum libri tredecim,* bk. 7, chap. 10.

each circle we see not only the false covering of virtue each vice cloaks itself in but the moment when each sinner deceived him- or herself into becoming part of that deception. Thus Francesca gives us the image of courtly love she still thinks she and Paolo embody and the occasion she was transformed into its language: "Amor condusse noi ad una morte." For the reader, however, the phrase reveals that Francesca continues to delude herself; we remember the "bufera infernal, in loco d'ogne luce muto" [the infernal whirlwind in a place where all light is mute], which ceaselessly changes the position of the carnal sinners but never changes them, just as by depriving Francesca of all chance for rest the tempest equally deprives her of all chance to satisfy her desire.

Since sin disrupts the commensurations of general and particular justice, Dante will also represent the unrepentant and the metaphysics of their condition in a manner that finally is aesthetic. Each sinner is an "imagine perversa"; each is "due e nessun." Hell is the surd space of unbecoming that confines them, the space where "before the flame a dark color moves across the paper, which is not yet black, and the white dies away." The *Inferno* is the graveyard of the broken proportions and interrupted coordinations that have left the damned forever separated from the selves they once had been.

Metamorphosis, however, is Dante's explicit punishment for theft, and it is among the thieves that he declares Ovid's language of change inadequate to describe them fully. It is to the thieves we must turn, therefore, to see how Dante incorporated the literature of metamorphosis into his aesthetics of nonbeing.

II

The crime of theft, according to Aquinas, has three major attributes: first, that it is contrary to justice; second, that it usurps someone else's property; third, that it is done surreptitiously (*S.T.* II–II.66.3). Because the thief takes from another what he has no right to, his deed necessarily destroys the level measure between people that justice upholds. It is fitting, therefore, that Dante's transformations of the thieves preserve a grim equality: there is no difference between them and the creatures they become. Because their intellectual soul no longer constitutes them as human, Vanni Fucci and the others can bring only an unperfected materiality, which already has made them less men than beasts, to their constant loss and recovery of form. This unnatural equity between themselves and the things they turn into makes their exchange of matter a depraved imitation of justice, which requires the due coordination of one person to another, so that all acts of restoration be rightfully proportionate with the nature of the person to whom something unjust was done. The thieves, as we have seen, are not coordinated as one person to another but as human to nonhuman; for them, no act of restoration is possible.

Dante sets up a similarly ironic equation when he says the thieves were ready to exchange their matter ("amendue le forme / a cambiar lor matera fosser pronte"). He seems to imply that they are willing participants in their transformations, just as they once had been willing to appropriate goods that did not belong to them. The thieves, however, have lost the power to determine their actions, since human will for Dante is by definition appetite informed by understanding (*Purg.* 18.19–39; cf. *S.T.* I.82.2–3). In them, as in all the damned, understanding is defective. "Fosser pronte," therefore, must strictly mean the thieves were prepared to undergo their exchange of matter, but such preparedness can do no more than parody an act of will. This had to be the case because justice is itself is act of will: according to the jurists it is the "lasting and constant will [perpetua et constans voluntas] of rendering to each one his right."[35] Justice, consequently, presupposes a firm and stable disposition on the part of those who practice it.[36] Thieves, of course, deprive others of what is theirs by right; in their constant mutations, they have therefore been rightfully deprived of anything of their own that is firm or stable. They have no disposition at all. By exposing their deficient wills, the metamorphoses also reveal the contrariety of their crime to justice.

This radical dissociation of the thieves from both justice and humanity is ultimately what differentiates their metamorphoses from Ovid's. Dante's sinners obviously have lost the ownership of their own bodies, a fitting consequence in light of the fact that theft was distinguished from sins against the person such as homicide or adultery because it involved the surreptitious usurping of another's property (*S.T.* II–II.66.3). To compensate for the property they seized, they have had

---

35. In human beings the will can be lasting only with respect to the object it desires, as when someone wills to do something always (*S.T.* II–II.58.1 ad 3).

36. As does any act that is virtuous: for Aquinas, "it must be voluntary, and spring from a firm and stable disposition" (*S.T.* II–II.58.1).

seized from them the proper power of the soul that makes them human, which God had given them freely as a gift of his love. Now to the extent that the thieves are defined more by their surface corporeality than by an inner essential form, Dante's transformations of them stand as the limit of Ovid's. But when Dante says that the Roman poet never transmuted two natures "a fronte a fronte," he points to paradigms of change Ovid never dreamed of. For by facing "front to front," the thieves and snakes profanely recall Paul's translation to the third heaven. Fourteen years ago, Paul knew a man in Christ who was rapt to paradise, "whether in the body, I know not, or out of the body, I know not: God knoweth" (2 Cor. 12.3). There he heard things that cannot be spoken and saw, in the words of Augustine's commentary on the rapture, "facie ad faciem" (2 Cor. 13).[37] Because Paul's emphasis on the impossibility of human understanding is accompanied by an attenuation of the body to the point where it becomes immaterial, in all senses of the word, his transport seems especially appropriate here. His rapture was, after all, a kind of theft; "raptum" is cognate to "rapina." And in its way, Paul's experience was as much a transgressive metamorphosis as Marsyas's was when he was drawn "from the sheath of his limbs" [de la vagina de le membra sue (*Par.* 1.21)] and became a god. Of equal import is Paul's experience on Malta, where he was bitten by a viper, yet remained unharmed (Acts 28.1–6). When the people saw the viper fastened to his hand, they said that though Paul escaped from the sea, vengeance ("ultio") had not allowed him to live. But when Paul did not swell up, as they expected ("illi existimabant eum in tumorem convertendum"), and suddenly fall down and die, they changed their minds and called him a god ("convertentes se, dicebant eum esse deum"). Both incidents foreshadow the soul's transfiguration in heaven; their wording makes us realize that Paul is the preeminent figure of Christian conversion, of which the thieves' metamorphoses are the grossest parody.

In a sense, then, the relations Dante establishes between metamorphosis and theft, justice, the impairment of the intellectual soul, conversion, and the Resurrection form the intellectual context of the poetic contest with Ovid. Dante foreshadows these relations in the extended simile that stands as prelude to the cantos of the thieves.

---

37. On Augustine's commentary, see F. X. Newman, "St. Augustine's Three Visions and the Structure of the *Commedia*," *MLN* 82 (1967): 56–78.

In quella parte del giovanetto anno
che 'l sole i crin sotto l'Aquario tempra
e già le notti al mezzo dì sen vanno,
quando la brina in su la terra assempra
l'imagine di sua sorella bianca,
ma poco dura a la sua penna tempra,
lo villanello a cui la roba manca,
si leva, e guarda, e vede la campagna
biancheggiar tutta; ond' ei si batte l'anca,
ritorna in casa, e qua e là si lagna,
come 'l tapin che non sa che si faccia;
poi riede, e la speranza ringavagna,
veggendo 'l mondo aver cangiata faccia
in poco d'ora, e prende suo vincastro
e fuor le pecorelle a pascer caccia.
Così me fece . . .

(Inf. 24.1–16)

[In that part of the youthful year when the sun tempers his locks
beneath Aquarius, and already the nights have moved toward half
the day, when the hoarfrost copies on the ground the image of her
white sister, but her pen keeps its point a little while, the peasant
who lacks fodder rises and looks out and sees the plain all white,
wherefore he slaps his thigh, returns to his house, and grumbles to
and fro, like the wretch who does not know what to do; then he
comes back outside, and again gathers up his hope, seeing the world
has changed its face so soon, and takes his staff and drives his sheep
to pasture. So I did . . .]

As critics have noted, this simile contains a natural, a linguistic, and an
interpretive metamorphosis: the landscape changes; meaning changes
in the "rime equivoche" of "tempra" and "faccia"; and Dante and Virgil seem to shift position as the description proceeds—first one, then
the other can be equated with the peasant.[38] What has not been noticed,

---

38. *Dante's Inferno,* trans. Mark Musa (Bloomington: University of Indiana Press,
1971), 201; see as well Lawrence Baldassaro, "Metamorphosis as Punishment and
Redemption in *Inferno* XXIV," *Dante Studies* 99 (1981): 89–112, who provides a summary
of the comment on the simile. The following studies are of special note in that they, as I,
relate the simile to Dante's own idea of writing: David Baker, "The Winter Simile in
Inferno XXIV," *Dante Studies* 92 (1974): 77–91; James Chiampi, "The Fate of Writing";

however, is that the simile is an allegory of Exod. 16.13–21. As they wandered through the desert the children of Israel murmured before the Lord that they did not have enough to eat. God directed Moses to say to them that in the evening they should eat flesh and in the morning they should have their fill of bread. In the evening the quails came up and in the morning dew lay round about the camp.

Cumque operuisset superficiem terrae, apparuit in solitudine minutum, et quasi pilo tusum in similitudinem pruinae super terram.

[And when it had covered the face of the earth, it appeared in the wilderness small, and as it were beaten with a pestle, like unto the hoarfrost on the ground.]

When the children of Israel saw it they asked, "What is it?" Moses told them it was the bread that the Lord had given them to eat. He ordered each man to gather an amount according to the number of souls that dwelled in his tent ("iuxta numerum animarum vestrarum quae habitant in tabernaculo"). And when they had gathered, he who gathered more had nothing left over, and he who gathered less had no lack. Moses commanded them to leave no part of the manna till morning, but they did not listen; the part they kept began to be full of worms and putrefied. And Moses grew angry with them. And so, morning by morning they gathered, each as much as might suffice to eat; but after the sun grew hot, the manna melted.

Dante transforms this scene with its striking metamorphosis into a parable against theft: its entire point is "take no more than what you need, for God provides all." The thieves violate the equity of what is given and what received, the balanced measure of food to man established at the ingathering of manna ("et mensi sunt ad mensuram gomor: nec qui plus collegerat, habuit amplius: nec qui minus paraverat, reperit minus: sed singuli iuxta id quod edere poterant, congregaverunt" [Exod. 16.18]). They are worse than the stiff-necked in Moses' troop, who kept a part of the manna until morning. For thieves not only take their rightful share but appropriate in secret a portion

Derby-Chapin, "Io"; Peter Hawkins, "Virtuosity and Virtue: Poetic Self-Realization in the *Commedia*," *Dante Studies* 98 (1980): 1–18; Margherita Frankel, "Dante's Anti-Virgilian 'Villanello,'" *Dante Studies* 102 (1984): 81–109; Robert Hollander, "Dante's 'Georgic' (*Inferno* XXIV 1–18)," *Dante Studies* 102 (1984): 111–21.

from the common store that God freely and openly gives to everyone. They outrage both particular justice, which regulates one person's relation to another, and general justice, which governs the relation of a person to the common good. This is perhaps the chief reason why Dante chose the cantos of the thieves to present most clearly the metamorphosis of unbecoming in the damned.[39] Beyond this, they despise God's gift of bread, itself the miraculous transformation of insubstantial dew into "food for full-grown men," which feeds the "sodalizio eletto a la gran cena" in canto 24 of the *Paradiso*.[40] Indeed, to Augustine, the manna became an exhortation to metamorphosis, to become the body of Christ ("fiant corpus Christi"), the "benedetto Agnello" whose sacrifice is the source of the food the apostles and the blessed feast on.[41] The manna was commonly seen as a figure for both the Incarnation and the Eucharist, the two principles of spiritual generation that subtend the flesh-and-blood generation of human beings that Statius has described.[42] And so Dante devised metamorphoses for the thieves by which they are set apart from themselves and the community of men: like the putrescent manna, they began to teem with worms ("scatere coepit vermibus"), with whom they keep continuous company. Or,

---

39. In the exegetical tradition, the giving of manna was also associated with justice. Augustine comments on the Jews murmuring after Jesus says that he is the living bread that came down from heaven (John 6.41–59), an incident that closely follows the multiplication of the fishes and loaves (John 6.5–14). These Jews, Augustine says, did not know how to hunger after the bread of heaven, which seeks the hunger of the inner man ("interiori hominis quaerit esuriem"). Thus Matthew says (5.6): "Blessed are they that hunger and thirst after justice [iustitiam], for they shall have their fill." St. Paul, however (1 Cor. 1.30), says that Christ is justice ("iustitiam . . . esse Christum"). Therefore he who hungers for this bread hungers for justice ("iustitiam"). Augustine, *In Iohannis Evangelium tractatus* CXXIV 26.1 (*Corpus christianorum series latina* 36 [Turnhout: Brepols, 1954]). Cf. Rabanus Maurus, *Commentaria in Exodum*, PL 108.79, who also associates the manna with justice: "Si quid enim hic boni operis acquiras, si quid justitiae . . . hoc tibi in futuro saeculo erit cibus."

40. See again Augustine, *Confessions*, 7.10; and Freccero's comment in "Dante's Prologue Scene," in *Dante:The Poetics of Conversion*, ed. Rachel Jacoff (Cambridge, Mass.: Harvard University Press, 1986), 7.

41. Augustine says the manna was only a shadow, which becomes an injunction to participate in the Incarnation. The faithful only know the body of Christ if they do not neglect to be the body of Christ ("si corpus Christi esse non negligant. Fiant corpus Christi, si uolunt uiuere de Spiritu Christi"). Augustine then continues in terms that recall those I have argued must be applied to the thieves: just as all have a spirit and a body, and the body lives by the spirit, so to live by the spirit of Christ, one must be in the body of Christ ("In corpore esto Christi") (*In Iohannis . . . tractatus* 26.13).

42. For manna as a figure for the Incarnation and the Eucharist: in addition to Augustine, see Rabanus Maurus, *Commentaria*, PL 108.81.

more precisely, they become like the murmuring children of Israel in the counterpart of this scene that one finds in Num. 21.5–6. There the stiff-necked grumbled they had neither bread to eat nor water to drink; "wherefore the Lord sent among the people fiery serpents, which bit them and killed many of them."[43] In this the thieves recall the serpent who underwent the first transformation as punishment for inducing Eve to eat the forbidden fruit. They are food turned rotten; they therefore are set apart as well from communion with God, and from the Eucharist, the food that for Dante transforms things of the world into the substance of spirit.

In all their doings, of course, the thieves stand in contrast to the lowly "villanello," who also undergoes something like a metamorphosis. He is like the children of Israel in that he grumbles out of want of food.[44] Yet he is also like Moses, the shepherd who leads that flock, for after he returns outside and sees that the frost has melted, he gathers up his hope and drives forth his own sheep to pasture. What has enabled the transformation of his resentment into his complaisance is the fact that he was no thief, that he was among those who followed the commandment, in Italian: "non desidare la roba d'altri," thou shalt not covet thy neighbors' goods. What he did not take from another, he is given; as the sun grows warmer, he "gathers up his hope." "Ringavagna" literally means "puts back in his basket" [gavagno].[45] The word is precise in its overtones; it makes us recall the multiplication of the two fishes and five loaves, the leftovers of which were gathered in twelve baskets. The peasant's food is the food of hope, even as Jesus provided food for those who came to him like a hungry flock ("sicut oves non habentes pastorem" [Mark 6.34]). And since the multiplication of fish and loaves is, in its way, a metamorphosis of number, it resonates ironically in the thieves' reduction to quantity as their chief formal principle. It is no accident, then, that the "villanello" regains hope as the direct result of a metamorphosis, the "world's having changed its face so soon." His responsiveness to the change in nature looks toward not only the coordinated generation of body and soul in man

---

43. This passage perhaps is the ultimate biblical source for the form of the thieves' punishment. The connection between the passages in Exodus and Numbers was often noted. See, for example, the Book of Wisdom, 16.1–7; Rabanus Maurus (*PL* 108.78).

44. "Roba" means fodder here but generally can be extended to food of any sort, as is clear from *Purgatorio* 13.61.

45. See *The Divine Comedy*, trans. Charles Singleton, *Inferno 2*, Commentary, 409.

but to the "doppia vesta" and "bianche stole," the effulgence of the soul and resurrected body, that is the final transfiguration of the blessed, which Dante speaks of in his examination on hope in canto 25 of the *Paradiso.*

It is altogether appropriate, therefore, that with his opening poetic flourish Dante also announces his contest with Ovid, the poet of metamorphosis. We notice, of course, that Dante calls specific attention to nature's act of writing; the hoarfrost's pen keeps its point only a short time. This metaphor is as perplexing in its implications as it is exact in its effect. As the pen loses its point, its ink would fade and disappear, just as the manna melted in the warmth of the sun. But when the ink has run out, the white that remains on the page (for the metaphor asks us to think the plain is the page nature writes on) would make it the image of hoarfrost on the field, which is as white as snow. Yet the letters the pen has already written also would cover the page, as snow covers a field. Nature, it would seem, writes with white ink; inscription begins to converge with the blank page. The contrast with the thieves is ironic. In their changings they will be compared, we remember, to paper written on with an "ink" that destroys it. They are the brown that precedes the flame where the white dies off—matter, in other words, no longer there as it once was. Unlike the thieves, however, both the snow and the page do await further change. The hoarfrost in the morning, like the snow it copies, will eventually melt. The white page, on the other hand, whether Dante's or nature's, awaits an ink equally evanescent, an ink that reminds us that the peasant's regaining hope of food corresponds to the melting of the manna.

However mysterious these intricacies, it seems clear that Dante wants to implicate his own poetry in his prelude to the metamorphoses of the thieves by establishing some correspondence between his writing and nature's based on the dissolving and survival of signifiers common to both. (Snow, after all, is more lasting than hoarfrost, and ink does, for a time, fix letters on the page.) This impression is buttressed by the explicit allusion to the prologue scene that launched Dante's journey. Soon after the pastoral simile, Virgil comforts his charge: he turns to Dante with the sweet look the pilgrim first saw at the foot of the mountain. Dante then undergoes his own change of heart in concert with the change of expression he sees in his guide. Dante takes these pains to introduce his contest with Ovid by calling attention to the qualities of his own poetical allegory because it is precisely the interplay between the literal and inner senses of his scripture that distinguishes his metamorphoses from Ovid's. In its allegorical refashioning of Exodus, Dante's pastoral interlude demonstrates how mortal language can be turned into the "pane de li angeli."[46]

When letters change into the blank page awaiting further inscription, or when the hoarfrost thaws to reveal the face of the earth, the transformation is thoroughly Ovidian, an alteration of surface to surface. In medieval terms, signifiers have been resolved into matter whose potentiality is directed entirely toward further signification. But when Dante invites us to watch his letters melt to reveal the history of Exodus beneath, his poetry becomes allegorical, and his stance toward Ovid necessarily changes.[47] In the *Convivio* (2.1.9–11), Dante had said that the allegory of poets differs from that of theologians chiefly in two senses: the literal and the anagogical. For poets, the letter of their text is a fiction; for exegetes, it is history, which is the medium the Bible uses to convey that "sovrasenso" Dante calls the anagogic, which refers to "the supernal things of eternal glory." Because history is no fiction, the literal sense cannot be discarded in the quest for deeper, spiritual meaning; just as with anything that has an inside and an outside ("che ha dentro e di fuori"), the allegorical must be arrived at through the literal. So too, Dante continues, just as the literal sense constitutes the subject matter ("subietto e materia") and the allegorical senses the form ("forma") of Scripture, one cannot gain knowledge of the latter without first knowing the former, in the same way that "it is impossible to

---

46. See Psalm 77.25: "panem angelorum munducavit homo," where the bread of the angels is an explicit reference to the manna. Compare *Par.* 2.11 and *Convivio* 1.1.17: "O beati quelli pochi che seggiono a quella mensa dove lo pane de li angeli si manuca! e miseri quelli che con le pecore hanno comune cibo!" [Oh how blessed those few who sit at that table where the bread of the angels is eaten. And how wretched those who have common fare with sheep]. In this respect, as in many others, as we shall see, the simile that begins *Inferno* 24 revises previous assertions Dante had made in the *Convivio*. A number of studies have recently pointed out how the *Comedy* stands as a palinode to the *Convivio*. See, for instance, Frankel, "Dante's Anti-Virgilian Villanello": 101–2, and the bibliography she provides.

47. We should note that in the exegetical tradition the giving of the manna was seen as a call to allegorical interpretation. Rabanus speaks of those whose hearts were too dense and thick to feel what was minute, subtle, and spiritual in the word of God, which is what the manna stands for ("Nihil enim in verbo Dei minutum, nihil subtile, nihil sentiunt spirituale, sed totum pingue, totum crassum. Incrassatum est enim cor populi illius" [*PL* 108.79]). Augustine (*In Iohannis . . . tractatus* 26.11) speaks of those who ate manna, yet died (John 6.49). But there are many who ate and are not dead because they understood the visible food spiritually ("uisibilem escam spiritualiter intellexerunt").

arrive at the form of gold if the matter is not digested and prepared" [si come impossibile la forma de l'oro è venire, se la materia, cioè lo suo subietto, non è digesta e apparecchiata (*Conv.* 2.1.10–11)]. Dante's words seem to forecast not only his allusion to the giving of manna in his prologue to the metamorphoses of the thieves but also the connection he will make between it and Statius's account of the bodily digestions that precede God's creation of the intellectual soul as the body's form.

Once Dante posits that the same dialectic of inner and outer, of form and matter, that characterized the thieves in Hell also characterizes access to the meaning of scriptural writing, we realize that metamorphosis could capture the essence of theft only by becoming a figure of theological allegory. In Dante's formulation, the allegory of theologians is in fact a kind of justice, in which an equitable balance between the external and the hidden senses of the Bible is established.[48] By violating justice, the thieves have robbed themselves of the possibility of allegory, of becoming signs of God's eternal glory. Instead of experiencing the translation of flesh to spirit, which is the change allegory effects in the inner understanding of the word, the thieves undergo metamorphoses that reveal them as a kind of matter at once too hard and too amorphous to receive lasting formal inscription. Dante therefore rewrites Ovidian metamorphosis to show that under God's inspection, its sole ethical import consists in the fact that its transformations are only superficial, that they have no inner meaning but continually look to further change. To Dante, Ovidian metamorphosis derives its value from the impermanence of its literal sense, from the fact that it never seeks to be more than hoarfrost that momentarily covers a field like

---

48. One might in fact say that in its allegorical and moral senses, allegory deals with particular justice: how one disposes oneself within to deal uprightly with others. Dante gives two examples, both of which, significantly enough, involve metamorphoses. In the *Convivio*, Dante says that Jesus took only three apostles up the mount on which he was transfigured to teach that we should take few companions in the most secret things. Assuming that the *Epistle to Can Grande* is his, Dante says the moral sense of Psalm 113 is the conversion of the soul from the grief and misery of sin to a state of grace. The anagogic sense, on the other hand, deals with general justice: how each participates in the common good. Dante's example again is Psalm 113, which foretells the greatest metamorphosis of all: the departure of the sanctified soul from the servitude of this corruption to the liberty of eternal glory. Dante recalls here Romans 8.21: "Ipsa creatura liberabitur a servitute corruptionis in libertatem gloriae filorum Dei." As Aquinas says in his commentary (ad. q.I, quoted in *Convivio*, ed. Giovanni Busnelli and Giuseppe Vandelli [Florence: Le Monnier, 1964], 100), for "creatura" we should read "homo iustus."

snow. To represent the thieves adequately, however, or to explain the meaning of their condition, the letter of the text must be more than a fiction: it must have the substantiality of history, the power to make the change of dew into manna something more than a metaphor.[49]

Dante's linking of theft, metamorphosis, and allegory, therefore, is not arbitrary; neither is it without precedent. Augustine himself, as we saw, located his Edenic sin in an orchard. From the moment he stole the pears, Augustine's life became biblical, a journey from the garden of sin to the garden of redemption, from the region of want he had transformed himself into to the prophesied paradise of the fig tree, which he throws himself under just before his conversion. Indeed, the metamorphosis of conversion is the motor that has driven the entire allegory of Augustine's life; his theft was a perverse imitation of God's gratuitous grace, which in the end turned the sinner into a saint.

Augustine may well have provided a context for the thieves' metamorphoses; Dante's audacious silencing of Ovid, however, proclaims that these cantos are fundamentally moments of revisionary literary history. But Dante does more than reject the traditional allegorized reading of Ovid, something he had himself employed in the *Convivio*. As much as the long simile that opens canto 24 transforms classical poetry, it also testifies to an alteration in Dante's understanding of his own poetry.

In the last "canzone" of the *Convivio* ("Le dolci rime d'amor"), Dante had denounced the idea that true gentility derives from possessions.

---

49. As Dante's reading of Orpheus in the *Convivio* (2.1.3) shows, Ovid's metamorphosis could never be more than metaphors. According to Augustine, however, metaphors are signs where "things that we signify by proper terms are usurped [usurpata] by others signifying something else" (*De doctrina christiana* 2.10.15). Metaphor therefore bears an inherent resemblance to theft, which Thomas, as we have seen, defined as the usurping of someone else's property in violation of justice ("contrariatur justitiae, quae unicuique tribuit quod suum est, et ex hoc competit ei quod usurpat alienum" [*S.T.* II–II.66.3]). But as a figure for justice, metamorphosis must be more than a metaphor. The equality that Ovidian metamorphosis suggests between two things is essentially convertible; like metaphor, it is a trope of the surface. For Dante, however, metamorphosis is an allegory of inner change. Dante therefore refashions Ovid's literal sense, giving metamorphosis the depth of history, so that it can figure the condition of the thieves. And in so doing, Dante would deny as inappropriate the allegorical readings of Ovid that were so common in the Middle Ages, just as he would in the next canto deny the traditional allegories that had been attached to Ulysses. In this regard, see, for instance, John Freccero, "Dante's Ulysses: From Epic to Novel," in *Dante: The Poetics of Conversion*, ed. Rachel Jacoff (Cambridge, Mass.: Harvard University Press, 1986), 136–51; and Giuseppe Mazzotta, *Dante, Poet of the Desert*, 70–106.

Only the vulgar, he says, equate nobility with having been rich a long time; this sort of fatuousness has led to the still worse error of calling someone "gentle" merely because he is the son, or grandson, of a man of rank.

To combat these noxious beliefs, Dante imagines himself a farmer of the intellect. "Just as grass [erba] multiplies and overruns an uncultivated field, and covers the ear of wheat so that from a distance it appears as if there is no wheat at all, and the fruit [frutto] is lost in the end, so it is with bad opinions in the mind." How grand the undertaking of his "canzone," Dante exclaims, "to want to hoe a field so wild with clover" [a volere omai così trifoglioso campo sarchiare (4.7.3–4)]. Just as he resolves to separate the wheat from the tares by means of reason, however, Dante suddenly becomes overwrought at the thought of a person who continues to believe a man is noble for reasons he knows are false.

> Ma vilissimo sembra, a chi 'l ver guata,
> cui è scorto 'l cammino e poscia l'erra,
> e tocca a tal, ch'è morto e va per terra!

> (38–40)

[But to one who regards the truth, he seems most base who wanders from the path after it has been shown to him: such a one has reached the point that he is dead, and walks on earth!]

To illustrate the vileness of such a man, Dante asks us to picture a plain with well-marked paths. Except for these narrow ways ("fuori de li suoi stretti sentieri"), however, the plain is a field filled with hedges, ditches, stones, undergrowth, and all kinds of similar impediments. It has snowed, and the snow covers everything, making all vistas look the same ("e rende una figura in ogni parti"), so that one cannot see the markings of any path. Someone comes from one part of the countryside; he wants to go to a dwelling on the other side. Guided solely by his industry, knowledge, and wit ("e per sua industria, cioè per accorgimento e per bontade d'ingegno, solo da sé guidato"), he makes his way along the straight path ("diritto cammino") to where he wanted to go. Another man comes who wishes to go to the same place. He need only follow the footsteps left by the first traveler, but nevertheless he loses the track and struggles amid thorns down steep slopes ("e tortisce per li pruni e per le ruine") where he should not be (4.7.6–7).

The ways in which Dante changed this scene when he introduced the thieves constitute perhaps the greatest metamorphosis of the metamorphoses cantos.[50] In the journey toward salvation, no one, whatever his genius, can guide himself; as Ulysses proves, all true guidance comes from above. The "villanello" demonstrates that there is no path to blaze until the sun, which leads men aright by every path ("che mena dritto altrui per ogne calle" [*Inf.* 1.18]), melts the hoarfrost that has copied the image of her white sister. Or, as Dante will say, when he reflects on that access of ultimate grace that allowed him his utmost vision, "Così la neve a sol si disigilla" (*Par.* 33, 64). As snow is unsealed by the sun, so Dante, as he nears his experience of having seen God face-to-face, will not register what he saw but rather the disappearance of the mediating agencies of his vision. In his lowliness, therefore, in his rustic befuddlement, in his not knowing what to do, the peasant reveals the effrontery of Dante's earlier hope to hoe the mind by reason and philosophy. Only God, not human endeavor, gathers the wheat that has fallen to the ground and died, so that it might bring forth much fruit (John 12.24–25). Only by the willing sacrifice of the Lamb is the "sodalizio" fed. Because he returns to his house and waits, because he does not set off across the field in search of shelter, the "villanello," not Dante the philosopher-poet of the *Convivio,* is the better shepherd, the more able to lead others to good food.

In silencing Ovid, therefore, Dante also silences himself. At the beginning of the *Comedy,* Dante pictures himself wandering from a "diritto cammino" that the sun had as surely pointed out to him as the footsteps in the snow marked it for the traveler in the *Convivio.* For all the literary virtuosity of Dante's descriptions of the thieves' metamorphoses, these cantos do not represent a break in the poem's style. Rather Dante makes of his brashness a brazen serpent for the sun to unseal. When the murmurers in the desert were struck by fiery serpents, God commanded Moses to forge a brazen serpent and set it up for a sign ("pro signo") that "whosoever being struck shall look on it, shall live" (Num. 21.8). This verse was given its gloss in the Book of

---

50. For another reading of the association of this passage from the *Convivio* with the thieves, see Hawkins, "Virtuosity and Virtue."

Wisdom (16.5–7): when the people were destroyed by the bitings of crooked serpents ("perversorum colubrorum"), God's wrath did not endure forever; he gave them "a sign of salvation" [signum . . . salutis], "for he that turned to it was not healed by that which he saw, but by thee the Saviour of all" [qui enim conversus est, non per hoc quod videbat sanabatur, sed per te omnium salvatorem]. To the exegetes, the brazen serpent was, of course, a symbol of Christ; Dante, however, makes brazen claims for his verse, so that his readers should look at it as it effaces itself and see that it is set up as a sign of salvation. In the *Inferno*, metamorphosis therefore changes from fiction to a figure of allegory, the soul's impaired form, justice, conversion, the Incarnation, and the Resurrection. Even Ovid, if he could silence his amusement, might stand in awe of that.

III

For Dante, however, far more than artistic pride is at issue in this contest with Ovid; he has equally staked his historical identity and his ultimate salvation as a poet on its outcome. One of the reasons Dante makes the metamorphoses cantos the forerunner of his interview with Donati and Bonagiunta is that in the "tenzone" he had accused both Forese and his father of being thieves. Anyone bearing a purse would say of Forese, "Questi c'ha la faccia fessa / è piùvico ladron negli atti sui" (74.7–8). "Scarface there is obviously a known thief" is Foster and Boyde's translation. But even this double insult—the social humiliation of the scarred face is piled on the public opprobrium of thievery—is not enough for Dante:[51] with one blasphemous fusillade, he goes on to indict Simone Donati for larceny and brand his son a bastard.

> E tal giace per lui nel letto tristo,
> per tema non sia preso a lo 'mbolare,
> che gli appartien quanto Giosepp' a Cristo.
>
> (74.9–11)

[And there's one [i.e., Simone] who lies in bed distraught for fear that he'll be caught in the act of thieving, who has as much to do with him [i.e., Forese] as Joseph with Christ.]

---

51. According to the legal and literary documents Barbi cites, Dante's contemporaries thought facial wounds were among the worst that could be inflicted: see Dante, *Rime della Vita Nuova e della giovenezza*, ed. M. Barbi and F. Maggini (Florence: Le Monnier, 1956), 356.

If Dante's pen errs ("se fior la penna abborra" [*Inf.* 25.144]), it errs here and not in the circle of the thieves, where silencing Ovid becomes the first step in transforming poetic rivalry into the aesthetics of being that reconciles Dante with Forese. From the vantage of Purgatory, the unknown (and unknowable) sinner Dante and Virgil encounter when they first enter the seventh "bolgia" simultaneously epitomizes the motives of the "tenzone" and stands as a memorial to the consequences that would have followed from it had it remained unrepented; his voice "ill-suited for forming words," this soul "seemed to be moving as he spoke" [ma chi parlava ad ire parea mosso (*Inf.* 24.69)].[52] As he suffers the unchanging changes of God's "vendetta" (*Inf.* 24.120) in this "fierce gullet" [gola fiera (*Inf.* 24.123)], this shadow has lost its ability to speak meaningfully—a hell for any slanderer. He is like Vanni Fucci, who raised his hands against God "with both the figs" [con amendue le fiche (*Inf.* 25.2)]; their intent to malign with malice aforethought may remain, but both will go signifying their unintelligibility.[53] It is with good reason, then, that Dante reforms the "disconvenevole parlare" he had had with Donati. On the terrace where the gluttons redeem the faults of their "gola fiera," their bodies so transformed that their faces are inscribed with the "M" of humanity, the two walk as one, so that "neither did speech make their going more slow, nor the going their speech" [Né 'l dir l'andar, né l'andar lui più lento / facea (*Purg.* 24.1–2)]. Their words and their actions now in concert, Dante makes his peace with Forese when he signifies his reformation as a poet of the "stil novo" to Bonagiunta.

We should therefore not be surprised to discover that, besides the "tenzone" and the *Convivio*, the cantos of the thieves are also the setting for an equally profound transformation of perhaps the last "canzone"

52. Many manuscripts have this soul "moved by anger" [ma chi parlava ad ira [rather than "ad ire"] parea mosso] instead of "moving as he spoke." "Ad ira" is the reading of the vast majority of early commentators, including Lana, L'Ottimo, and Benvenuto; Dante's son Pietro, however, specifically says "ad ire" was what his father wrote. Commentators who see this figure moved by anger have tended to identify him as Vanni Fucci. I prefer to take the sinner as a separate shade, though his anger, if it exists, coupled with the "voice ill-suited for forming words," would also make him a fitting emblem of the emotions that propelled the "tenzone" and punishment for it. On the manuscript crux, see *The Divine Comedy,* trans. Charles Singleton, *Inferno 2,* Commentary, 413–14.

53. Dante can neither understand the sounds that the unknown sinner in the "bolgia" of the thieves makes nor see who is uttering them. It is worthwhile recalling at this point that Dante recognizes Forese not by sight but by means of his "voce" and Cacciaguida by neither sight nor word.

Dante wrote as a stilnovist.[54] In "Amor, da che convien pur ch'io mi doglia," the exiled poet depicts himself obsessed by a "beautiful but wicked" woman ("bella e ria"), whose cruel delight in his suffering causes his soul to disintegrate. The poem begins with Dante asking Love to give him the skill as well as the will to lament. He complains that his soul, working to its own harm, portrays his lady in his imagination, "thus giving shape to its own torment" [così dipinge, e forma la sua pena (89.19–21)]; when his rational soul gazes at the image, it rages against itself ("incontro a sé s'adira" [24]) for the desire the image kindles. But his anguish causes such a tempest, no argument of reason can restrain him. So great is the desire, it makes him seek the real woman who causes it, even though this is like "snow going to the sun" [Ben conosco che va la neve al sole (37)] or a man whose own two feet take him to the place where he is killed ("fo come colui / che . . . va co' suoi piedi al loco ov'egli è morto" [38–40]). As he nears his lady, he is so struck, he is rendered lifeless. When his rational soul returns to his heart, he realizes that "unknowing and forgetfulness were with it all the time it was away" (49–51). He rises and trembles in fear; his pale visage shows what lightning ("trono") it was that struck him (51–60). Dante then ends his "montanina . . . canzone," which he most likely composed in the Casentino in 1307 or 1308, by addressing it. "If you should ever enter Florence, my land that, void of love and stripped of compassion, shuts me out, say: 'Now my maker can make war on you no longer: he is so chainbound in the place I come from, even were your ferocity to relax, he is not free to return here."

"Amor, da che convien" is as remarkable for its bitter recuperation

---

54. Because Dante directed "Amor, da che convien" to Moroello Malaspina, critics have agreed that it was, if not the final "canzone" he wrote, one of the very last. The "congedo," however, with its double fantasy, first that Florence might revoke Dante's banishment and then that Dante would not be able to return even if it did, is hard to understand, both politically and as an extension of the literary conceits of "canzone" itself (especially if the "donna senza pietà" is an allegory for Florence). These difficulties have caused Guglielmo Gorni recently to conjecture that "Amor, da che convien" was composed before Dante went into exile, then adapted after 1302 for allegorical purposes that remain obscure and as such "palmed off to Moroello and provocatively addressed to Florence" (136). See Guglielmo Gorni, "La canzone 'montanina' *Amor, dacché convien pur ch'io mi doglia* (CXVI)," *Letture classensi* 24 (1995): 129–50. In light of the use I think Dante made of "Amor, da che convien" in the metamorphoses cantos, I am not entirely persuaded by Gorni's conjecture, weighty and balanced though his arguments are. Ultimately, however, my argument here does not depend on when Dante wrote the "canzone."

of the psychologism of the *Vita nuova* as it is for the way Dante will make it subtend the metamorphoses of the *Inferno*. Even in Cavalcanti phantasm and spirit had never ravaged a soul more than they do here. In the second and third stanzas, Dante literally unknots ("snoda") his unconfinable anguish, which "pours out audibly in breath" from his mouth ("L'*angoscia*, che non cape dentro, *spira* / fuor de la bocca" [28–29]), by describing what happens when he looks at the eyes that slay him:[55]

Qual io divengo sì *feruto*, Amore,
sailo tu, e non io,
che rimani a veder me sanza vita;
e se l'anima torna poscia al core,
ignoranza ed oblio
stato è con lei, mentre ch'ella è partita.
Com'io risurgo, e miro la ferita
che mi disfece quand'io fui percosso . . .

(46–53)

[What I become when so stricken, you know, Love, not I—you who stay to see me lifeless. And though in time the soul returns to the heart, unknowing and forgetfulness were with it while it was away. When I get to my feet, and gaze at the wound that unmade me when I received the blow . . .]

As Foster and Boyde say, the effects of the lady are such that Dante's rational soul is "as good as dead." To explain this state, they point to those passages from the *Convivio*—the work Dante was writing during these years—in which he equates reason and being human ("vivere ne l'uomo è ragione usare") and contends that the man in whom the rational soul is disabled is not a man but a beast ("non rimane più uomo, ma

---

55. "Pours out audibly in breath" is Foster and Boyde's translation for "spira": they gloss Dante's use by referring to two other "canzoni," "E' m'incresce" ("sento . . . raccoglier l'aire del sezza' sospiro" [5–6]) and "Amor, che ne la mente mi ragiona" ("messi . . . pien di desiri, / che prendon aire e diventan sospiri" [35–36]). In both cases Dante is describing the production of sighs, which strengthens the parallel I draw below between "Amor, da che convien" and the metamorphosis of Vanni Fucci. "Spira" also links Dante's "canzone," as we shall see, to his dialogue with Bonagiunta in *Purgatorio* 24.

cosa con anima sensitiva solamente, cioè animale bruto" [*Conv.* 4.7.10–15]).[56] There is good reason to think this reading is right, for the same "unknotting" of the soul Dante describes in the "canzone" characterizes the metamorphosis of Vanni Fucci, the "mule" whose "vita bestial" bespeaks the impairment of intellect I have argued deforms the thieves and all the sinners in Hell.

The serpent that makes Fucci a burnt offering strikes him where the neck is joined ("s'annoda," [24.99]) to the shoulders; after his ashes have resumed his shape, Dante describes his confusion.

> E qual è quel che cade, *e non sa como,*
>
> . . . .
>
> *quando si leva,* che 'ntorno *si mira*
> tutto smaritto de la grande *angoscia*
> ch'elli ha sofferta, e guardando *sospira.*
>
> (24.112–17)

[And as one who falls and knows not how . . . who, when he rises, stares about him, all bewildered by the great anguish he has suffered and, looking, sighs.]

Both the thief in Hell and Dante in love are struck and wounded, both fall into unconsciousness; each awakes confused and struggles to his feet; each looks about, bewildered and in anguish. Nor are these the only parallels between the "canzone" and the *Inferno.* After identifying himself, Vanni Fucci turns toward Dante, his soul and face colored with dismal shame ("drizzò verso me l'animo e 'l *volto,* / e di trista vergogna si *dipinse*" [131–32]; cf. "Amor": "così *dipinge*" [21]); he says his pain is greater now that Dante has caught him undergoing his wracking transformations than it was when he died ("Più mi *duol* che tu m'hai *colto* / ne la miseria dove tu mi vedi" [133–34]). But to avenge himself for his humiliation, he commands that Dante hear ("odi") him. The White Guelfs will help drive the Blacks from Pistoia, but they will themselves be driven from Florence and defeated at Campo Piceno: "Mars draws a vapor from the Val di Magra . . . and with impetuous and bitter storm ["*tempesta* impetüosa e agra" (147); cf. "Amor": "*tempesta*" (27)] a thunderbolt suddenly shall rend the clouds so that every White shall be

---

56. *Dante's Lyric Poetry,* 2:334–35.

struck by it" [ond' ei repente spezzerà la nebbia, / sì ch'ogne Bianco ne
sarà *feruto* (149–50)]. "E detto l'ho perché doler ti debbia": "and I have
said this that it may grieve you." Commentators both early and late
identify the Mars that Fucci refers to as Moroello Malaspina. Dante
stayed with Malaspina in the Lunigiana—the site of the Val di Magra—
in the autumn of 1306. In a letter *(Epistle IV)* Dante wrote to Moroello
soon after, he excuses himself for neglecting his lord's service: passion-
ate love for a woman, Dante says, overwhelmed him when he came to
the river Arno, as his "dominus" can plainly see if he reads the "canzone" that accompanies the letter.[57] Since that "canzone" is "Amor, da
che convien," it seems more than appropriate that with Fucci's spiteful
invocation of Mars, the defeat of the Bianchi, and their banishment
from Florence, Dante also invokes the earlier description he sent to
Moroello of how love threatened his very existence as a poet.

> Amor, da che convien pur ch'io mi doglia
> perché la gente m'*oda*,
> e mostri me d'ogni vertute spento,
> dammi savere a pianger come voglia,
> sì che 'l *duol* che si *snoda*
> portin le mie parole com'io 'l sento.
> Tu vo' ch'io muoia, e io ne son contento:
> ma chi mi scuserà, s'io non so dire
> ciò che mi fai sentire?
> chi crederà ch'io sia omai sì *colto*?
> E se mi dai parlar quanto tormento,
> fa', signor mio, che innanzi al mio morire
> questa rëa per me nol possa udire:
> ché, se intendesse ciò che dentro ascolto,
> pietà faria men bello il suo bel *volto*.

(89.1–15)

[Love, since after all I am forced to grieve so that others hear me and
to show myself bereft of all resistance, grant me the skill as well as
the will to lament so that my words might carry the grief that

---

57. Few readers today question the letter's authenticity or that it was addressed to
Malaspina. See Boyde and Foster's helpful note, *Dante's Lyric Poetry*, 2:330–31. No one to
my knowledge has noticed the connection between "Amor, da che convien" and Vanni
Fucci's baleful prophecy.

unknots itself just as I feel it. You wish me to die, and I am satisfied: but who will excuse me if I cannot put into words what you make me feel? Who will believe that I am now so caught by another? But if you give me speech to match my pain, see to it, my Lord, that this cruel woman may not hear it from me before I die; for were she to hear what I listen to within, pity would make her fair face less fair.]

In the "canzone," however, the stilnovists' trope of the lover's soul divided against itself is so strong, it dominates the political context that the "congedo" offers as an analogy: Dante's expulsion from "la mia terra, / che fuor di sé mi serra" [my land, that shuts me out from her (77–78)] may be like the soul's evacuation from the body, but the first loss is completely subordinated to the greater loss of the second. The peace Dante would make with his city ("non vi può far lo mio fattor più guerra" [81]) is the palest image of the death he experiences when, like snow going to the sun, he returns to see his lady. By contrast, in the *Inferno* the civil war that divides Florence is the political counterpart of the dissolution of soul in the damned; both are equally unnatural and both equally irreparable. The fire of the thunderbolt that will strike the Bianchi is generated from the same Mavorial source as the water that forms the clouds it breaks from; but the antagonism of the elements assures their immediate disunion and separate dissipation. Unlike the hoarfrost and its sisterly snow in the sun, there is no possibility or hope of transformation into an integrated "corpus novum." In the earthly Florence that Fucci evokes, all bonds have been severed; it is a place where the body politic has been permanently alienated from its unifying soul. Even a flock with the lowliest "villanello" to lead it is a truer community than this; Dante's Florence has become the city of Dis, and the mulish sibyl of its dismemberment, who has lost his own coherence and humanness, is its most representative citizen. Only when Cacciaguida glosses Fucci's words in the heaven of Mars will Dante hear of a Florence when it was "the sheepfold of St. John" [l'ovil di San Giovanni (*Par.* 16.25)]. And Dante shall enter this Florence only because he reconstituted himself in body and soul as Love's poet.[58]

---

58. In an interesting note, the Anonimo commentary also connects "Amor, da che convien" with *Purgatorio* 24. We are told that the "Gentucca" Bonagiunta mumbles was the name of the "donna gentile" whom Dante loved after Beatrice's death! Still later, Dante fell in love a third time with "una di Casentino," about whom he wrote in a "canzone" that the Anonimo then quotes. Boccaccio also knew "Amor, da che convien"; it appears in his two autograph manuscripts, Chigiano L V 176 and Toledano 104, 6.

By incorporating the tissue of recalls and parallels from "Amor, da che convien" into the text of Vanni Fucci's metamorphosis and prediction, Dante reveals that the "stil novo," no less than the philosopher's self-reliance or the controversialist's exaltation of himself over his opponent, could be in need of reform. The ideas of the unknotting ("snoda") of grief that Dante breathes forth from within ("che non cape dentro, spira / fuor de la bocca") align the "canzone" with Dante's description of his meeting with Bonagiunta. For the mature poet, the concentrated self-absorption of the lover is indistinguishable from the decision of the damned to put themselves before God: as Francesca confirms, both at heart are a kind of idolatry. Perhaps Dante's most passionately solipsistic poem, "Amor, da che convien" exemplifies the waywardness Beatrice accuses Dante of after she had died.[59] As her comparison to Malehaut implies, no poetry, in the new style or otherwise, can incarnate knowledge and love unless it is put in the service of signifying the transformation of flesh into the spiritual body.

IV

It has become something of a commonplace to see the "tenzone" as the opposite or even the "annulment" of the "stil novo"; Giorgio Petrocchi speaks for many others when he locates Dante's entire experience as "viator" in the *Comedy* between the literary limits of these two discourses.[60] Yet we have seen the author Dante equate the "stil novo" and the "tenzone" not once but three times. In the cantos of the thieves, Vanni Fucci's venom, which causes even prophecy to degenerate into unjustifiable vituperation, is the archetype of the motives that produced Dante's and Forese's gratuitous vilifications, but it is "Amor, da che convien" rather than the sonnets of the "contentio" that gives Fucci's foretelling its form. In the *Paradiso*, Dante counterbalances the hellish juxtaposition of genres by their marriage in heaven: Beatrice's transumptive "cough" is as much Nella Donati's as it is Malehaut's.

---

59. *Purg.* 30.124–26: "As soon as I was on the threshold of my second age and had changed life [mutai vita], this one [i.e., Dante] took himself from me and gave himself to others." This "traviamento," as Italian critics have called it, has been variously interpreted. I agree with those who, like Contini and Petrocchi, read Dante's "vagrancy" as primarily stylistic, a wandering into modes such as the "tenzone." (See Giorgio Petrocchi, *Vita di Dante* [Rome: Laterza, 1983], 51–55). Dante quite possibly exchanged his sonnets with Forese at the same time he was finishing the *Vita nuova*.

60. Petrocchi, *Vita di Dante*, 51.

Clearly, either style can lead to the underworld or to the empyrean; as Bonagiunta acknowledges to Dante and Forese in Purgatory, everything depends on how closely the pen's wings follow the analogies that are the dictation of Love.[61]

By placing both the "stil novo" and the "tenzone" under the sign of metamorphosis in the *Inferno*, Dante suggests that whenever contentious sonnets or amatory "canzoni" present themselves as the reified objects of their own narcissism, they become Ovid's offspring. Once the death of the soul, which is a conceit in "Amor, da che convien," becomes Vanni Fucci's permanent condition, Dante's thief finds himself forever the wretch of irony, Ovid's trope of existence in the *Metamorphoses*. Like Daphne, Vanni Fucci discovers that his affirmation of an "I" is canceled by a transformation that declares him to be "Not-I."[62] Unlike Ovid's nymph, however, whose "I" persists in the "Not-I" she changes into, Fucci has lost the principle on which his "I" was based. Not-human before his cremation, beast after it, he undergoes alterations that, like the alterations of all the damned, can never be more than imaginary; their conversions are always a fiction. In disenchanting the high style of passion's egoism by transforming it into the negations of antiphrasis, Dante therefore silences Ovid. And, ironically enough, by silencing him, Dante condemns as well the self-aggrandizement that comes from talking one's adversary mute, which is the gratification that the "tenzone" holds up as its alluring prize.

For the "stil novo" and the "tenzone" to effect substantive change, they must become the stepchildren of Virgil by taking on the depth of history and the polysemy of allegory. From what Bonagiunta says, nothing in either the content or the formal organization and inner consonance—the "bellezza" as Dante calls it—of "Donne ch'avete intelletto d'amore" differentiates it from "Amor, da che convien." What does distinguish the two "canzoni" is that Dante makes "Donne ch'avete" a point of conversion in his life. The discovery of the "stilo de la loda" was an epiphany of snow and rain, the emergence of a new voice even as the old one continued to sound. In his declaration to Bonagiunta, Dante likewise announces a new, fully embodied style of

---

61. See again Ascoli's important reassessment of palinode as a structure of thought in Dante: "Palinode and History in the Oeuvre of Dante," 155–83.

62. For a more extended discussion of the connection between irony and allegory, see my "Chaucer's Canterbury Poetics: Irony, Allegory and the *Prologue* to *The Manciple's Tale*," *Studies in the Age of Chaucer* 18 (1996): 55–90.

praise that does not abolish the older one but fulfills it. The two moments of "Donne ch'avete" are thus discrete and separate events that allow Dante to trace his history from the *Vita nuova* to the *Comedy* according to the trajectories of allegory. Yet in a very real sense the two moments of "Donne ch'avete" are also the same moment, not merely because they share the same structure but because in each otherness underwrites identity and identity otherness. This sort of dialectical recursiveness, which is the recursiveness of analogy, is grounded in the solidity of experience; it is what enables Christian allegory to be a theory of bodies as well as souls in time and space. Compared to it, the objectified "spiriti" of "Amor, da che convien" are no more than projections of images of the self into a material world where they cannot survive—snow going to the sun. Their death and resuscitation are phantoms of a real resurrection, a failed search for a tactile history, for a corporeal form that can "go signifying" the changes in their motions, their love, their pain. Because the spirits of "Amor, da che convien" are solely "of imagination compact," they are Ovidian. But when they acquire a local habitation in the world and become susceptible to embodied development, as they do in "Donne che avete," they become Virgilian. And when they are transposed into allegories of salvation, when "auri sacra fames" changes from Polydorus's curse into an exhortation that prompts Statius's conversion, they become Dante's. For Dante's Virgil, as much as Dante's Ovid, is a version of himself. It is in the tension between his transformation of the one and his metamorphosis of the other that Dante begets his aesthetics of being.

It was a commonplace in the Middle Ages that human beings stood midway between heaven and earth. People partook of the qualities of both realms. For Dante, the proper medium to represent such creatures was poetry; by speaking for the mind and the senses at once, thought that walks in beauty at the same time bespoke humankind's unique nature, flesh joined to soul, in the image of their maker. By constituting his poetry as a discourse of analogy, Dante made it the language of aesthetics as well. But from the *Vita nuova* to the *Comedy*, as we have seen, aesthetics undergoes a remarkable transformation. Though it never ceases to comprehend that which is between the body and the intellect, ultimately it transcends both. Through Hell, Purgatory, and Paradise it becomes the way the love that moves the sun and other stars expresses itself in human terms.

Bibliography

Sources and Ancient Texts

Alan of Lille. *Rhythmus de incarnatione Christi.* In *Patrologia Latina (PL),* edited by J. P. Migne, 210.577A–80A.

———. *Rhythmus alter. PL* 210.579A.

Albert the Great. *Alberti Magni . . . Opera Omnia.* Edited by August Borgnet and Emile Borgnet. Paris: Ludovicum Vives, 1890–99.

Alighieri, Dante. *Convivio.* 2 vols. Edited by Giovanni Busnelli and Giuseppe Vandelli. 2d. ed. Edited by A. E. Quaglio. Florence: Le Monnier, 1964.

———. *Dante's Lyric Poetry.* 2 vols. Edited and Translated by Kenelm Foster and Patrick Boyde. Oxford: Clarendon, 1967.

———. *De vulgari eloquentia.* Edited by Pier Vincenzo Mengaldo. In *Opere minori,* vol. 2. Milan-Naples: Riccardo Ricciardi, 1979.

———. *De vulgari eloquentia.* Translated by A. G. Ferrers Howell. London: Kegan Paul, 1890.

———. *La Divina Commedia.* 3 vols. Edited by Umberto Bosco and Giovanni Reggio. Florence: Le Monnier, 1979.

———. *La Divina Commedia secondo l'antica vulgata.* 4 vols. Edited by Giorgio Petrocchi. Società dantesca italiana. Milan: Mondadori, 1966–67.

———. *The Divine Comedy.* Translated with a commentary by Charles Singleton. Princeton: Princeton University Press, 1970–76.

———. *Il Fiore e Il Detto d'Amore* (attribuibili a Dante Alighieri). Edited by Gianfranco Contini. Milan: Mondadori, 1984.

———. *Rime della Vita Nuova e della giovanezza.* Edited by Michele Barbi and F. Maggini. Florence: Le Monnier, 1956.

———. *Vita nuova.* Edited by Domenico de Robertis. Milan and Naples: Riccardo Ricciardi, 1980.

———. *Vita nuova.* Edited by Francesco Mazzoni. Tallone: Alpignano, 1965.

Aquinas, St. Thomas. *Aristotle's De anima in the Version of William of Moerbeke and the Commentary of St. Thomas Aquinas.* Translated by Kenelm Foster and Silvester Humphries. New Haven: Yale University Press, 1954.

———. *Commentary on the Nichomachean Ethics.* 2 vols. Library of Living Catholic Thought. Translated by C. I. Litzinger. Chicago: Regnery, 1964.

———. *Summa theologiae* (Latin text and English translation). Blackfriars Edition. New York: McGraw-Hill, 1964.

———. *De unitate intellectus contra Averroistas* (On the unity of the intellect against the Averroists). Translated by Beatrice Zedler. Milwaukee: Marquette University Press, 1968.

Aristotle. *The Complete Works of Aristotle.* 2 vols. Edited by Jonathan Barnes. Princeton: Princeton University Press, 1984.

Augustine, St. *Confessionum libri tredecim.* Edited by P. Knöll, Corpus scriptorum ecclesiasticorum latinorum. Prague, Vienna, Leipzig: Geroldi, 1896.

———. *Confessions.* Translated by R. S. Pine-Coffin. New York: Penguin, 1961.

———. *De doctrina christiana.* Corpus christianorum series latina 28. Turnhout: Brepols, 1970.

———. *On Christian Doctrine.* Translated by D. W. Robertson, Jr. Indianapolis: Bobbs Merrill, 1958.

———. *In Iohannis Evangelium tractatus.* Corpus christianorum series latina 36. Turnhout: Brepols, 1954.

Averroes. *Commentarium magnum in Aristotelis De anima libros.* Edited by F. S. Crawford. Cambridge, Mass.: Medieval Academy of America, 1953.

Boethius. *The Consolation of Philosophy.* Translated by R. H. Green. Indianapolis: Bobbs Merrill, 1962.

Cavalcanti, Guido. *The Poetry of Guido Cavalcanti.* Edited and translated by Lowry Nelson, Jr. New York: Garland, 1986.

Cicero. *De officiis.* Edited and translated by W. Miller. Loeb Classical Library. Cambridge, Mass.: Harvard University Press, 1928.

Commento alla Divina Commedia d'anonimo fiorentino del secolo XIV. Dartmouth Dante Project. Robert Hollander, Director. telnet library.dartmouth.edu.

Guillaume de Lorris and Jean de Meung. *Le Roman de la Rose.* Edited by Daniel Poirion. Paris: Garnier-Flammarion, 1974.

Guinizelli, Guido. *The Poetry of Guido Guinizelli.* Edited and translated by Robert Edwards. New York: Garland, 1987.

Hugh of St. Victor. *De unione corporis et spiritus.* PL 177.285–94.

Jacobus de Pistorio. *Quaestio de felicitate.* Translated by Paul Oscar Kristeller. In "A Philosophical Treatise from Bologna dedicated to Guido Cavalcanti: Magister Jacobus de Pistorio and his *Quaestio de felicitate*," 2:425–63. *Medioevo e Rinascimento: Studi in onore di Bruno Nardi.* 2 vols. Florence: Sansoni, 1955.

Lambert of Auxerre. *Property of Terms.* Translated by Norman Kretzmann and Eleonore Stump. In *The Cambridge Translations of Medieval Philosophical Texts.* Cambridge: Cambridge University Press, 1988.

Latini, Brunetto. *Li livres dou tresor*. Edited by F. J. Karmody. Berkeley and Los Angeles: University of California Press, 1958.

———. *Tesoretto*. In *Poeti del duecento*, edited by Gianfranco Contini, 2:169–284. Milan and Naples: Riccardo Ricciardi, 1960.

Ovid. *P. Ovidii Nasonis Metamorphoses*. Edited by W. S. Anderson. Leipzig: Teubner, 1977.

Patrologiae cursus completus (PL). Edited by J. P. Migne. Paris, 1844–64.

Plato. *Timaeus*. Edited and translated by R. G. Bury. Loeb Classical Library. Cambridge, Mass.: Harvard University Press, 1941.

Poeti del Dolce stil nuovo. Edited by Mario Marti. Florence: Le Monnier, 1969.

Poeti del duecento. 2 vols. Edited by Gianfranco Contini. Milan and Naples: Riccardo Ricciardi, 1960.

Proclus. *Commentary on the First Book of Euclid's Elements*. Translated by G. R. Morrow. Princeton: Princeton University Press, 1970.

Rabanus Maurus. *Commentaria in Exodum*. PL 108.9–246.

Suger of St. Denis. *De rebus in administratione sua gestis*. Translated by Edwin Panofsky. In *Abbot Suger on the Abbey Church of St.-Denis and Its Art Treasures*, translated by Edwin Panofsky. Princeton: Princeton University Press, 1979.

Virgil. *P. Virgili Maronis Opera*. Edited by R. A. B. Mynors. Oxford: Clarendon, 1969.

Modern Works and Studies

Agamben, Giorgio. *Stanzas: Word and Phantasm in Western Culture*. Translated by Ronald Martinez. Theory and History of Literature 69. Minneapolis: University of Minnesota Press, 1993. Originally published as *Stanze*. Turin: Einaudi, 1977.

Ahern, John. "The New Life of the Book: The Implied Reader of the *Vita Nuova*." *Dante Studies* 110 (1992): 1–16.

———. "The Reader on the Piazza: Verbal Duel in Dante's *Vita Nuova*." *Texas Studies in Language and Literature* 32 (1990): 18–39.

Allen, Judson. *The Ethical Poetic of the Later Middle Ages*. Toronto: University of Toronto Press, 1982.

Andrea, Antonio d'. "Dante, la mémoire et le livre: Le sens de la *Vita Nuova*." In *Jeux de mémoire*, edited by Bruno Roy and Paul Zumthor, 91–97. Montreal: University of Montreal Press, 1985.

Armour, Peter. "Brunetto, the Stoic Pessimist." *Dante Studies* 112 (1994): 1–18.

Ascoli, Albert. "Palinode and History in the Oeuvre of Dante." In *Dante Now: Current Trends in Dante Studies*, edited by Theodore Cachey, 155–86. Notre Dame: University of Notre Dame Press, 1995.

Baker, David. "The Winter Simile in *Inferno* XXIV." *Dante Studies* 92 (1974): 77–91.

Baldassaro, Lawrence. "Metamorphosis as Punishment and Redemption in *Inferno* XXIV." *Dante Studies* 99 (1981): 89–112.

Balthasar, Hans Urs von. *The Glory of the Lord: A Theological Aesthetics.* 3 vols. Edited by Joseph Fessio and John Riches. San Francisco: Ignatius Press, 1982.

Barański, Zygmunt. "Allegoria, storia e letteratura nella *Commedia.*" In *Dante e le forme dell'allegoresi,* edited by Michelangelo Picone, 79–97. Ravenna: Longo, 1987.

———. "Dante's (Anti-)Rhetoric: Notes on the Poetics of the *Commedia.*" In *Moving in Measure: Essays in Honour of Brian Moloney,* edited by Judith Bryce and Doug Thompson, 1–14. Hull: Hull University Press, 1989.

———. "Dante's Biblical Linguistics." *Lectura dantis* 5 (1989): 105–43.

———. "The Poetics of Meter." In *Dante Now: Current Trends in Dante Studies,* edited by Theodore Cachey, 3–41. Notre Dame: University of Notre Dame Press, 1995.

———. " 'Significar *per verba*': Notes on Dante and Plurilingualism." *Italianist* 6 (1986): 5–18.

Barberi, Squarotti. "Le poetiche del Trecento in Italia." In *Momenti e problemi di storia dell'estetica,* 1:255–91. Milan: Marzorati, 1959.

Barbi, Michele. "Con Dante e coi suoi interpreti: II: Francesca da Rimini." *Studi danteschi* 15 (1932): 5–36.

Barolini, Teodolinda. *Dante's Poets.* Princeton: Princeton University Press, 1983.

———. *The Undivine Comedy.* Princeton: Princeton University Press, 1992.

Boyde, Patrick. *Perception and Passion in Dante's Comedy.* Cambridge: Cambridge University Press, 1993.

Branca, Vittore. "Poetics of Renewal and Hagiographic Tradition in the *Vita nuova.*" *Lectura Dantis Newberryana* 1 (1988): 123–52.

Brownlee, Kevin. "Phaeton's Fall and Dante's Ascent." *Dante Studies* 102 (1984): 135–44.

———. "Why the Angels Speak Italian: Dante as Vernacular *Poeta* in *Paradiso* XXV." *Poetics Today* 5 (1984): 597–610.

Bruyne, Edgar de. *Études d'esthétique médiévale.* 3 vols. Bruges: De Tempel, 1946.

Bundy, Murray W. *The Theory of Imagination in Classical and Mediaeval Thought.* Urbana: University of Illinois Press, 1928.

Burrell, David. *Analogy and Philosophical Language.* New Haven: Yale University Press, 1973.

The Cambridge History of Later Medieval Philosophy. Edited by Norman Kretzmann, Anthony Kenny, and Jan Pinborg. Cambridge: Cambridge University Press, 1982.

The Cambridge Translations of Medieval Philosophical Texts. Edited by Norman Kretzmann and Eleonore Stump. Cambridge: Cambridge University Press, 1988.

Carruthers, Mary. *The Book of Memory: A Study of Memory in Medieval Culture.* Cambridge: Cambridge University Press, 1990.

Casella, Mario. Review of *Il dolce stil nuovo*, by Fernando Figurelli. *Studi danteschi* 18 (1934): 105–26.

Cervigni, Dino. "I canti di Cacciaguida: Significato della storia e poetica della lingua." In *Dante Alighieri 1985, in memoriam Hermann Gmelin*, edited by R. Baum and W. Hirdt, 129–40. Tübingen: Stauffenburg, 1985.

Chiampi, James. "The Fate of Writing: The Punishment of the Thieves in the *Inferno*." *Dante Studies* 102 (1984): 51–60.

Chiappelli, Fredi. "Proposta d'interpretazione per la tenzone di Dante con Forese." *Giornale storico della letteratura italiana* 142 (1965): 321–50.

Chiarini, Eugenio. "Tenzone con Forese." In *Enciclopedia dantesca*, 5:562–63. Rome: Istituto dell'Enciclopedia Italiana, 1976.

Contini, Gianfranco. *Un'idea di Dante*. Turin: Einaudi, 1970.

———. *Letteratura italiana della origini.* Florence: Sansoni, 1970.

Copeland, Rita. *Rhetoric, Hermeneutics, and Translation in the Middle Ages.* Cambridge: Cambridge University Press, 1991.

Copleston, Frederick. *A History of Philosophy.* Vol. 2. *Medieval Philosophy.* Part 2. Garden City: Doubleday, 1962.

Cornford, Francis. *Plato's Cosmology.* London: Routledge and Kegan Paul, 1952.

Corti, Maria. *La felicità mentale: Nuove prospettive per Cavalcanti e Dante.* Turin: Einaudi, 1983.

———. "Il modello analogico nel pensiero medievale e dantesco." In *Dante e le forme dell'allegoresi*, edited by Michelangelo Picone, 7–20. Ravenna: Longo, 1987.

Costa, Elio. "Il *Tesoretto* di Brunetto Latini e la tradizione allegorica medievale." In *Dante e le forme dell'allegoresi*, edited by Michelangelo Picone, 43–58. Ravenna: Longo, 1987.

Croce, Benedetto. *Aesthetic.* Translated by Douglas Ainslie. New York, Noonday Press, 1955.

Cudini, Piero. "La tenzone tra Dante e Forese e la *Commedia* (*Inf.* XXX; *Purg.* XXIII–XXIV)." *Giornale storico della letteratura italiana* 159 (1982): 1–25.

Curtius, Ernst Robert. *European Literature and the Latin Middle Ages.* Translated by W. Trask. 1953. Reprint, New York: Harper and Row, 1963.

Dante e le forme dell'allegoresi. Edited by Michelangelo Picone. Ravenna: Longo, 1987.

Dante Now: Current Trends in Dante Studies. Edited by Theodore Cachey. Notre Dame: University of Notre Dame Press, 1995.

Demats, Paule. *Fabula.* Geneva: Droz, 1973.

Derby-Chapin, D. L. "Io and the Negative Apotheosis of Vanni Fucci." *Dante Studies* 89 (1971): 19–31.

Derla, Luigi. "'I' mi son un, che quando / Amor mi spira, noto . . .': su *Purg.* xxiv, 49–61." *Aevum* 58 (1984): 274–76.

Durling, Robert, and Ronald Martinez. *Time and the Crystal.* Berkeley: University of California Press, 1990.

Eagleton, Terry. *The Ideology of the Aesthetic.* Oxford: Blackwell, 1990.

Eco, Umberto. *The Aesthetics of Thomas Aquinas.* Translated by Hugh Bredin. Cambridge, Mass.: Harvard University Press, 1988.

———. *Art and Beauty in the Middle Ages.* Translated by Hugh Bredin. New Haven: Yale University Press, 1986.

Enciclopedia dantesca. Edited by Umberto Bosco and Giorgio Petrocchi. 6 vols. Rome: Istituto dell'Enciclopedia Italiana, 1970–78.

Favati, Guido. "Guido Cavalcanti, Dino del Garbo e l'averroisimo di Bruno Nardi." *Filologia romanza* 2 (1955): 67–83.

———. *Inchiesta sul Dolce Stil Nuovo.* Florence: Le Monnier, 1975.

Fiedler, Wilfried. *Analogiemodelle bei Aristoteles.* Studien zur antiken Philosophie 9. Amsterdam: B. R. Gruner, 1978.

Foster, Kenelm. *The Two Dantes and Other Studies.* London: Darton, 1977.

Frankel, Margherita. "Dante's Anti-Virgilian 'Villanello.'" *Dante Studies* 102 (1984): 81–109.

Freccero, John. *Dante: The Poetics of Conversion.* Edited by Rachel Jacoff. Cambridge, Mass.: Harvard University Press, 1986.

Ghisalberti, Fausto. "Arnolfo d'Orléans: Un cultore di Ovidio nel secolo xii." Reale Istituto Lombardo di Scienze e Lettere (Milan). *Memorie* 246, no. 4 (1932): 157–234.

———. "Giovanni del Virgilio espositore delle 'Metamorfosi.'" *Il Giornale Dantesco* 34, n.s., 4 (1933): 3–110.

———. "L''Ovidius Moralizatus' di Pierre Bersuire." *Studi Romanzi* 23 (1933): 5–136.

Gilbert, Allan H. *Dante's Conception of Justice.* Duke University Publications. Durham: Duke University Press, 1925.

Ginsberg, Warren. "Chaucer's Canterbury Poetics: Irony, Allegory and the *Prologue* to *The Manciple's Tale.*" *Studies in the Age of Chaucer* 18 (1996): 55–90.

———. "Ovid's *Metamorphoses* and the Politics of Interpretation." *Classical Journal* 84 (1989): 222–31.

———. "Ovid and the Problem of Gender." *Mediaevalia* 13 (1987): 20–25.

———."Preaching and Avarice in the Pardoner's Tale." *Mediaevalia* 2 (1976): 77–99.

Glunz, Hans H. *Die Litterarästhetik des europäischen Mittelalters.* Frankfurt: Klostermann, 1963.

Gorni, Guglielmo. "La canzone 'montanina' *Amor, dacché convien pur ch'io mi doglia* (CXVI)." *Letture classensi* 24 (1995): 129–50.

———. *Il nodo della lingua e il verbo d'amore.* Florence: Olschki, 1981.

Gross, Kenneth. "Infernal Metamorphoses: An Interpretation of Dante's Counterpass." *MLN* 100 (1985): 42–69.

Guglielminetti, Marziano. *Memoria e scrittura.* Turin: Einaudi, 1977.

Harrison, Robert. *The Body of Beatrice.* Baltimore: Johns Hopkins, 1988.

Hawkins, Peter. "Virtuosity and Virtue: Poetic Self-Realization in the *Commedia.*" *Dante Studies* 98 (1980): 1–18.

Hollander, Robert. "Dante and Cino da Pistoia." *Dante Studies* 110 (1992): 201–31.

———. "Dante's 'Georgic' (*Inferno* XXIV 1–18)." *Dante Studies* 102 (1984): 111–21.

———. *Studies in Dante.* Ravenna: Longo, 1980.

Holloway, Julia. *Twice Told Tales: Brunetto Latini and Dante Alighieri.* New York: Peter Lang, 1993.

Honess, Claire. "Expressing the Inexpressible: The Theme of Communication in the Heaven of Mars." *Lectura Dantis* 14 (1994): 42–60.

Iannucci, Amilcare. "Dante's Theory of Genres in the *Divina Commedia.*" *Dante Studies* 91 (1973): 1–25.

Klein, Robert. *Form and Meaning.* Translated by Henri Zerner. New York: Viking, 1979. Originally published as *La forme et l'intelligible* (Paris: Gallimard, 1979).

Kolve, V. A. *Chaucer and the Imagery of Narrative.* Stanford: Stanford University Press, 1984.

Kristeller, Paul Oscar. "A Philosophical Treatise from Bologna dedicated to Guido Cavalcanti: Magister Jacobus de Pistorio and his *Quaestio de felicitate.*" In *Medioevo e Rinascimento: Studi in onore di Bruno Nardi,* 2:425–63. 2 vols. Florence: Sansoni, 1955.

Landry, Bernard. *La Notion d'Analogie chez saint Bonaventure et chez saint Thomas d'Aquin.* Paris: Loinvain, 1922.

Leeuw, Geraldus van der. *Sacred and Profane Beauty: The Holy in Art.* Translated by David Green. Nashville: Abingdon Press, 1963.

Lesher, J. H. "The Meaning of '"NOYS' in the Posterior Analytics." *Phronesis* 18 (1973): 44–68.

Lonergan, Bernard. *Verbum: Word and Idea in Aquinas.* South Bend, Ind: University of Notre Dame Press, 1967.

Lyttkens, Hampus. *The Analogy between God and the World.* Uppsala: Almqvist and Wiksells, 1952.

Marigo, Aristide. *Mistica e scienza nella Vita nuova di Dante.* Padua: Drucker, 1914.

Maritain, Jacques. *St. Thomas and the Problem of Evil.* The Aquinas Lecture, 1942. Milwaukee: Marquette University Press, 1942.

Marti, Mario. "Rime realistiche (la tenzone e le petrose dantesche)." *Nuove letture dantesche,* 8:209–30. Florence: Le Monnier, 1976.

Martinez, Ronald L. "The Pilgrim's Answer and the Poetics of the Spirit." *Stanford Italian Review* 3 (1983): 37–63.

Mattalia, Daniele. *Il Canto XXV dell' Inferno.* Florence: Le Monnier, 1962.

Mazzoni, Francesco. "Brunetto Latini." In *Enciclopedia dantesca,* 3:579–88. Rome: Istituto dell'Enciclopedia Italiana, 1976.

Mazzotta, Giuseppe. *Dante, Poet of the Desert.* Princeton: Princeton University Press, 1979.

———. *Dante's Vision and the Circle of Knowledge.* Princeton: Princeton University Press, 1993.

———. "The Language of Poetry in the *Vita nuova.*" *Rivista di studi italiani* 1 (1983): 3–14.

———. "Why Did Dante Write the Comedy." In *Dante Now: Current Trends in Dante Studies,* edited by Theodore Cachey, 63–79. Notre Dame: University of Notre Dame Press, 1995.

Menocal, María Rosa. *Writing in Dante's Cult of Truth from Borges to Boccaccio.* Durham and London: Duke University Press, 1991.

Minnis, A. J. *Medieval Theories of Authorship.* London: Scolar Press, 1984.

Musa, Mark. *Dante's Inferno.* Bloomington: Indiana University Press, 1971.

———. *Dante's Vita nuova.* Bloomington: Indiana University Press, 1973.

Najemy, John. "Brunetto Latini's 'Politica.'" *Dante Studies* 112 (1994): 33–51.

Nardi, Bruno. *Dante e la cultura medievale.* Bari: Laterza, 1983.

———. "Noterella polemica sull' averroismo di Guido Cavalcanti." *Rassegna di filosofia* 3 (1954): 47–71.

———. *Studi di filosofia medievale.* Rome: Edizioni di storia e letterature, 1960.

Newman, F. X. "St. Augustine's Three Visions and the Structure of the *Commedia.*" *MLN* 82 (1967): 56–78.

Noakes, Susan. "Hermeneutics, Politics, and Civic Ideology in the *Vita Nuova:* Thoughts Preliminary to an Interpretation." *Texas Studies in Language and Literature* 32 (1990): 40–59.

Nolan, Barbara. "The *Vita Nuova* and Richard of St. Victor's Phenomenology of Vision." *Dante Studies* 92 (1974): 35–52.

Owen, G. E. L. "Logic and Metaphysics in Some Early Works of Aristotle." In *Aristotle and Plato in Mid-Fourth Century,* 163–90. Gotenburg: Symposium Aristotelicum, 1960.

Owens, Joseph. "Faith, Ideas, Illumination, and Experience." In *The Cambridge History of Later Medieval Philosophy,* edited by Norman Kretzmann, Anthony Kenny, and Jan Pinborg, 440–59.

Panofsky, Edwin. *Abbot Suger on the Abbey Church of St.-Denis and Its Art Treasures.* Princeton: Princeton University Press, 1979.

Paratore, Ettore. *Tradizione e struttura in Dante.* Florence: Sansoni, 1968.

Parodi, E. G. Review of "Studi di Dante: La conoscenza del futuro e del presente nei dannati danteschi," by G. Surra. *Bulletino della Società Dantesca Italiana NS* 19 (1912): 169–83.

Pertile, Lino. "Canto—Cantica—Comedia e l'epistole a Cangrande." *Lectura Dantis* 9 (1991): 105–23.

———. "Dante's *Comedy* beyond the *Stilnovo.*" *Lectura dantis* 13 (1993): 63–68.

———. "Il nodo di Bonagiunta, le penne di Dante, e il Dolce Stil Novo." *Lettere italiane* 46 (1994): 44–75.

Petrocchi, Giorgio. *Vita di Dante.* Rome: Laterza, 1983.

Pézard, André. *Dante sous la pluie de feu (Enfer XV).* Paris: J. Vrin, 1950.

———. "Volgare e latino nella Commedia." *Letture classensi* 2 (1966–67): 95–111.

Picone, Michelangelo, "Immagine e somiglianza: dai Siciliani a Dante." *Versants* 12 (1987): 63–71.

———. "La *Vita nuova* fra autobiografia e tipologia." In *Dante e le forme dell'allegoresi,* edited by Michelangelo Picone, 59–69. Ravenna: Longo, 1987.

———. "Strutture poetiche e strutture prosastiche nella *Vita nuova.*" *Modern Language Notes* 92 (1977): 117–29.

Pouillon, H. "La beauté, proprieté transcendentale chez les scolastiques (1220–70)." *Archives d'histoire doctrinale et littéraire du moyen âge* 15 (1946): 263–327.

Priest, Paul. "Looking Back from the Vision: Trinitarian Structure and Poetry in the *Commedia.*" *Dante Studies* 91 (1973): 113–30.

Robertis, Domenico de. *Il libro della Vita Nuova.* Florence: Sansoni, 1961.

Ross, Sir David. *Aristotle.* London: Methuen, 1966.

Rubenstein, Nicolai. "The Beginning of Political Thought in Florence." *Journal of the Warburg and Cortauld Institutes* 5 (1942): 198–227.

Santayana, George. *The Sense of Beauty: Being the Outline of Aesthetic Theory.* New York: Dover, 1955.

Savarese, Gaetano. "Una proposta per Forese: Il memorar presente." *Rassegna della letteratura italiana* 94 (1990): 5–20.

Schnapp, Jeffrey. "Dante's Ovidian Self-Correction in *Paradiso* 17." In *The Poetry of Allusion: Virgil and Ovid in Dante's "Commedia,"* edited by Rachel Jacoff and Jeffrey Schnapp, 214–23. Stanford: Stanford University Press, 1991.

———. "Sì pïa l'ombra d'Anchise si porse": *Paradiso* 15.25." In *The Poetry of Allusion: Virgil and Ovid in Dante's "Commedia,"* edited by Rachel Jacoff and Jeffrey Schnapp, 145–56. Stanford: Stanford University Press, 1991.

———. *The Transfiguration of History at the Center of Dante's Paradise.* Princeton: Princeton University Press, 1986.

Scott, J. A. "Dante's Use of the Word 'Intelletto.'" *Italica* 40 (1963): 215–24.

Shaw, J. E. *Guido Cavalcanti's Theory of Love.* Toronto: University of Toronto Press, 1949.

Simonelli, Maria. "Bonagiunta Orbicciani e la problematica dello stil nuovo (*Purg.* XXIV) 65–86." *Dante Studies* 86 (1968): 65–84.

Singleton, Charles. *Dante Studies 2: Journey to Beatrice.* Cambridge, Mass.: Harvard University Press, 1967.

———. *An Essay on the Vita Nuova.* 1949. Reprint, Baltimore: Johns Hopkins, 1977.

———. "The Use of Latin in the *Vita Nuova.*" *MLN* 30 (1946): 108–12.

Skulsky, Harold. *Metamorphosis: The Mind in Exile.* Cambridge, Mass.: Harvard University Press, 1981.

Spargo, E. J. M. *The Category of the Aesthetic in the Philosophy of St. Bonaventure.* Philosophy Series 11. New York: Franciscan Institute of St. Bonaventure, 1953.

Stäuble, Antonio. "La tenzone di Dante con Forese Donati." *Letture classensi* 24 (1995): 151–70.

Steneck, Nicholas. "Albert on the Psychology of Sense Perception." In *Albertus Magnus and the Sciences: Commemorative Essays, 1980,* edited by James Weisheipl, 263–90. Pontifical Institute of Medieval Studies. Toronto: University of Toronto Press, 1980.

———. "Albert the Great on the Internal Senses." *Isis* 65 (1974): 193–211.

Stephany, William. "Erysichthon and the Poetics of the Spirit." In *The Poetry of Allusion,* edited by Rachel Jacoff and Jeffrey Schnapp, 173–80. Stanford: Stanford University Press, 1991.

Stillinger, Thomas. *The Song of Troilus.* Philadelphia: University of Pennsylvania Press, 1992.

Stone, Gregory. "Dante's Averroistic Hermeneutics: (On 'Meaning' in the *Vita Nuova*)." *Dante Studies* 112 (1994): 133–59.

Templer, Margherita de Bonfils. "Amore e le visioni nella *Vita Nuova.*" *Dante Studies* 92 (1974): 19–34.

Took, J. F. *Dante, Lyric Poet and Philosopher.* Oxford: Clarendon, 1990.

———. "'L'etterno piacer": *Aesthetic Ideas in Dante.* Oxford: Clarendon, 1984.

Trimpi, Wesley. *Muses of One Mind.* Princeton: Princeton University Press, 1983.

Wack, Mary. *Lovesickness in the Middle Ages.* Philadelphia: University of Pennsylvania Press, 1990.

Werge, Thomas. "Dante's Tesoro: *Inferno* XV." *Romance Notes* 7 (1965–66): 203–6.

Williams, Raymond. *Keywords.* Fontana: Croom Helm, 1976.

Wingell, Albert. "The Forested Mountaintop in Augustine and Dante." *Dante Studies* 99 (1981): 9–48.

Index